PROPHETS
WITHOUT VISION

PROPHETS WITHOUT VISION

Subjectivity and the Sacred
in Contemporary American Writing

Hedda Ben-Bassat

Lewisburg
Bucknell University Press
London: Associated University Presses

Associated University Presses
440 Forsgate Drive
Cranbury, NJ 08512

Associated University Presses
16 Barter Street
London WC1A 2AH, England

Associated University Presses
P.O. Box 338, Port Credit
Mississauga, Ontario
Canada L5G 4L8

The paper used in this publication meets the requirements of the American National Standard for Permanence of Paper for Printed Library Materials Z39.48-1984.

Library of Congress Cataloging-in-Publication Data

Ben-Bassat, Hedda, 1946–
    Prophets without vision : subjectivity and the sacred in contemporary American writing / Hedda Ben-Bassat.
        p.   cm.
    Includes bibliographical references (p.) and index.
    ISBN 0-8387-5433-3 (alk. paper)
    1. American fiction—20th century—History and criticism.   2. Religious fiction, American—History and criticism.   3. Religion and literature—History—20th century.   4. Postmodernism (Literature)—United States.   5. Subjectivity in literature.   6. Holy, The, in literature. 7. Prophecies in literature.   I. Title.
PS374.R47 B46   2000
813'.509384—dc21   99-054765

CONTENTS

Acknowledgments

I wish to thank a number of institutions for assistance extended while I was at work on research on the book: The United States Israel Educational Foundation, for awarding me a Career Development Grant; The American Council of Learned Societies, for a Fellowship of American Studies; Tel Aviv University, for sabbatical leave.

On a more personal note I would like to express gratitude to colleagues and friends abroad and in Israel. To David Jasper for inspiration and sustained interest. To Hana Wirth-Nesher and Robert Griffin, who read earlier versions of the manuscript and offered acute comments. To Sacvan Bercovitch and Werner Sollors for advice and encouragement.

My deepest gratitude to Zephyra Porat, who has been my guide and mentor for many years, and who has left me in her debt both by suggesting avenues for exploration and by drawing out the implications of my arguments.

Finally I wish to thank my husband Dan and my daughters Anat and Tamar for their unfailing patience and support.

The poem "Reassurance" is quoted from *Revolutionary Petunias & Other Poems* by Alice Walker. Used by permission, Harcourt Inc.

PROPHETS
WITHOUT VISION

.

1

Introduction: Pilgrims and Strangers: Postmodernism, Scriptural Faiths, and the Vanishing American Self.

Personal Identity is not what matters

—Derek Parfit, *Reasons and Persons*

Why should personal identity matter?

—W. B. Michaels, *Our America*

I am not what I am

—Karl Barth, *The Epistle to the Romans*

Who is it that I ain't?

—William Faulkner, *Light in August*

I

My book is about crises of ideology and identity in the fiction of five contemporary American writers—John Updike, Flannery O'Connor, Grace Paley, James Baldwin, and Alice Walker. These writers construct fictional characters modeled on competing voices in the multicultural American scene. At the same time, the hybrid or hyphenated historical identities they construct (and, by the same token, deconstruct) break down in scenes of self-questioning and judgment.[1] The effect of self-questioning is not to entrench African Americans, gender-specific Americans, or religious-specific Americans in their respective group identities. Nor, on the other hand, does the fading of group identity reduce these fictional characters to nonidentity, signifying the "death of the subject." In the fiction of Updike, O'Connor, Paley, Baldwin, and Walker, scenes of identity breakdown do not reduce the subject to nothing, but rather render him or her politically invisible, that is, unreadable by reference ex-

11

clusively to the political or historical. In Ralph Ellison's *Invisible Man*,[2] for example, the protagonist's invisibility is, on one level, readable as the effect of power politics whose ideology and institutions remove representatives of minority groups from official visibility. But on another level, vanishing selfhood can be explained by "the technologies of self" practiced by American self-examiners from Edwards through Emerson to Ellison. Puritan notebooks and personal narratives make the sinful historical self appear in order, by the act of confession, to make it disappear.[3] My book examines traditional technologies of producing a vanishing self as they are deployed by contemporary American writers. In the acts of writing and the acts of reading they evoke, Updike, O'Connor, Paley, Baldwin, and Walker make the historical selfhood of reader and protagonist disappear, but do not thereby reduce their selfhood to nothing.

Reading postmodern crises of identity in contemporary American fiction through pre-modern lenses of traditional prophetic faiths reveals structures of ethically beneficial breakdowns in narrative identities and the ideological narratives in which they are inscribed.[4] How does their traditional faith contribute to the techniques of self-construction and deconstruction which Updike, O'Connor, Paley, Baldwin, and Walker deploy in their fiction? Why should we as readers be interested in the drama of the dissolution of their readable fictional characters? What do practices of prophetic faiths contribute to American aesthetics of disappearing identity?

Paul Ricoeur's analysis of vanishing selfhood in Musil's *Man Without Qualities* helps clarify the questions that guided my reading. Ricoeur argues that "a non subject is one figure of the subject" in modern and postmodern imaginary writing:

> A non subject is not nothing. . . . The plea for selfhood . . . begins to shift into its opposite when . . . readers in quest of identity find themselves confronting the hypothesis of their own loss of identity. . . . To be sure, this nothingness is not the nothingness of which there is nothing to say. Quite the contrary. . . . [T]he most dramatic transformations of personal identity pass through the crucible of this nothingness of identity. . . . So many conversion narratives attest to such nights of personal identity. In these moments of extreme destitution . . . personal identity is not what matters. . . . [H]ow, then, are we to maintain on the ethical level a self which, on the narrative level, seems to be fading away?[5]

Fading selfhood, Ricoeur observes, lends itself to opposite interpretations, depending on the reader's ideology. Postmodern readers interpret disappearing subjects in postmodern fiction as reflecting the death of the subject. But for readers who still adhere to Biblical faith,[6] self-fading is the fictional representation of mystic dark nights of the soul, paving the way to religious and or moral transformation. For these readers the gap between narrative identity and ethical selfhood is the gap between two very different cognitive structures. A narrative that does not answer the question "who?" is one structure. A newborn self who nevertheless answers a call to awakening is another structure. In fictions of self-fading, the constant question, for religiously-oriented readers, is why not "make the gap separating narrative identity and moral identity work for the benefit of their living dialectic?" Where narratives answer to questions of identity breakdown, ethical responses to calls of responsibility may break through. In the structure of call and response, the question "who am I?" does not matter. What matters is the obligation to reply "Here I am!" in response to the call of the Other, human or divine.[7]

Contemporary American fiction, philosophy, and criticism has been infiltrated by the philosophers of self-fading that dominate the European conversation. Here, the problems of fading subjectivity frequently take the form of critiques of narrative identities, which together compose the multifaceted and elusive "American self." The aim of New Americanist[8] criticism is not to use the fading of narrative identity to the benefit of ethical selfhood (individual and collective). On the contrary, the brunt of New American criticism is aimed against Old American constructions of an ideal American self, whose ethical excellence is exemplary. This ethical self (democratic, humanistic, libertarian) is seen as an instrument of repression and oppression, denying the wide variety of minority and marginal groups, preventing them from forging their own narratives of identity and contributing to the portrait of American self.

The debate between the Old and the New versions of self-vanishing, featured in American narratives of estrangement in the wilderness, seems to resolve itself into an either/or proposition: either look closely at the historical and political conditions of identity production, or focus on the trans-historical, universal values of identity production. New Americanists accuse Old Americanists of sacrificing political identities to ethical abstractions. Old Americanists accuse New Americanists of sacrificing meaning, message, and depth to political ideologies.

My methodology replaces either/or propositions with dialectical relations of both/and. Conversion narratives feature both concrete political historical anchorage and its traumatic loss for the benefit of ethical awakening. Political narratives must be broken down, and the narrative identities they produce must be shattered, in order that prophetic awakening may be staged and communicated. That is the main argument of the following chapters, which center on the gap, in contemporary American fiction, between narrative identities and prophetic identities (or lack thereof), and the ways this gap displays traces of several prophetic traditions.

To situate my own reading between Old and New Americanism, let me briefly rehearse the positions in the American conversation. Once the two rival alternatives are clear I will propose a third alternative, inspired by contemporary theories of pre-modern traditions traceable in post–World War II American writing and the fading self they deliberately construct and deconstruct. Not all Americanist scholars can be classified as either Old or New. Indeed my own search for a third alternative, combining old traditions with new political and historical awareness, is inspired by the work of Emily Miller-Budick. In *Fiction and Historical Consciousness, Engendering Romance,* and *Nineteenth-Century American Romance,*[9] Miller-Budick combines an illuminating analysis of aesthetic (romance) and philosophical (skeptic) traditions, with incisive analysis of feminist, Jewish, and African American constructions of identity. Her philosophical methodology is openly indebted to the American philosopher Stanley Cavell, himself neither an Old nor a New Americanist.[10] Particularly illuminating for my purposes is a passage Miller-Budick cites in her latest book, from Cavell's *Senses of Walden.* The passage opens with the figure of the reader as stranger. Here, as elsewhere in Cavell, respecting one another's and one's own strangeness, outside of politics, produces positive ethical effects:

> The reader's position is that of a stranger. To write to him is to acknowledge that he is outside the words. . . . The conditions of meeting upon the words are that we—writer and reader—learn how to depart from them, . . . and then return to them, finding ourselves there again.[11]

Applying Cavell's models to her study of romance as genre, Miller-Budick reads the American corpus of romance fiction as open to moral explorations. In her earlier works, Miller-Budick's literary analysis traces the origins of romance fiction and the fictional selves it produces, in the scriptural paradigms of Adam and Isaac. Miller-

Budick deploys critical categories that are neither exclusively Old Americanist nor New Americanist but both. She carefully explores the contemporary political conditions of literary production in African-American and Jewish women writers. But she also reads for ethical and religious traditional values and meanings. The latter reading is closer in spirit to Old Americanist positions.

II

Unlike Miller-Budick and myself, New Americanists do not allow for a position midway between ethical/universal and political/history-specific readings. On the contrary, New Americanists such as Donald Pease, Jonathan Arac, and Jane Tompkins charge Old Americanists, such as Matthiessen and Trilling, with ethical and ideological obsessions resulting in oblivion to the real conditions and issues of literary production and consumption. Old American celebrations of an ideal American self, the New Americanists argue, feature tacit "exceptionalism." Reading for absolute universal values and meanings results in an essentialism which can only benefit the power politics of repression and exclusion.[12]

I agree that narratives of American selfhood have always been politically and historically anchored. But I ask, why would narratives of ethical awakening necessarily exclude or repress the political and historical issues that require ethical recognition? In all the contemporary texts examined in this book, the characters are strongly anchored in class, gender, and ethnic affiliations. Yet at crucial moments in the action, these characters of many qualities experience a fading-out and breakdown of their political identifications, along with a breaking-in of an ethical call.

It is from this stance that I will select the points of the New Americanist position which have contributed most to my own dialectical model. Among the prominent New Americanist critics, I found Walter Benn Michaels and Donald Pease particularly helpful. For a defense of Old Americanist readings, I relied on the work of Frederick Crews and Miller-Budick, neither of whom, however, can be pigeonholed as Old Americanists.

The keynote of the New Americanists' opposition to Old Americanist readings is pluralism. Their readings embrace the minority voices they claim that Old Americanists erase. They attack the old canon, from which these voices have been excluded by official academic liberalism. In the name of an ideological shift from liberal formalist universalism to poststructuralist historicism, New Americanists denounce the Old as representing only "white middle class non-immigrant northern families."[13]

The "adversarial reductiveness" practiced by contemporary critics such as Pease, Michaels, Tompkins and Arac, says Frederick Crews in "Whose American Renaissance?," finds fault with Old Americanist authors and critics for complicity with racism, sexism, and homophobia.[14] They find particular fault with the Old Americanists' attempts to portray the fictional American self as a universal individual. Working on the poststructuralist principle that narrative or fictional identity is not the referent of narrative but its product, New Americanists argue that the more narratives we have, the more complex and elusive portraits of American selfhood must become. Furthermore, the New Americanists' argument, according to Crews, shifts the ideological focus to the political, social, and historical conditions of literary production, requiring a parallel shift away from problems of individual identity to that of groups, classes, or nations.

Setting up a relation of mutual exclusion between Old and New Americanists, each repressing the other, Crews takes clear sides against the latter. His most saving denunciation of their "severely impoverished premises" reads as follows:

> All the liabilities of the New Americanist enterprise that I have touched upon—its self-righteousness, its tendency to conceive of American history only as a highlight film of outrages, its impatience with artistic purposes other than "redefining the social order," and its choice of critical principles according to the partisan cause at hand—suggest that there may be yet a role for other styles of reading American literature.[15]

As for the Old Americanists, with whom he obviously sympathizes, Crews praises Matthiessen and his Old Americanist colleagues where New Americanists blame them, for presenting a "vision of universal brotherhood," and for demonstrating that major American writers had "transcended the politics of their age."[16]

I agree with the objections Donald Pease raises to Crews' charge of impoverishment. In "National Identities, Postmodern Artifacts, and Postnational Narratives," Pease observes that the national focus of Matthiessen, Trilling, and Chase produced a fictional self neither individual nor collective, let alone concretely embodied in historical conditions.[17] The universality of national identity thus produced, molded as its subjective correlative an I "dependent for its integrity upon its capacity to exclude externals as well as to integrate an identity."[18]

I do not agree, however, that any universalist reading as such is necessarily exclusionist. Therefore, I am particularly interested in questioning the argument which Walter Benn Michaels proposes in *Our America: Nativism, Modernism and Pluralism*. Michaels amasses a wealth of illuminating material in support of his dual claim, that in America any universalism boils down to racism, and that therefore, ethically speaking, nonidentity is better than an Old Americanist universal one. In my reading of Updike, O'Connor, Paley, Baldwin, and Walker, I show that fading away or estrangement from collective American identities is cultivated for ethical purposes. Michaels claims, on the other hand, that mutual estrangement invites aggression.

Michaels convincingly shows that pluralist American identity-construction essentializes radical racism, thus breeding hostility and alienation. While aliens may gain citizenship, they remain estranged from the nativist model of American selfhood. Politically defined aliens inspire hostility by their very difference.[19] Thus Jewish immigrants are seen as one prototype of the hated aliens, who "represent the greatest threat to America and in fact to the very idea of America."[20] Aliens, Michaels emphasizes, are hated not because of their inferiority to "Americanness," but simply because of their difference from it.[21] The wholly different unassimilated stranger, whether Jewish, African-American, or Native American, Michaels suggests, is seen by American pluralists as "tragic," not because of the nature of her own distinctive culture, but because it encloses her and separates her from "Americanness": "The tragedy consists in the inability . . . to adapt 'culturally' and 'historically' to 'American institutions'."[22]

Michaels ends his study with a critique of the racist nature of American cultural pluralism resulting precisely from the very definition of culture as pluralized, rather than preferring one set of practices to another.[23] Implicitly aggressive, American cultural pluralism creates and contrasts a model of American selfhood on the one hand, and hostility-inspiring alien groups on the other.

Updike, O'Connor, Paley, Baldwin, and Walker would ask, how can a writer invent a sphere for friendly relations among strangers outside of politics without relinquishing the quest for identity? For Michaels this question does not seem worth asking: "this effort to give a more persuasive answer to the question of who we are does not answer the question . . . Why should it matter who we are?"[24]

To Updike, O'Connor, Paley, Baldwin, and Walker, and to their readers, the question does matter. Identity itself continues to exist as a pressing question even when no satisfying answers are available. Taking the questionability of political selfhood as their point of departure, the fictional characters in the writers studied here discover that nights of narrative identity nurture the dawn of ethical responsiveness.

It takes at least two readings to follow the gaps that separate the narrative identities of my writers' protagonists from the prophetic stranger by whom they are shattered and doubled. One reading would characterize the contemporary conflict in which their sociopolitical and historical conditions engage them. The other reading would have recourse to the prophetic models that each in his or her way invokes. It might be objected that the doubled and divided fictional self in Updike, O'Connor, Paley, Baldwin, and Walker can be ascribed to what is called, in postmodern criticism, political and cultural schizophrenia; why then appeal to prophetic origins? My answer is that the writers I examine—not only the outspokenly religious ones like Updike and O'Connor, but even an outspokenly secular writer like Paley—appeal to prophetic origins. Each in her or his way, and resorting to diverse hereditary intertexts, textually represents "the soul's mumps and measles and whooping-coughs,"[25] not only as a contemporary disease of the postmodern subject, but as a hereditary dis-ease of their respective religious selves.

III

"Who is it that I aint"? This is the question that Byron Bunch, a central character in Faulkner's *Light In August* (1932) asks Lena Grove at the beginning of his loss-of-self-to-find-his-soul experience.[26]

To be or not to be Byron Bunch is the question that Bunch asks on the threshold of what Cavell, in another context, has called his conversion-aversion experience.[27] From that point on, guided by the religion of salutary self-alienation, Bunch practices Christian and comic technologies of self-doubling self-loss. Faulkner represents Bunch's ethics of going beyond questions of historical identity as neither exceptionalist nor essentialist, neither nativist nor universalist. According to the New Americanists, essentialism in one way and exceptionalism in another repress painful political or sociological issues. Byron Bunch does not repress but rather transcends, while remaining anchored in the historical situation of the novel. He remains engaged in the political action of the novel, but is not of it. Politically, he rises to the rescue of victims of racist and male-chauvinist violence. However, the question concerning the deconstruction and renewed construction of Bunch's selfhood is not raised in political-historical categories, nor is it staged in a political space. For Byron Bunch, as for Henry Thoreau, seeking transcendent selfhood is for Sunday, when and where one wonders, as a lapsed believer in prophetic promises, "Who is it that I ain't?"

My book is not about Faulkner. It is about writers who cannot easily go back to Old American literary roots for ways of transcending the New Americanist politics of hyphenated, pluralistic identity, and its multicultural group-recognitions. The texts I examine feature strangers with double selves. They are not only hyphenated horizontally on the political and cultural level. They are also conflicted vertically on the metaphysical ladder of a self cut by what Ricoeur in *Oneself As Another* calls "the Kantian knife."[28] They are thus structured because they are troubled by two opposite questions. The first is, "Who am I?", and the second, "Is 'who am I' the only question?" They are confronted by these questions because they are textually constructed as living in two discursive worlds. One world is political and accessible to our new or modern categories. The other discursive world is prophetic and requires theological, metaphysical categories of subject construction and/or deconstruction for its analysis.

Updike, O'Connor, Paley, Baldwin, and Walker represent salutary self-alienation as being more ambiguous than in Faulkner. For one thing, the experience is rarely justified by clear and unquestioned religious paradigms. Secondly, and perhaps therefore, the anguish and possible amorality of losing group identity often verges on a sense of having betrayed the group, especially in the cases of Walker and Baldwin. And yet, even without the overt Old Americanist scriptural affiliation, the authors I discuss continue to write about pilgrims and strangers as exemplary Americans. Pilgrimages, journeys to foreign (imaginary or metaphysical) spaces, consistently feature searching for who the protagonist "ain't"; that is, for a self other than his or her own historical anchorage. Like Faulkner's Bunch, so Baldwin's Peter (in "Previous Condition") and Walker's Fanny (in

The Temple of My Familiar) are citizens of two worlds,[29] and bearers of two selves. In one world their recognizable identity is determined by racial, ethnic, gender, and class identification marks. But in the other world, their aesthetically produced self-as-other is deliberately alienated from that very political world and the self it produces. For their peers in the political world, and even to themselves, Peter and Fanny appear to be fugitives, responsibility shirkers, even traitors. But for their other-worldly imaginary or prophetically-produced self they are represented as having become strangers to themselves for salutary purposes.[30]

As shown above, on the political, historical level, and for the empirical self constructed there, the alien is a negative, hostility-inspiring element. My purpose is to show that, from an ethical or religious point of view, not all self-alienation or estrangement is represented as negative. My claim is, on the contrary, that we only experience the anxieties of alienation if we no longer have ears to hear or memory to recall the Old Americanist prophetic discourse of not being oneself, or being "otherwise than being," or "oneself as another."[31] The theoretical work done in the present and in the following chapters is designed to recall to our modern ears the still small prophetic voice, whispering on one register of the texts written by Updike, O'Connor, Paley, Baldwin, and Walker. We do not have to be retrained to hear the many political, cultural, and social voices that sing on the historical level of these authors' texts. New Americanist criticism has rendered us competent for such responses. But the habit of excluding religious rhetoric and accusing it of exceptionalism has taught us to disregard or dismiss as politically tyrannical myths the prophetic voice that urges us not only to find our politically situated self but also to lose it.

Politically interpreted, having an alien identity and being metaphorically invisible to others is clearly an insult and injury requiring resistance and subversion of repressing ideologies. Ideologically biased narratives not only exclude aliens from social visibility, but thereby deny them their right to produce their own narratives and narrative identities. Yet, ethically interpreted, from the perspective of a prophetic tradition running from Edwards to Emerson and from Emerson to Ellison, estrangement, alienation, and invisibility can be reversed into scenes of illumination and initiation. In Ellison's *Invisible Man*, as in Musil's *Man Without Qualities*, the fading of subject on the historical level of text occasions the question, "What does [visible] identity matter?" I hear a call to responsibility, and here I am! Perhaps this ethical reversal of invisibility or fading is more accessible in Ellison's *Invisible Man* (as in Baldwin's "Previous Condition," Walker's *The Temple of My Familiar,* and O'Connor's *The Violent Bear It Away*), than in Musil's *Man Without Qualities,* because the prophetic legacy is more pronounced in American fiction. At any rate, prominent American literary critics, cultural historians, and philosophers appeal to prophetic categories in addressing the constructions and deconstructions of subjectivity in American fiction, poetry, philosophy, and films. Though fading subjectivity is often presented as a postmodern structure, Sacvan Bercovitch, Stanley Cavell, and Harold Bloom trace, in diverse ways, nineteenth- and twentieth-century productions of vanishing American selfhood to classic prophetic precursors.

In their very different readings of the American tradition, from the Puritans through the Transcendentalists to our own day, Bercovitch, Cavell, and Bloom argue that the elusive or disappearing subject which American writing features is not a non-subject, let alone a dead one. In their eyes, disappearing American selfhood is not "nothing," and the question "Who is it that I ain't?" is not an empty question. Each in his way reconstructs an American prophetic tradition of beneficial estrangement, and represents, ethically and aesthetically, beneficial disappearance as the effect of an indigenous prophetic legacy.

For Sacvan Bercovitch, elusive selfhood is structured as doubled and divided rather than as disappearing. In *The Puritan Origins of the American Self* and *The American Jeremiad,* Bercovitch traces prophetic self-division in American selfhood to Puritan origins, which he locates on both the scriptural and the secular historical levels of cultural discourse. Dwelling on ideological and symbolic strategies of constructing narrative identity, Bercovitch highlights a tightly integrating interrelation between individual and collective selfhood thus produced. To be sure, Bercovitch observes the existence of alternative cultural strategies, which precisely divorce the prophetic subject from the community, but he does not stress them.

In *The Puritan Origins of the American Self,* Bercovitch persuasively exposes the "profound Puritan ambivalence towards selfhood," which he terms "auto-machia."[32] He underlines, moreover, the "relentless psychic strain" that such inner war engendered between an external, transcendent God and the "I-ness" of the individual believer. The psychological conflict located God's judgment (krisis) in the Puritan's trial of the self, thus perpetuating a state of self-questioning (*Puritan Origins*, 22). However, the structure and dynamics of auto-machia do not form the center of Bercovitch's analysis. His focus is rather on sociopolitical symbolic practices, whereby the founders of Puritan communities produced well-integrated private/ public narrative identities. In Bercovitch's model, prophetic inroads into political historical identities do not dissolve the historical narratives by which they are produced. Instead the two identity-producing types of narrative and history intertwine. Bercovitch cites the Puritan dictum that "Prophesie is Historie antedated; and Historie is post-dated Prophesie. The same thing is told in both."[33]

Not only Puritan auto-machias and the self in question they produce are marginalized in *Puritan Origins*. Also marginalized is an opposite model of prophetic identity, assimilated by Emerson into his version of prophetic American selfhood. Bercovitch comments in passing on the mutual exclusiveness of Puritan self-deflation, and Promethean self-inflation. But he argues that, nevertheless, both Jonathan Edwards' auto-machias and Emerson's Promethean auto-generations claim American legitimacy as heirs of a prophetic tradition. Such a "hermeneutics bridges the considerable gap between Christic auto-machia and Promethean self-creation" (*Puritan Origins*, 157). Bercovitch sees two successive strains of prophetic discourse as merging. One is Puritan and the other, Romantic, indeed German Romantic. Bercovitch himself dissolves the plurality and perhaps even incompatibility of varieties of prophetic selfhood. He claims that for all their obvious differences, Edwardsian auto-machias and Emersonian Prometheanism both serve to incorporate individual identities into a corporate American myth. As representative American, Emerson "annihilates division":

> By projecting himself in his hero, he recasts Romantic autobiography into auto-American-biography, creates himself as symbol of a corporate teleology. . . . The rhetoric he inherited enabled him to dissolve all differences between history and the self—as well as all differences within the self (civic, natural, prophetic)—and so to overcome political disenchantment by revealing himself as the representative American. (*Puritan Origins*, 170, 173)

This does not mean to imply that Bercovitch represents Emerson's prophetic persona as conforming to the pattern of a citizen in the city on a hill, let alone as undertaking a mission to the wilderness.[34] On the contrary, he stresses Emerson's commitment to the

Romantic-Promethean ideal of prophetic genius. Bercovitch knows that Emerson's genius-prophet invents himself in sublime isolation from the community. Nevertheless, Bercovitch does not read prophetic selfhood as being born out of a break in historical identity. On the contrary, he says that Emerson dissolves the differences between history and the self, as well as all differences within the self:

> Against the "double consciousness . . . of the Understanding and of the Soul" which he termed "the worst feature of our biography," Emerson chanted the prophetic self, a "dualism" emptied of two-ness, of the alien or the unknown—personal and national identity twinned in the bipolar unity of auto-American-biography.[35]

Similarly, Bercovitch himself dissolves all differences into a collective model of Puritan prophetism, and goes as far as to argue that the Emersonian self represents "the myth of America" (*Puritan Origins*, 165).

IV

Like Sacvan Bercovitch, Stanley Cavell sees Emerson as heir to America's indigenous prophetic tradition. In *The Senses Of Walden*, Cavell defines "prophetic poetics" as a means of discarding the writer's and reader's historical selfhood, in order to find it elsewhere. Cavell reads Thoreau's *Walden* as a "sacred text" reverberating with the spirit of Old Testament prophets like Ezekiel and Jeremiah, who portray themselves in situations of limitation or loss. In Thoreau's awareness that "he will not be hearkened to, and his interpretation of it," Cavell finds "immediate identifications with Jeremiah and Ezekiel."[36] St. Paul's model of prophecy as initiating "Christ's giving 'gifts unto men' " (*The Senses*, 29), serves Cavell as further evidence of Thoreau's prophetic vocation.

According to Cavell the difference between the appeal to prophecy made by the Puritan forefathers, and the adaptation of prophetic strategies by the Transcendentalists, lies in a difference in the Puritan texts themselves. Puritans feature both a communal turn to a city on a hill as well as a withdrawal to the wilderness, while in Emerson and Thoreau, Cavell claims, the communal element is repressed.[37] Thoreau's discourse "directly disobeys the cardinal motivation of Puritan preaching—that the word be spoken and confessed aloud. The time for such prophesying is absolutely over" (*The Senses*, 29). Cavell further argues with the idea that the Puritan conception of the city on a hill, as the foundation of a community of saints, can be simply taken for a model of national self-congratulation.[38] On the contrary, to his mind the city can serve as a horizon for self-criticism, and inspire the feeling that "(t)here were prophets but there was no Zion."[39] Cavell remarks that the first step towards finding a prophetic self is recognizing that we have lost our access to it: "The writer comes to us from a sense of loss . . . like any American, he has lost a nation and with it the God of the fathers. . . . The object of hope . . . is to be found in the true acceptance of loss" (*The Senses*, 50).

Cavell's readings of the scriptural/prophetic intertext in Emerson and Thoreau focus on narratives of foreign journeys[40] and the salutary self-estrangement that they figuratively endorse. Such narratives of pursuing, through loss, a further "unattained but attainable self," are interpreted by Cavell as inviting philosophical analysis in general, and skeptic analysis in particular. The skeptic tradition, Cavell argues, generates figures of elusive, unapproachable selfhood. The recurrent features of such a doubt-haunted self are strangeness, uncanniness, and newness. Cavell reads encounters with newness, strangeness, and phantom doubles as scenes of instruction postulated on loss of recognizable anchorage. Doubling, splitting, and estrangement spell for Cavell poetic variations on the traditional theme—one must lose historical anchorage in order to allow newness.[41]

Though my own reading is more theologically oriented than his, I am deeply indebted to Cavell for my thesis that writers and readers of American texts must lose their historically and politically anchored subject-positions in order to explore the prophetic potential of the American self. How to elude the historical and political identities by which they are imprisoned? Although Cavell does not say so explicitly, he hints that the American self qua prophetic is elusive in principle, and that therefore, as I understand it, it is only by embracing loss that one can overcome it. "The fate of having a self," he insists, "is one in which the self is always to be found" (*The Senses*, 51). Cavell quotes Thoreau as insisting on the reader's withdrawal to "the ocean of one's being alone," where he or she experiences the process of losing the self in order to find it: "Not till we are lost, in other words, not till we have lost the world . . . do we begin to find ourselves" (*The Senses*, 49). Thoreau's pilgrims, Cavell argues, are not partakers of a communal errand. Rather, whether writers or readers, they are strangers who "realize that they have lost the world, i.e. are lost to it" (*The Senses*, 51).

Cavell selects for quotation from *Walden* passages in which Thoreau represents himself and the reader as being "beside ourselves in a sane way" (*The Senses*, 100). Through such experiences, Cavell remarks, "it is the double who is the spectator, and I who am the scene of occurrence" (*The Senses*, 100). How then, Cavell asks, is the elusive "I" of an American writer or reader produced in the act of reading and writing?:

> The writer specifies my relation to the double as my being beside it. Being beside oneself is the dictionary definition of ecstasy. To suggest that one may stand there, stay there in a sane sense, is to suggest that the besidedness of which ecstasy speaks is my experience of my existence, my knowledge "of myself as a human entity," my assurance of my integrity or identity. This condition—the condition of "having" a self, and knowing it—is an instance of the general relation the writer perceives as "being next to." (*The Senses*, 103)

In seeking our elusive unapproachable American self, Cavell remarks, "our first resolve should be toward the nextness of the self to the self; it is the capacity not to deny either of its positions or attitudes . . ." (*The Senses*, 107). This capacity to tolerate multiple dualities renders selfhood "something, towards which I can stand in various relations, ones in which I can stand to other selves . . ." (*The Senses*, 51–52).[42]

In the preface to *The Senses of Walden*, Cavell notes the process of estrangement from self and others as part of a positive rather than hostility-provoking dynamic between writer and reader, despite or because of their mutual estrangement

> [Thoreau] has had to establish himself as a neighbor; which next means to establish himself as a stranger; which in turn means to establish the concept and the recognition of neighbors and strangers; this will mean establishing his reader as his stranger. (*The Senses*, vi)[43]

Where does the self encounter the stranger-self or other? This is the question which guides the journeys towards uncanny rebirth, which Cavell traces in Emerson as well as in Thoreau.[44] He goes for answers outside American philosophical thought, and finds close analogies between the figurative loss of self in scriptural prophetic discourse

and the conceptual transcendence of the self in the philosophy of
Kant, Heidegger, and Wittgenstein. Cavell associates Emerson's
"ideas of loss and turning," as well as his "finding of founding as
finding" with the work of Heidegger and Wittgenstein.[45] The mysterious stranger encountered by Emerson's and Thoreau's seeker beyond historical identity, is not miraculously supernatural, Cavell
argues, but imaginatively uncanny; not an object of faith but of the
transcendental and skeptical imagination. William James has shown
that the uncanniness of a divided and double self can be traced to
religious sources as old as Augustine or Bunyan, and as modern as
Tolstoi.[46] But Cavell chooses to trace uncanny experience to philosophical sources, especially to the Kantian model of self-division.
Reading *Walden* as situated between philosophy and literature, Cavell applauds Thoreau's claim that "the uncanny vision [is] essential
to philosophy," that his own text partakes of the fantastic, and that
the reader "is [the other that inhabits the realm of] the fantastic."
As uncanny readers of uncanny texts "we are each of us double and
each must learn 'to be beside oneself in a sane way'."[47]

Beside oneself, but where? one still wonders. In a city of words,
a "pure pool of words," Cavell would answer (*Conditions*, 8–9). He
suggests that in the act of reading itself, reader and writer experience being beside themselves. Borrowing the trope "city of words"
from Plato's *Republic* (book 9), and of course Kant's *Critique of Practical Reason*, Cavell invokes a space which exists nowhere except in the
imagination and ethical faith of writer and reader, released by acts
of reading and writing from the constraints of their empirical situations and selfhoods.[48] Just as Bercovitch's Puritans were citizens of
two cities (earthly and heavenly), so Cavell's transcendental skeptics
are citizens of two worlds (ordinary and strange). Whether self-es-
tranged by faith, as in Bercovitch, or by the uncanny imagination, as
in Cavell, a prophetic subject is twice divided. As Cavell puts it in
philosophical terms: "We are halved not only horizontally but vertically . . . each of us seeking that of which we were originally half"
(*Conditions*, 59). In Cavell, prophetic self-estrangement functions
positively as a space of conversion. Experiencing its own otherness,
the self can overcome doubts about other minds. Prophetic experience transcends the world in order to return to it.[49]

V

Cavell believes that the function of "prophetic poetics" is to dis-
engage writers and readers from their political and historical condi-

tions in order to re-engage them. I agree, but in order to cope with the multiple dualities of Updike, O'Connor, Paley, Baldwin, and Walker I found it necessary to use also models that have a stronger political orientation than Cavell's. Particularly helpful for me is the work of Jean-Paul Sartre. Like Cavell he appeals to the Kantian ethics of citizenship in two worlds in defining the relation between literature and politics, but with a much stronger political emphasis. In *What Is Literature?*, Sartre argues that the writer's task is not to bury the reader in his or her historicity, but to release him or her into a transcendent space of words. "Lacking the wherewithal," he claims, "the city of ends lasts for each of us only while we are reading."[50]

While we are reading, in other words, we imaginatively reenter a universal, ethical city, which exists nowhere in history or politics. Sartre believes that the politics of identity must be imaginatively eluded, to enable moving towards an ethics of ideal citizenship. For Sartre, as for Plato and Kant, words generate an ideal space where human beings can recognize one another as ends in themselves. However, in Sartre, entry is through political action, not beyond it: "A man puts himself entirely into his project for emancipating the Negroes or restoring the Hebrew language to the Jews in Palestine . . . and thereby realizes the human condition in its universality" (*Literature*, 236). In such imaginary transcendent spaces political communities and conversations among readers are exchanged for a community of readers and writers, recognizing the human right to be ends rather than means—humanity for humanity's sake:

> Let us bear in mind that the man who reads strips himself in some way of his *empirical* personality, and escapes from his resentments, his fears, and his lusts, in order to put himself at the peak of his freedom. This freedom takes the literary work, and through it mankind, for absolute ends. . . . Thus, by its very exigence, the reader attains that chorus of good will which Kant has called The City of Ends. (200, my italics)

Shattering horizontal empirical selfhood, by introducing the vertical ascendance into ethical selfhood, the writer risks being considered a sinner and a traitor by his group, class, ethnic community, or nation.[51] And the reader, for her or his part, is at the risk of falling prey to the oppressive "paradox of ethics" still predominant in contemporary conversation. Sartre notes that the reader who fulfills his ethical duties may neglect "the injustices of the age, the class struggle, colonialism, anti-Semitism etc., and finally take advantage of oppression in order to do good" (191). Likewise, any overt political activity may result in relating to most men as mere "means." The task of the writer is to set up a city (of ends or words), where hybrid readers—both victims and victimizers, oppressed and oppressors—can treat, in universal categories, every stranger (to their group of affiliation), as an absolute "end."[52]

Unlike the more secular Sartre, Cavell confronts the question whether humanity's universal hopes require theological categories for their support. In *Conditions Handsome and Unhandsome* Cavell asks: "Kant's price is to leave religion with its corner on hope, hence as something whose object is elsewhere, something theology may well itself wish to contest—but why without the help of philosophy?" (20) Since my focus is on the prophetic origins of elusive American selfhood, I reversed Cavell's question and asked why not use religious categories, particularly when working with prophetic American materials?

VI

To pursue this rhetorical question I consulted Harold Bloom, who insists that there is no exhaustive appreciation of American poetics that does not include an analysis of American religion.[53] Like Bercovitch and Cavell, Bloom sees prophetic poetics as central to the construction and deconstruction of the subject in American letters. But the prophetic tradition that Bloom reconstructs derives neither from Cotton Mather and Edwards, nor from Kant and Wittgenstein, but from Marcion and Valentinus. Bloom's aesthetic religion is anchored in the gnostic heresy according to which the estranged self is redeemed through vertical, trans-historical alienation.

Though the *origins* of Bloom's American self differ from those postulated by Bercovitch and Cavell, the *structure* of prophetic subjectivity he exposes shares features in common with theirs. The heart of prophetic experience in the New World, says Bloom, and in this he concurs with Bercovitch and Cavell, is Newness. As a prooftext he cites, in *Poetry and Repression*, an entry in Emerson's Journal dated April 1846. The passage is carefully selected by Bloom for its linking of newness with disappearance, just as Cavell had sought passages in Thoreau that link newness with loss. Emerson writes:

> He or That which in despair of naming aright, some have called the *Newness* . . . lurks, he hides, he who is success, reality, joy, power. . . . This is

He that shall come; or if He come not, nothing comes: He that disappears in the moment when we go to celebrate Him. If we go to burn those that blame our celebration, He appears in them. The Divine Newness.[54]

For Bloom the notorious elusiveness of the American self is subservient to repressing precursors and resisting their demonic influence. Cultivated loss of others results in partial loss of self, but only in order to father or mother a self of one's own. In Whitman, Bloom claims, "Newness is even more splendidly elusive," because Whitman represents himself as "carrying the crescent child that carries its own full mother in its belly" (*Poetry and Repression*, 263–64). The American self is more sublimely elusive in Whitman than in Emerson because Whitman disappears more radically. As Bloom puts it: "Emerson says: *'I and the abyss'*; Whitman says: *'The Abyss of My Self.'* The second statement is necessarily more Sublime and, alas, even more American" (*Poetry and Repression*, 266).

Curiously enough, when dealing with the prophetic voice in Blake, Bloom speaks of the prophet as founder, rather than loser—as public orator in the city—and maintains that Blake could not find his prophetic voice.

A biblical prophet may wander when he is cast out into the desert, when his voice becomes a voice in the wilderness, but he does not wander when he goes through the midst of the city . . . through Jerusalem the City of God. There his inspired voice always has a purpose and his inspired feet have a destination. (*Poetry and Repression*, 37)

At the same time Bloom observes that Blake does not exactly silence that prophetic voice, but rather experiences it as hiding. Walking in the city, Blake admits: "I am not Ezekiel I am not a prophet, I am too fearful to be the prophet I ought to be, I am hid" (*Poetry and Repression*, 37). Bloom finds that Blake's prophetic poetics expresses "a terrible nostalgia for a lost prophetic *voice*, the voice of Ezekiel and religious logocentrism" (*Poetry and Repression*, 40).[55]

But this tribute to prophetic double-voicedness in Blake is hardly the crux of Bloom's insights into the prophetic origins of American poetics and selfhood. On the contrary, Bloom's preferred models are frankly and unambiguously solipsistic. In *The American Religion* Bloom traces a predominantly gnostic tradition that highlights a form of solipsism, diametrically opposed to the traditional concept of the Biblical prophet:

And the American Religion, for its two centuries of existence, seems to me irretrievably Gnostic. It is a knowing, by and of an uncreated self, or self-within-the-self, and the knowledge leads to freedom, a dangerous and doom-eager freedom: from nature, time, history, community, other selves. (49)

My readings of Walker and Baldwin analyze their respective strategies of self-estrangement as fictional variations on gnostic paradigms. In his seminal book *The Gnostic Religion,* Hans Jonas cites the wide array of gnostic allegories. Particularly pertinent to my narrative of pilgrims and strangers in American prophetic tradition is the Valentinian tale of the captive spark awakened by a call of an alien stranger. The call reveals to the spark her estrangement in the world of deceiving matter, and her true origin in the Absolute.[56]

For Bloom, reducing the historical self to a mere shadow and responding to the gnostic stranger is tantamount to self-deification:

"What works and is" is the stranger god, or even alien god, within. . . . Self-reliance, in Emerson as . . . in Valentinus the Gnostic, is the religion that celebrates and reveres . . . a whatness which from the perspective of religious orthodoxy can only be the primal Abyss.[57]

Thus, what orthodox Christians dread as the "primal Abyss," neo-gnostic elusive subjects desire as their own alienated divinity.

Surprisingly, Bloom does not relate to African-American adaptations of gnostic allegory. He does not include in his canon of gnostic American prophets any African-American reversal of Christian estrangement tales into occasions of metaphysical rebellion against Jehovah and His word. My sense is that Bloom's theory would benefit by extending the American corpus in which traces of gnostic prophetism may be found. My analyses of Baldwin and Walker amplify Bloom's models of American Gnosticism to include features which Bloom's confinement to a white corpus neglects. My claim is that Baldwin and Walker find in the different schools of gnostic heresy, rather than in variants of orthodox religious discourse, appropriate strategies for constructing/deconstructing their elusive prophetic selfhoods. I will show that Baldwin and Walker resist the official prophetic tradition of oppressing white institutions, by deploying time-honored gnostic heretical strategies of subversion. What Gnostics wanted to subvert more than anything else was the anxiety of guilt. Not surprisingly therefore, there are no moral Jeremiads in this tradition.

VII

Such a radically amoral and anti-moral model cannot exhaust the complexities of the prophetic selfhood in Walker and Baldwin, nor, for that matter, in Updike, Paley, and O'Connor. All five writers have preserved the old-fashioned Jewish and Christian prophetic sense of right and wrong, and the prophetic pursuit of justice for all members of the community. For Protestant (Updike) and Catholic (O'Connor) writers in particular, a prophetic anxiety of guilt is painfully pronounced. The models of Bloom, Cavell, and Bercovitch do not address the anxieties of guilt haunting such twentieth-century American readers and writers. I therefore found indispensable in this respect the works of the Protestant theologian and philosopher Karl Barth and the Jewish theologian and philosopher Emmanuel Levinas. Each in his own way analyzes modern anxiety in terms of a breakdown or crisis of selfhood, which unconsciously revives the anxieties of guilt and judgment suffered by prophetic subjects.

Each theologian reads the crisis of disintegrating subjectivity that followed in the wake of Holocaust history, as overtures to religious awakening and rebirth. An individual must lose his/her certainties of historical or narrative identity in order to find the uncertainty of self-under-judgment and grace. Theologically regarded, the breakdown of subjectivity is at once a sign and a symptom of the breaking-in of divinity.[58]

For Updike and O'Connor, no Christian philosopher defines the theological gain in losing historical self-assurance more clearly than Karl Barth.[59] Each self-professed Christian writer, in his or her way, evokes Barthian models in constructing their respective versions of guilt-shattered American selfhood. It therefore seems imperative to offer a somewhat lengthy quotation from Barth, in which the main elements of his Crisis Theology and psychology, and their Scriptural origin, are compressed:

> By faith we are what we are not. Faith is the predicate of which the new man is the subject. Projected into the midst of human life, the new man seems no more than a void, his "passionate motions of eternity" (Kierke-gaard) are invisible. Seen from the human side, he is incomprehensible, a mere negation; and yet it is this which marks him for what he is. He is the zero point between two branches of a hyperbola stretching to infinity; and being this he is in unimaginable fashion both end and beginning. The new subject, being that which is radically and absolutely

'other' must therefore be contrasted with what I am. It is in fact what I am not.[60]

Like Bloom's Transcendentalists, Barth's prophetic subject represents new subjectivity as being born of the symbolic death of "what I am." As newborn subject, I am what I am not. Yet Barth's radically elusive new self shatters the pretensions of a Promethean or titanic self. The "titanic element [in] . . . human consciousness," Barth claims, is "subjected to the destructive judgement of God" (*Romans*, 483). The effect of divine "inbreaking" with its correlative breakdown of historical selfhood and its Promethean pretensions is an experience of being cut through vertically, from an infinitely transcendent and invisible gaze which knows me otherwise than I, delusively, know myself. This transcendent gaze

> cuts down vertically from above through every particular human status.
> . . . The historical framework is broken through . . . [at] the invisible
> point of observation. . . . The judgement exercised by my infinite upon
> my finite existence . . . set beyond time, beyond visibility, beyond all fi-
> nite and concrete events of my life. . . . A point outside that identity from
> which I may know myself, or rather from which I may be known. (*Ro-
> mans*, 139, 198)

Barth's dynamics of crisis and judgment, whereby Promethean identity is reduced to nothing and an other, strange, new self is born, will be further examined in my chapters on John Updike and Flannery O'Connor. Both these Christian writers construct and deconstruct elusive characters along Barthian lines of breakdown and breakthrough. They reduce sublimely elusive American subjects to zero, and thereby produce a "point outside identity," where the selves of writers and readers find their sense of American selfhood put in question.

For purposes of the present introduction suffice it to observe once again that a subject in question is not necessarily nothing. Whether we read identity crises and collapses as "death of the subject," or as rebirth of prophetic subject called to respond to judgment, depends on the theoretical lenses through which we are reading.

VIII

Whereas Christian writers invite us to read through New Testament lenses when confronted by breaks in narrative identity, Jewish writers invite us to read through Old Testament lenses. For example, discussing the conflict between Sara and her father, Reb Smolinski, in Anzia Yezierska's *Bread Givers*, Walter Benn Michaels cites a passage which refers to the assimilation-resisting father as "an ancient prophet that [has] just stepped out of the Bible."[61] Politically interpreted, the prophetic reference in Yezierska seems insignificant. But read as encoding a conflict of rival prophetic identity-models, the passage, I believe, also suggests that old Jewish models of prophetic selfhood cannot easily be assimilated to new American ones.

I chose the father-daughter and parent-child description in Grace Paley's stories as a test case for examining alternative ways to interpret the resistance of Jewish parents' generation to assimilation. Political or multicultural readings of Paley's tales of generational conflicts suggest that the older generation is barred from the conversations of the younger by their linguistic heritage and its ideological luggage. But I hope to show in my chapter on Paley that in her stories the old Jewish model of prophetic faith refuses to dissolve its difference from the New American Promethean model. My reading will add that Paley stages an irreconcilable argument between traditional scriptural prophetic voices and the official voice of Promethean prophetism. In other words I agree with Paley's critics that the "Jewish" affiliation of her characters is cultural, linguistic rather than religious.[62] But beyond her multicultural dialogic techniques, Paley can also be read as a seismograph of cultural exile due to religious and ethical incompatibilities between the self-for-other of old Jewish prophets, and the self-for-self of new (politically motivated) prophets.

In stories where she invokes scriptural intertexts, Paley does not dissolve the differences between the diverse models of prophetic ideology and identity-construction available in her complex American and European heritage. Emerson, as Bercovitch has shown, dissolves the differences between Promethean and Puritan models of prophetic identity. By contrast, Paley sharpens differences. Whereas the different models melt into a single voice in Emerson, in Paley the voices are sorted out, and the "argument" between them is polarized. By staging dialogues among speakers from different generations, language systems, races, and genders, Paley does more than admit manifold voices to a synchronic, contemporary, multicultural conversation. In "Faith In the Afternoon,"[63] for example, the protagonist, Faith, crosses synchronic multicultural lines comfortably and without feeling that her ideology and identity are broken down.

But when she crosses generational lines, Faith's sense of ideological identity is put in question. In another story, "Enormous Changes At the Last Minute," Alexandra's avant-garde lover traces the origin of his pop-poetry to the Bible and declaims it in an "enraged prophetic voice." (*Collected Stories*, 218). I feel tempted to ask, scriptural or prophetic according to what model? Bloom's model of the Promethean sublime might permit a one-word poem on the theme of "I! I! I!" (*Collected Stories*, 216), to pose as prophetic. But Alexandra herself has her doubts, and reads by other categories. She would probably be more comfortable with the love poetry Paley attributes to one of her elderly Jewish characters, Faith's father (*Collected Stories*, 158), although avant-garde poet-prophets would dismiss it as incompatible with American newness. On the other hand, when Faith's Jewish interlocutors—her parents or their acquaintances—mumble fragments of Jewish imperatives, such as "don't be selfish," "don't argue with your father," "care for your children," Faith's response is split. On the one hand her Jewish breeding prompts her spontaneous obedience. On the other hand, her American education makes her feel critical of and distant from her old-fashioned parents. Either way, whether the prophetic status is claimed by a young avant-garde, pop-Promethean, or whether prophetic commands are declaimed by old-fashioned Jewish parents, the differences between the two prophetic voices cannot be dissolved in Paley's stories. One represses the other, and the alienation of old and new is beyond reconciliation.

Jewish parents are excluded from contemporary conversations and resist assimilation into new American culture, not only because they are immigrants who have not mastered the language. Their Jewish code of filial obedience, for example, is incompatible with Promethean American cult of filial disobedience. Their Jewish code of respect for the past is incompatible with the characteristically Promethean American anxiety of influence. The voice of the old and the voice of the new, which blend so easily in Emerson, according to Bercovitch, are replaced in Paley by a sharp separation of voices. The answer to the question of what constitutes prophetic ideology and identity is radically split between two positions that her fictional dialogues represent as mutually exclusive. In Paley's stories, such as "Faith In the Afternoon" and "Dreamer in a Dead Language," old Jews are outsiders not only because they are unassimilated and speak English "with an accent." They are also outsiders because they reminisce about the Old World, and cling to its alien ideologies. For help in conceptualizing the irresolvable differences between scriptural and Promethean models of prophetic selfhood in Paley, I turn to Emmanuel Levinas.

In *Beyond the Verse, In the Time of the Nations*, and *Outside the Subject*, Levinas argues that Jews are reviled and resented by their non-Jewish host-cultures because Jews are aliens in ethical principle and not only by political and historical mishap.[64] Levinas explains xenophobic anti-Semitism as a response to Jewish commitment to universal ethical values irrespective of political and national differences.[65] This does not mean that their prophetic faith allows Jews to evade responsibility for the sufferings and injustices of history. On the contrary, their prophetic tradition holds that entrance to the city of justice on the universal level of faith demands passing through the cities of political injustice, on the particular level of history and politics. According to Levinas, their prophetic ethic obliges Jews to serve as willing hostages of history. They are commanded to open their historical selfhood towards their suffering neighbors in the full light of historical visibility.

Barth would read the breaking-in of prophetic vocation as a breaking down of the historical ego entirely, and lifting the shattered subject above history to some invisible point in eternity. By deliberate contrast with Christian models, Levinas represents prophetic self-estrangement as drawing the self out of solipsistic invisibility, and placing the newborn subject squarely face-to-face with concrete historical strangers. Thus called out from self-enclosure by faces of suffering historical strangers, Levinas's prophetic subject is not thereby drowned in history. On the contrary, in *Beyond the Verse* he writes: "We are no longer submerged by events, we . . . enter into an order where the other man is finally visible."[66] This prophetically enjoined responsibility towards our fellow human beings, be they ever so alien, Levinas wryly notes, is "a strange and uncomfortable privilege" (*Beyond*, 198).

Paley's Jewish characters are neither isolated from history in some invisible solipsistic asylum, nor, conversely, are they so buried in history that they lack the distance from which to judge and grieve over it. Exiled to Jewish old-age homes, on the margins of contemporary American culture, the old people's distance could be described, borrowing Levinas' categories, as diachronic. In drawing distinctions between his own ethics of dialogue and the philosophies of dialogue in Buber and Gabriel Marcel, Levinas says that for traditional Jews the *dia-* in dialogue is *dia-* in diachrony.[67]

Levinas's self-for-other is not on the same conversational plane with his/her human or divine interlocutor. Still less are the dynamics between word and hearer reducible to the structure of an interior dialogue: "It is not the internal speech of the well-known dialogue of the soul with itself, doors and windows closed." It is, rather, "the original diachrony of time."[68] In relation to the unapproachable anteriority of ethical commands, Levinas's prophetically-summoned subject is practically dragged to judgment without choice or appeal. In *Beyond the Verse*, Levinas writes:

> But in the responsibility for others—the subject, the self—I am summoned to appear rather than simply appearing, replying to a subpoena that cannot be declined and seizes me precisely in my non-interchangeable identity by calling to me. . . . This anteriority of responsibility must be understood in relation to freedom as the very authority of the absolute . . . [as] a pure "susceptibility"; an obligation to answer preceding any questioning. . . . [O]bedience precedes the order that has furtively infiltrated the soul that obeys. [The subpoenaed self] is seized by "a traumatizing" order coming from a past that was never present, since my responsibility is answerable to the freedom of others. (127–28)

In diachronic relations the other is not an equal interlocutor but an absolute authority whose "subpoena" I am not free to resist: "l'absolument Autre c'est Autrui."[69] Nothing can be stranger and more shattering to a Promethean or imperialist subject than being obliged to obey, in advance, the call of another, Levinas repeatedly maintains.[70]

Precisely for this reason, he claims, Jewish prophetic faith extends hope of relief from the prison-house of tragic self-enclosure. Levinas's subpoenaed self is liberated from the bondage of "metaethical tragic man" (*In the Time*, 152), simply by taking the absolute authority of human others for granted.

Levinas recruits "the feminine" in the relentless war he wages against the imperial subject of Western philosophy. The function of femininity, Levinas claims, makes gender itself a further category of ethically beneficial self-estrangement. This function is to release the self from its narcissistic shadow (or giant as Emerson would call it).[71] The task of the feminine "caress of consolation," Levinas writes in "Judaism and the Feminine,"[72] is to break down masculine self-sufficiency and enable feminine gentleness, compassion, and loving-kindness to break through.

Levinas claims that a woman's caress can release virile, imperial subjects from the tragedy of self-enclosure:

> [T]he plane of *eros* allows us to see that the other par excellence is the feminine. . . . [Feminine duration] resolves the tragic involved in being. . . . The enchainment to oneself is the impossibility of getting rid of oneself. . . . The hero is overwhelmed by himself. Therein lies what is tragic in him.[73]

Levinas's feminine redeemer transports the self "elsewhere by the movement of a caress." This consoling caress "can only come from elsewhere, while everything in the subject is here. . . . This alterity comes to me only from the other."[74]

In "Judaism and the Feminine," the name of the liberating caress is not alterity. Her "name is woman":

> To light eyes that are blind, to . . . overcome an alienation which ultimately results from the very virility of . . . the all conquering *logos* . . . should be the ontological function of the feminine, the vocation of the one 'who does not conquer.' Woman does not simply come to someone deprived of companionship to keep him company. She answers to a solitude inside this privation.[75]

I will not deal with the question of Paley's feminist affiliation. My topic being the prophetic tradition, I will focus on the analogies between Paley's stories of Jewish responsiveness to strangers in need and Levinas's definition of prophetic subjectivity as a self open to the stranger at the core of its identity.

In Paley, as in Levinas, obeying the command, "love the stranger as thyself!", and answering the call of strangers before you are even called, is the practice of any ethical subject, regardless of gender. It is not only Paley's female character, Faith, who listens to strangers regardless of their strangeness, or perhaps because of it. In Paley's story "Zagrowsky Tells," an old Jewish father more strangely still adopts a colored[76] child born to his mentally disturbed daughter. In this often discussed story,[77] Paley tells a twice-told tale of mutual estrangement. On the political and multicultural level, she tells a tale of ethnic rivalry and enmity among what Scripture would call enemy-brothers. On the prophetic level she tells a tale of an elderly Jewish person's response to the appeal of an estranged child.

On the political plane of ethnic rivalry, Zagrowsky is not unjustly charged with racism. On the same plane, his Jewish wife is abused by an African-American, who refuses to answer her call for help, because his race has been made to suffer more than hers.[78] But on the other level, mysteriously seized by what Levinas would call a command from elsewhere, Zagrowsky subverts and inverts his potentially tragic self into a prophetically subpoenaed self-for-other. Why? readers have frequently asked. The Old Testament names (Esau, Emanuel) that Zagrowsky invokes hint at the Jewish tradition behind his response to the silent appeal of a "brown baby. . . . A perfect stranger" (361).

Paley's Romantic American heritage[79] may account for Faith's mishearing of Zagrowsky's reference to "Isaac's other son"—"It was Abraham, she interrupted" (*Collected Stories*, 359). Influenced by a non-Jewish intellectual climate, Faith is more familiar with tales of Isaac and Ishmael than tales of Jacob and Esau. An American reader's acquired literary instincts would prompt her to recall "Call me Ishmael." But Zagrowsky is heir to an older, less familiar cultural tradition. His cultivated instincts to adopt a stranger date from older prophetic writings to which Faith could hardly have had access. The Old Testament and Talmudic commandment "love the stranger!", Levinas informs us, is grounded in Talmudic interpretations of scriptural texts. One exemplary tale whose interpretation he cites is the story of Jacob and Esau's rivalry being transformed into fraternity in the ethical sense. From this tale the Talmud draws the corollary that the Jewish people must treat as fraternal neighbors the nation of Edom whom Esau fathered.[80] Framed by this Jewish prophetic intertext, Zagrowsky's act seems less strange and unreadable than it appears to Faith and her friends.

Levinas's reading of Isaiah's prophesies about peace with the nations of the worlds, even with Rome, make less baffling Paley's choice of Emanuel for the adopted grandson's name. In Christian Scriptural hermeneutics Isaiah's prophetic promise concerning Immanuel (Isaiah 7:14) prefigures the Christian Messiah. In Jewish interpretations of prophetic texts, Levinas writes, the times of the Messiah will differ from the times of secular history only in two, at once political and ethical, respects. First, the order of war among enemy nations will be replaced by peace, a peace of universal brotherhood grounded in mutual recognition of the human as human. Secondly, universal democracy will grant each individual the absolute right to his or her unique difference for reasons that were prophetic and ethical long before they became politically and legally instituted.[81]

"Can democracy and the 'rights of man' divorce themselves without danger from their prophetic and ethical depths?", Levinas asks in *Beyond the Verse* (xv). When those universalist "prophetic ethical depths" are repressed by reductive political readings, can nonallergic exposure to the other's radical strangeness honor his or her absolute claim to my prompt response "Here I am!"? Making Samuel's "Here I am" (I Samuel 3:4) the linchpin of prophetic subjectivity, Levinas maintains that "Who am I?" is not the ethical question, nor for that matter is "Who is it that I ain't?"[82] In prophetic ethics the problem of identity is not framed as a question to which there may be no answer. Rather, it is framed as a call to which answering is obeying, caring, and responding. It is as subpoenaed by the other that one's ethical identity is what it is.

Unlike Ricoeur,[83] Levinas does not say in his words that answering a question is one thing, responding to a call is another. Instead he cites and interprets Amos:

"The Lord God has spoken; who can but prophesy?" The reading of the prophetic text is still to a certain extent prophetic, even if all human beings are not open with the same attentiveness and the same sincerity to the Word which speaks in them. And who, nowadays, embraces tradition? (*Beyond*, xiii–xiv)

Levinas observes that the traditional "who" of prophetic calling is as subject to dissemination, polysemy, and infinite opening, as the "who" of postmodern theories of subject construction and deconstruction. In "The Rights of Man and the Rights of the Other" he cites again a Talmudic Midrash rather than speak in philosophical concepts:

The rights of man manifest the uniqueness or the absolute of the person, despite his or her subsumption under the category of the human species, or because of that subsumption. This is the paradox, or mystery, or novelty of the human in being. . . . It [is] suggested by a remarkable talmudic [sic] apologue, which I quote: "Behold man, who strikes coins with the same die and gets coins all alike; but behold the King of kings, the Holy-Blessed-Be-He, who strikes all men with the die of Adam and not one is the same as another. That is why each is obliged to say: The world was created for me!"[84]

IX

Most American readers who trace the elusive American self to prophetic origins seek a master narrative—Christian, skeptic, gnostic,

Romantic. By contrast, contemporary American fictions produce polysemous, polyvocal, doubled-layered imaginary worlds inhabited by double and divided characters. On the political-historical layer of these fictions, many different voices ask "Who am I?" and offer many competing answers. On the ethical prophetic layer, the stranger encountered is diversely described, depending on religious intertexts to which the writer alludes.

In tracing a polyvocal discourse of prophetic ethics, transmitted from Old Americanist to New Americanist dramas of self-fading, my aim is not to offer one more master narrative. On the contrary, my foregoing analysis argues that the diachronic depths of American fiction feature their own polysemic pluralism. In the following chapters I show that the fiction of Updike, O'Connor, Paley, Baldwin, and Walker has absorbed a diversity of prophetic modes from a diversity of religious and philosophical sources. Rather than being reducible to one or another dominant mode (Christian, Jewish, Gnostic), the character of American thought and its fictional correlatives is a dynamic among them all. This dynamic involves conflict as well as reciprocity, and always invites new reader responses.

2

John Updike's Postmodern Apocalypse at Midpoint: Bloom's Giants and Their Barthian Double

To seem a creature, to subdue / my giant solipsism to a common scale.
—John Updike, *Midpoint and Other Poems*

I

Why do readers of John Updike frequently dismiss him as "a gifted stylist with little to say"?[1] If he has anything to say, why so quietly as to be almost inaudible? The following chapter examines whether the break of communication between Updike and academic critics is the fault of the writer, or perhaps of readers not attuned to hear Updike's quiet message. What anticipations of readers does Updike expect to disappoint even at the cost of being misread?

The following analysis suggests that Updike invites misreadings by writing against the grain of two paradigms of prophetic rhetoric examined in the previous chapter. One is the paradigm of the prophetic sublime, introduced by Bloom; the other is the paradigm of collective prophetic selfhood introduced by Bercovitch. Bloom rightly claims that "the American Sublime will never touch [Updike's] pages," despite his religious "mewings."[2] Bercovitch might remark that Americanus and his auto-machias are conspicuously absent from Updike, whatever errand in the wilderness his protagonists or narrators might undertake. If Updike belongs in the prophetic tradition, as he repeatedly hints,[3] his cultural precursors are neither Bloom's prototypes nor Bercovitch's. Rather, his theology of Cross and Crisis sends him across the Atlantic to Kierkegaard and Barth.[4] His figures are highly complex hybrids of American models he criticizes, and European models which he transplants to American cultural soil.

41

American culture, as Matthiessen aptly defined it, is as much heir to Renaissance Humanism as to primitive Christian faith. American Protestantism in general, and Puritanism in particular, did not preach self-despair and self-annihilation. On the contrary, from John Cotton, through Jonathan Edwards, to Tillich and Niebuhr, it has shared the Renaissance humanistic view of a self-confident, God-reliant, God-supported subjectivity. This is conspicuous in Puritan prophetic histories—secular chronicles, read, written, and rewritten from a theological perspective. These texts, as Bercovitch shows, are sagas of the communal errand into the wilderness, undertaken by heroically suffering saints and their legendary ministers.[5]

Updike seems to object to such an interpretation of God-reliance, which exalts human beings instead of reducing them to nothingness. His texts, though equally prophetic histories, debunk and parody, rather than praise, the delusions of grandeur of self-reliant Americans. Not even Jonathan Edwards's "Sinners in the Hands of an Angry God" can provide Updike with a satisfactory, indigenous-American model for a prophetic call to awakening. Edwards's implied addressees are as self-confident as their spiritual descendent Emerson would be; as certain that God's light is in their conscience, and that their righteous self-reliance is God-reliance. Not for them the Lutheran grace that abounds only for those penitent and confessed sinners, whose "self-criticism," Karl Barth asserts, leaves "no hope of covering the conscience up and lulling it to sleep."[6] Nor is this promise of grace sought by Updike's fictional characters who, as grotesque parodies of Puritan history-making-ministers, prefer despair to grace and happy self-ignorance to tormenting self-examination. They embody the collective self of a community of self-confident hedonists, in passionate pursuit of pleasure and pleasant oblivion.[7]

Updike repeatedly argues that the God-reliance on which Puritan ethics were postulated in the seventeenth and eighteenth centuries, was the same God-reliance on which the great criminals of Rimbaud and Nietzsche were postulated in the nineteenth century, and on which Fascist and Nazi horrors were perpetrated in the twentieth century.[8] Concurring with Karl Barth, to whom he frequently appeals, Updike maintains that humanist-Protestant self-confidence is a stance that renders ethics impossible. Barth openly challenges liberal Protestantism, claiming that "there is no way from us to God— not even a via negativa—not even a via dialectica nor paradoxa. The god who stood at the end of some human way . . . would not be

God."[9] Against the humanistic notion of divine selfhood he rejects, Barth sets his concept of "God's pilgrim," whose model is "the great frontier crossing of Jesus." He advocates a "pilgrim theology that would cut right across all existing theological possibilities, right, left and center."[10] In a similar vein, contrasting Barth with Tillich, Updike criticizes liberal Protestantism, underpinning "the ambiguity, even futility" of Tillich's faith: "Terms like 'grace' and 'Will of God' walk . . . as bloodless ghosts, transparent against the milky background of 'beyond' and 'being' that Tillich, God forbid, would confuse with the Christian faith."[11]

Updike's prophetic model is inspired by Barth's confessional Lutheranism, which requires a negativity-bound self-knowledge that no American model offers.[12] Thus he cites Barth's prophecy of darkness, doubt, and abysmal self-despair: "The only part of our assertion of which we are *certain,* the only part we can *prove,* is that man is negatived, negated" (*Assorted Prose,* 219). With Barth's help Updike assaults three aspects of human narcissism. Barth would dismiss human pride of language with the question: "How can human utterance carry an irresistible and compelling meaning?" For the human pride of genius and creativity, Barth has nothing but scorn. The only creativity belongs to God: "The impassable frontier of death . . . is the boundary that separates and must separate . . . Creator from creation, the Holy One from sinners, the heavenly idea of the good from its . . . infinitely imperfect appearances." As for the heart of American cultural narcissism, namely titanism, Barth's denunciation is in the language of St. Paul's attacks against the inflated egos of his own time:

> It will always be necessary to tell the man who is puffed up by his culture his want of it, who in his morality or religiosity reaches toward heaven like a Titan, that he must . . . go from less to less, that he must learn to become small, to become nothing, that he must die.[13]

Barth had as his target for criticism a German audience who had witnessed the horrors of Fascist and Nazi titanism. Updike, by radical contrast, faces an audience of American individualists and/or exhibitionists, for whom human grandeur and sublimity remain a dream rather than a historical nightmare.

For the most eloquent celebration of giantism one may refer to Bloom's invaluable chapter on the American Sublime, in *Poetry and Repression.*[14] Bloom reads Emerson as the seer, namer, and prophet of the American Sublime, who "founds his Sublime upon a refusal of . . . literary history," and shows its distinction to be selfhood as "[n]ot merely rebirth, but the even more hyperbolic trope of self-begetting."[15] The Emersonian hyperbole Bloom foregrounds is the "giant" by whom Emersonian subjects are shadowed. "My giant," Emerson asserts, "goes with me wherever I go."[16] Bloom regards the giant figure not as a passing trope but as a central topos of American religion which he traces persuasively from Emerson to Whitman and then to Stevens. He attaches central importance to Whitman's passing observation that Emerson is the father of American giantism: "The best part of Emersonianism is, it breeds the giant that destroys itself."[17]

Updike agrees with Bloom that the giant who goes with Americans wherever they go is a key figure in the Emersonian prophetic paradigm. Unlike Bloom, he comes to bury this giant not to praise it; He buries the hyperbolic self on whom Promethean prophetic selfhood relies, and with it the Sublime as an aesthetic category for the grandeur of the Emersonian self. Unlike Barth, however, precisely because he is a Protestant on American soil, Updike never relinquishes the self-responsibility of the isolated subject. Nor does he require, let alone accomplish, the consummation of Christian life required by Barth, namely the total negation which only God can accomplish. One might add that Updike is not a theologian but an artist who, like Whitman, at best credits God with half his poetic creation and not with the very power of creativity. In his poetry and prose, therefore, Updike vacillates in a perpetual midpoint between the confidence of a self-reliant creator and the self-criticism of a Lutheran, crushed by the negating presence of an absent God.

As an American artist, Updike can renounce neither his aesthetic stance nor his sense of independent, creative selfhood. Therefore, he cannot fully endorse Barth's model of Christian prophet.[18] Instead, his dual voice constructs a confessional mode which shows that his poetics of subjectivity is neither fully Promethean nor Barthian. On the one hand, he criticizes with great irony the narcissistic existence of his characters and implied readers who refuse to examine themselves, let alone confess and expiate their frailties. On the other hand he portrays, with irony verging on revulsion, the incomplete process of his own personal awakening to reduced selfhood. While Updike subjects himself to minute self-examination, he can accept only halfheartedly his creaturely stance, and therefore can never repent and attain the final stage of the Barthian prophetic self. His voice forever stammers.

Between Barth and Bloom, Updike's aesthetics and ethics present a much more complex and paradoxical structure than critics have hitherto remarked. Neither sublime nor sordid, rather tempted by a giant on the one hand, yet committed to diminishing it on the other, Updike's self-contradictory confessions stutter in a double-coded voice. The purpose of the following analysis is to expose these dualities, not to explain them away.

Throughout his work Updike obeys opposite imperatives. To the Emersonian imperative "Obey thyself. That which shows God in me fortifies me. That which shows God out of me, makes me a wart and a wen,"[19] Updike counterpoints Barth's imperative, that "a drowning man cannot pull himself out by his own hair."[20] The effect of this double-coded, ethically, and aesthetically stammering voice is what deconstructionists would call undecidability and indeterminacy. No more than Updike himself, wavering between two models, are Updike's readers permitted to terminate the wavering of the two voices in his texts.

II

Perhaps the most accessible and self-reflexive example of the self-deconstructing models Updike fashions is one of his later stories, "Cruise,"[21] in which American tourists are paradoxically described now as giant-haunted God-like megalomaniacs, and now, more implausibly, as pilgrims. The narrative relates the itinerary of a cruise more in time than in space, to the sanctuaries of Greek and Roman giantism so famous in the annals of the American Renaissance. The pleasure-seeking protagonist Neuman (New Man), whom Updike casts as an American Everyman, was seduced by a voyage "marketed as a duplicate of the tortuous homeward voyage of Ulysses" (290).

The deconstructing intention of the implied author is flaunted quite openly by the observation that the pleasure seekers were entertained by lectures on deconstruction and feminism (291). Missing their target, the consumers of the "wry verbal deconstructionism," perhaps like Updike's readers, never dream that the shafts of deconstructing irony are aimed at their own American fantasies of self-deification. On the contrary, a nymphomaniac gorgon, or Calypso, seduces Neuman to oblivion precisely with the promise of divinity and eternal life: "*Aiae, aiae!* We are as gods. . . . Stay with me then and I'll make you divine. . . . With me you will be eternally youthful and never die" (291, 303). Only in Neuman's response does the discourse itself introduce what a Barthian witness would have to say of vain titanism. Neuman's words are a far cry from the Lutheran hyperboles Barth introduces at points of crossing the frontier between the human and the divine. A Barthian penitent would say, with God's grace, that he is nothing. More ironically and less humbly, Neuman is permitted to comment: "I am a mere man. Only gods and animals can withstand the monotony of eternity, however, paradisiacal" (303).

Bloom is therefore right to observe that the sublime in Updike is treated with churchwardenly mewings. Unlike Bloom, however, I find this a tribute to the complexity of Updike's art rather than a detraction. Though generally dismissive of Updike's discourse, critics seem to discard its complexities for opposite reasons. While for Bloom he is not sublime enough, for Vidal, his characters over-indulge in self-sublimation and therefore fail to pursue the path of self-examination. Actually each of these critics has perceived one of the two voices in Updike's contrapuntal text. Neither one credits him with counterpointed voice.[22]

Updike himself encourages and anticipates a split and dual reader response. One possible reading will cater to the oblivious Promethean prophetic paradigm. But the other, less likely response, will prompt an awakening to the Barthian reality of human vanity, if not nothingness. "Perhaps there are two kinds of people," Updike reflects in his memoirs, "those for whom nothingness is no problem, and those for whom it is an insuperable problem."[23]

Updike's novels invite one type of reader to enter "a world without guilt, one in which nobody makes a mistake." With an opposite, almost silently ironical voice, and for a less insouciant reader, Updike hardly pays relaxed guiltless dreamers the compliment of sublimity. Rather, he comments, they are "human lives that offer those who live them no alternatives and therefore pass as sheer glossy spectacle, like the existences of animals" (*Odd Jobs*, 356–57). To repeat, it is not the self-responsible self that Updike dismisses or deflates to animal stature, but only the lack of consciousness which self-inflated human beings share with animals.

The twofold focus of the narrative strategy, and the split portrait of the reader, occasionally responds to the split in the writer himself. Updike introduces this division between his grand "public, marketable self" and the shrunken "me" he fears the readership "is not understanding," since it is communicated in a language of illegible signs (*Self-Consciousness*, 250–51). Like the narrator in "Still Life,"[24] Updike fears he relates to his interlocutor by "exchanging, across a distance wider than it seemed, miscalculated signs." His divided voice, I believe, eludes critics and may account in part for (mis)readings which detect in his fiction "only the outside of things, the shell of the corporate existence we all have in being twentieth-century Americans."[25]

Critics overlook the distinction Updike frequently draws between the subjectivity inhabiting the glossy surface of American existence, and a more complex one, to which he directs his ideal reader: "To be a person is to be in a situation of tension . . . in a dialectical situation. A truly adjusted person is not a person at all, just an animal with clothes on or a statistic" (*Conversations*, 34).

Characteristically, he describes one of his most celebrated all-American characters—the protagonist of the Rabbit tetralogy—as "rejoining his animal self. Animals run without thinking, and he is for the moment free of all these bothersome moral worries" (*Conversations*, 224). Emerson's gigantic prophetic selfhood transformed to Rabbit's animal bathos represents Updike's recasting, ironically rather than reverently, the precursor whom Whitman held as "the giant that destroys itself." "Is not the self, as understood in the United States of the 'me decade'," Updike asks, "a precarious and luxurious invention?"[26] Elsewhere he replies to this rhetorical question by observing that the American Sublime could have been invented exclusively by "exultant egoism which only an American could have voiced" (*Hugging*, 109). Bloom defines the poetics of sublimity as an art of repressing the precursor. Ironically, Updike turns this definition against Bloom's giant, by his poetics of repressing sublime precursors, and reducing their ideology to a "doctrine of righteous selfishness" (*Odd Jobs*, 159). Further deflation is condensed in the definition of prophetic Sublime offered in Updike's essay "Whitman's Egotheism," as a "hunt . . . for power, the means to power is authenticity, and authenticity begins with the brute self" (*Hugging*, 107). In his essay on Emerson, Updike likewise piles up unflattering epithets such as "insouciance," and "reckless relaxation," so as to leave no doubt in the alert reader's mind that if the sublime does not touch Updike, it is not by chance (*Odd Jobs*, 161). Further deflations are explicit in statements such as "Emerson's great discovery, amid the ruins of the Puritan creed, was the art of relaxation and of doing what you wanted" (*Odd Jobs*, 159). In case the reader does not appreciate his de-sublimating meaning, Updike spells it out by observing that Emerson's innocence and disengagement constitute a "preparation for the notorious loneliness and callousness and violence of American life" (*Odd Jobs*, 162).

He stresses the need to repress, rather than re-express, the sublime theme of American poetics of prophecy, which has induced his characters' callousness:

> The writer's strength is not his own. . . . Beginning with the wish to make an impression, one ends in wishing to erase the impression . . . to make of oneself a point of focus purely, as selfless as a lens. (*Picked Up Pieces*, 54)

He explodes "giantism" as outdated and culture-specific, generated by the self-inflating geographical and sociological conditions in early nineteenth-century American frontier fantasy. In the twentieth century, he claims, the industrial and urban revolutions disproved this fantasy as, at least, a historical anachronism:

> By mid-nineteenth century the creed of American individualism was ascendent; the communal conscience of the Puritan villagers lay far behind and the cruel personal diminishments of industrialism were yet to be sharply felt. Our political institutions and our still vast unexploited territories permitted the enterprising individual an illusion of unlimited importance and sublime potential scarcely tasted since the Garden of Eden. Whitman developed a religious philosophy out of this geographical fact. (*Hugging*, 109–10)

Dismissing "giantism" as an anachronism is easier said than done, particularly for children of two World Wars beset by anxieties of death, violence, and cosmic catastrophe. Updike is fully aware of the appeal the American religion of self-confidence has, particularly at a period whose history encourages self-despair. As an American addressing Americans, he cannot follow the example of Karl Barth, and simply make the catastrophes of our time an occasion for sermons on human nothingness, creatureliness, and absolute God-reliance. Instead, he designs narratives which permit his protagonists to reach the edge of annihilation-anxiety, and then recoil from it into a stance of self-deifying self-confidence—a dual narrative of Bloom's titanism and Barth's penitent confessor.

In "Pigeon Feathers," to take an early example, the protagonist,

David, a young boy living among "giant pines" and haunted by frames of "gigantic cinder moons" of imagination, experiences a moment of horror—an "invitation to dread"—for which no brand of American religion can offer him consolation.[27] David stands for a brief moment at the Barthian point of crisis, aware for the first time of death as an experience of his creaturely existence: "Without warning David was visited by an exact vision of death: a long hole in the ground, no wider than your body, down which you are drawn while the white faces above recede" (88). The clergyman to whom David turns for guidance does not encourage Barthian self-criticism as a move towards the frontier crossing. Rather, he reiterates the affirmations of liberal theology: "David, you might think of Heaven this way: as the way the goodness Abraham Lincoln did lived after him" (95). David's mother likewise offers affirmations as an Emersonian nature enthusiast, for whom it is enough to know that "God has given us this wonderful April day" (97). The humanistic approach of the minister, expressed with "a coward's firmness," is more daringly and wholeheartedly voiced by the mother's affirmation that man is God's creator; to David's agonized question: "Then who made Him?", she replies happily: "Why, Man, Man" (97).

In "Pigeon Feathers" Updike deploys two strategies in his simultaneous narrative construction and deconstruction of empirical selfhood, which both liberal Protestants and Romantic Emersonians offer the protagonist as consolation. The mother is silenced in a brief catechism-like dialogue which resonates with Barth's observation that "The god who stood at the end of some human way . . . would not be God" (*The Word of God*, 204). Told that man is God's creator, David's answer is "that amounts to saying there is none." So much for liberal Protestantism. As for the Godlike human creator fashioned by Emerson, Updike's deconstruction is staged in an action required of David by his nature-loving mother. On the literal level, the mother, who is also a pragmatist, wants the pigeons who infest nature destroyed, and picks on her son as the obvious agent of destruction. To brace himself for the act David casts himself in the role of a human Maker and Master. His act of self-glorifying making is consummated in a gory massacre of pigeons, which does not bury "Caesar" but certainly diminishes him:

> Standing in the center of the floor, fully master now, disdaining to steady the barrel with anything but his arm, he killed two more [pigeons] that way. He felt like a beautiful avenger. . . . He had the sensation of a creator." (103)[28]

It is perhaps no wonder that an ear like Bloom's, attuned to the "in-rush of God in Emerson,"[29] would be deaf to Updike's debunking of that very posture.

In "George and Vivian,"[30] Updike presents a careless and callous American, on a visit to Italy and Ireland with his latest wife. They stop at the house and burial place of the writer D'Annunzio, who was greatly admired by Mussolini. Vivian is dismayed and tormented by the Fascist connection, and the monstrous catastrophes it instinc-tively evokes for her. While George admires the "gigantic centaur" decorating the burial area of D'Annunzio and his male companions, Vivian hates it for being "Nazi shrines." With Promethean uncon-cern George scornfully dismisses her protests, calls her repeatedly to "please relax," and admits to having great fun. He defends his re-laxed enjoyment by claiming that D'Annunzio had nothing to do with Nazism—"he was a poet, a *fin-de-siecle* dandy" who "had a good self-image. That's no crime. That doesn't mean Auschwitz" (173–77).

The portrayal of an American tourist's fascination with D'Annun-zio features a double-barreled satire aimed simultaneously at Ger-man and American giantism. Closely related to this fictional linkage of Fascist and transcendentalist ideology is the link Updike estab-lishes elsewhere between Emerson's "disengagement and distrust of altruism," and "Nietzsche's rapturous celebration of power and do-minion" (*Odd Jobs*, 162–63). More implicit but not less central is Up-dike's critique of the Emersonian self-reliant, imperial ego. Updike seems to castigate, where Emerson praises, the American narcissist who takes his giant with him wherever he goes. Indeed, George is the traveling fool, for whom the Italian landscape is reminiscent "of an American sacred place," and who expects to find in Ireland "America, its language and all its channels" (172, 181). Likewise, the pleasure George derives from the gigantic monster of D'Annun-zio's monument reflects his blithe acceptance of his own giant-self and dandyish "good self-image," which he is too blind to consider as sin, let alone give up.

It is interesting to see in this context a conceptual distinction in the respective use of "dandyism" which Updike and Foucault make when showing the contribution of aesthetic values to self-fashioning. Foucault draws a direct line from the stoic humanist aesthetics of self—the creation of selfhood through writing—to the existential construction of self as a work of art, epitomized in Baudelaire's "dandysme." The dandy "who makes of his body . . . his very existence, a work of art," Foucault adds, is diametrically opposed to "the man who goes off to discover himself . . . and his hidden truth."[31] In "George and Vivian" Updike criticizes Baudelaire's mode of dandyism, as celebrated by the solipsistic American self. Curiously, when he discusses Karl Barth's extreme anti-humanistic view, which presents man not as creator but as a creature, he refers to the theologian's concept of human nature as "Barthian dandyism" (*Self-Consciousness*, 153). The conceptual oxymoron—Barthian dandyism—might be an apt description of Updike's dual portrayal of himself. He is partly an American self, attuned to the demands of his readers who, like the traveling George, see dandyism in Baudelaire's sense. Yet Updike also admits to having a Christian self, afflicted with the sense of nothingness, guilt, and interminable subjection to judgment.

More severely than the American critics who question the ethical validity of Emerson's American Religion, Updike responds with what he describes as an "eerie sensation." He challenges American egotheism by wondering whether any ethics can emerge from a religion for which, as Emerson assumes, "there is no need of struggles, convulsions, and despairs." Updike's constructs of subjectivity polarize into almost schizophrenic conflict the Emersonian ego and the Protestant super-ego, which puts it in question. Emerson celebrates illusions as the space where the self awakens to finds itself confidently surrounded by the gods—"they alone with him alone."[32] By radical contrast, Updike's Protestant self admits to an anxiety of nothingness and unreality—"the fear of the identity being an illusion or being squelched"—and the terrifying discovery that, without God, the awakening self is a mere shadow or phantom.[33]

III

Woe to protagonists and readers who prefer soothing shadows to terrifying reality. In a 1993 interview Updike delineates the theological judgment to which his writing exposes the careless reader:

> I'm not trying to force a message upon the reader, but I am trying to give human behavior theological scrutiny as it's seen from above. . . . [T]o me, [my books] . . . are harsh perhaps, because the standards are otherworldly. I judge, in a way. I see my characters' confusion and rapacity and callousness against some kind of background of ideal behavior

that I suppose is part of my Christian background. . . . If nothing else, you're trying to read lessons in human vanity to your readers. (*Conversations*, 253–59)

Thus presented, Updike concedes, his work resounds with the rhetoric of an Ecclesiastes-like minister or priest (259). A skeptic priest, however, is one thing, and an inspired prophet, by any model, seems quite another. Although he is bent on destroying the Emersonian "giant that destroys itself," as a paradigm of prophetic selfhood, Updike does not replace it, for example, with Cotton Mather's "Americanus" as an alternative paradigm. Unable to "find affinity with the Puritan ethos" (*Conversations*, 94), and unwilling to reinvent its auto-American-biographies, Updike constructs a mode of rhetorical subjectivity that I would rather call confessional than prophetic. Updike's readers, as well as the protagonists with whom readers are expected to identify, are not members of an oppressed, marginal ethnic group. On the contrary, he invites a white, smug, blind majority to recognize with shame and penitence its inflated sense of selfhood, and the reality that it doggedly ignores.[34]

His model for the confessional subject can be reconstructed only indirectly by pursuing Updike's intertextual allusions to Karl Barth's Crisis Theology. From Barth's portraits of Christlike prophets at the frontier of self-annihilation, Updike borrows features of the creaturely self with which he hopes to conquer the giant that haunts American fantasy and historical fact. He is reluctant to use the term "prophetic" explicitly, not because he ignores the Emersonian delusions of grandeur from which American prophetic aesthetics and subjectivity suffer. On the contrary, he is well aware that his readers are secular, ideologically-committed Americans, bound to interpret the term "prophet" as exalted and titanic. Aware of the familiar models of American prophecy, he fears that even in his own day they can empower lunatic self-styled prophets to seduce indoctrinated and hallucinating would-be giants into political acts of mass destruction. In the European background Updike merely hints at the catastrophe emanating from the Romantic prophetic tradition in Germany—from "the Ubermensch to the Supermen of Hitler's master race" (*Odd Jobs*, 162). He is much more concerned with the destructive influence in America of self-ordained prophets, who are responsible for such mass disasters as witnessed in Waco and San Diego. In a recent novel, *In the Beauty of the Lilies*, he draws a parody of the Emersonian giant, a grotesque portrait of a Koresh-like "false prophet" (named Jesse), who is shot to death by a follower, awakened too late to save himself.[35]

How does Barth's paradigm of prophetic subjectivity serve Updike's attempt to deflate the titanism of American sublime, and offer an alternative model for twentieth-century American selfhood? Updike directs the reader, not explicitly but through intertextual allusions, to the experience of Barth's prophets and Kierkegaard's knights of faith. He wants his reader's blinkered eyes to open like Barth's confessing penitents, who see that "the primary and positive relation of man to God is brought out by a last wholly negative and annihilating crisis" (*The Word of God*, 170). Updike admits his adherence to "the crisis theology of Kierkegaard and Barth, which predicates a drastic condition of decay and collapse," and which summons the individual to awaken to the anxieties of his guilt and nothingness (*Odd Jobs*, 156).

Contemporary America is not free of anxieties, Updike comments. The climate is pervaded by "a failure of nerve—a sense of doubt as to the worth of any action" (*Conversations*, 14). He exploits his implied audience's anxiety in order to open a theological horizon less radically negative than Barth's. On the frontier of Creator and creature Barth postulates a great Negator, while Updike, on the same frontier, posits a "great Diminisher" (*Odd Jobs*, 455). Even less Barthian is Updike's refusal to relinquish an implied contact, no matter how diminishing, between creatures and their Creator: "I describe things not because their muteness mocks our subjectivity but because they seem to be masks for God" (*Conversations*, 45). As a critic of Emerson's religion of sublime confidence, Updike may have sympathized with Barth's proclamation that "it is simply that over against man's confidence and belief in himself, there has been written in huge proportions and with utmost clearness, a *mene, mene, tekel*" (*The Word of God*, 149). As a critic of Emerson, Updike would also have enjoyed the following assault Barth launches against any variety of transcendental ego:

We are tempted in Fichtean insolence to grasp for ourselves what does not belong to us. But we must once again be reminded . . . that man is not in a position to solve the ethical problem by his thought. . . . There is no way from us to God. . . . The god who stood at the end of some human way . . . would not be God. . . . One cannot speak of God simply by speaking of man in a loud voice. (*The Word of God*, 154, 177, 196)

No wonder that Updike chose Barth as the challenging double to the Emersonian model of prophetic selfhood. Just to illustrate the intriguing intertextual relation between Updike's dark Barthian double and his surface American unconcern, it is worth comparing the metaphor Updike uses to diminish the titan, with the very metaphor Barth uses in similar context. "We are in some deep way scared by how unthinkably small our place in the universe is," Updike claims. "We're almost creatures of gossamer, aren't we?" (*Conversations*, 204). Barth, likewise, highlights man's earthly existence in a "sick old world," in which "the whole network of life is hung upon thread like gossamer" (*The Word of God*, 188).

Moving from imagery to ideology increases our appreciation of Updike's apocalyptic moments. For Updike as for Barth, apocalypse does not correspond with the Second Coming of Christ at the end of time. Rather, it coincides with Christ's ritual resurrection every Easter, and with the psychological moment of awakening, marking for the individual believer the moment of identification with Christ. This Barthian standpoint is expressed by Updike in his poem "Seven Stanzas at Easter." The poem translates, in Barthian fashion, the theology of resurrection into a psychology of awakening. The scandalous fact of Christ's death and resurrection is seen as man's passage or conversion from the old (oblivious) to the new (awakened) self:

> Let us not seek to make it less monstrous,
> for our own convenience, . . .
> lest, awakened in one unthinkable hour,
> we are . . .
> crushed by remonstrance.[36]

The two states of sleep and awakening are encouraged by two opposite prophetic figures in Updike, as in Barth. The theologian distinguishes in contemporary existence between two prophet figures. The false prophet, who is "easy-going, someone you can live with as you are," serves the old and sinful man, who resists being awakened to judgment. The true prophet, by contrast, is "a man who most uncomfortably questions everything . . . about whom you are never sure, like a meteor of unknown whence and whither." He guides the individual in the choice between the uncaring life of the old man, and the anxiety of the crisis leading to the new man in God: "You cannot demand that I should tell you about God and also accept things as they are. This is impossible. You must choose one of the two: one, not both. Decide!"[37]

Updike would like to be able to force his readers to decide once and for all whether they are for or against God, for or against the "giant that destroys itself." However, the moment of crisis or radical decision requires a state of painful lucidity which American readers do their best to escape. Only once, to the best of my knowledge, does Updike use the strict theological term "Krino" (crisis), and only by way of an option that his protagonists evade as they cruise the world in pursuit of past gigantic civilizations ("Cruise," 301). To appreciate the moments of missed crisis or awakening that Updike stages, expecting to be misread, it is helpful to outline the Barthian model of Crisis Theology Updike alludes to only in passing. The moment of crisis is a point not in time, but in subjectivity. It is a personal experience of dread at the moment of awakening to the disastrous shattering of self, rather than a communal experience of historical apocalypse:

> For the *hour* of awakening, the striking of the last hour, the time of fulfillment, which is here announced, certainly does not mean some succeeding chronological hour. . . . It has nothing to do with any historical, or "telluric" or cosmic catastrophe. (*Romans,* 499–500)

Barth locates the prophetic perspective as a subjective point of observation, which is yet external and invisible to the subject—"a point outside that identity from which I may know myself, or rather from which I may be known" (*Romans,* 198). It is from this point, under the judgment of an unknown and invisible Observer, that the individual experiences a moment of diminishing humility, and awakens to his shame and guilt. Updike seems to endorse this perspective in his acute awareness of "a great Diminisher," and his sense of a "theological scrutiny from above."

Barth's model of prophetic crisis, which diminishes the self to nothingness, is diametrically opposed to the Sublime American self-confidence, which celebrates an expanded, exploring but not self-questioning self. To illustrate the contrast one can recall that, in order to figure the deified self, Emerson borrows the traditional symbol of God "as a circle whose center was everywhere and its circumference nowhere."[38] Barth deflates this very image and reduces the self-engrossed circular self to an ignorant creature, blind to invisible judgment: "What is this dynamic force which so powerfully and irresistibly drives me to recognize the closed circle in which I live?" (*Romans,* 198).

Misled by their own neglect of Updike's intertextual recourse to Barth, critics such as Vidal and Bloom completely miss the aesthetic and theological function of Updike's contrapuntal and even deconstructive style. Vidal merely notes that Updike plays word games with Barth and Kierkegaard, whose names "are often treated as one word, Barthegaard."[39] My obvious point is that Updike appeals to Barth for figurative and conceptual tools with which to clarify the ambiguities and dualities of prophetic selfhood in America. By recourse to Barth's dual model of the prophetic self Updike could give a dialectical shape to the rival models of Emersonian giantism and Lutheran no-me-ism, wrestling in the multiple origins of American selves.

Preaching to a Protestant audience, Barth could highlight the model of selfhood which reduces itself to nothing. He could, likewise, call his community of believers to stand on the frontier of crisis and judgment. By contrast, Updike knows that he writes for heedless readers, for whom he can foreground, though with fine strokes of non-flattering irony and satire, only that which they wish to hear. In this gap of non-admiration and diminishing portraiture, the reader who has followed Updike's use of Barth can grasp inklings of the frontier of crisis and judgment.

Critics have complained that Updike does not know how to end his stories.[40] My response is that were Updike an Emersonian, his hero would arrive at a sublime consummation; were he a Barthian, his protagonists would arrive at a terrifying self-negating consummation. Since Updike is stuck in an indeterminate and undecidable midpoint between the mutually exclusive alternatives, a point of consummating decision or ending cannot be reached. "I like middles," he tells an interviewer. "It is in middles that extremes clash, where ambiguity restlessly rules."[41]

IV

To put the same point as a question, can Barth's Crisis Theology and Updike's confessions of missed crisis account for the non-arrival of clear-cut endings? Barth's penitents look for a consummation on the other side of the grave, or frontier, where their negation will be compensated by an eternal state of awakening. Updike's protagonists, and even Updike himself, do not want to cross the threshold of death and self-negation. Updike welcomes the experience of diminished self-confidence not as a passage to death but as a passage to self-criticism which Barth would deem inadequate.[42] His protagonists are stuck in a still more inferior state of warding off not only death but even self-criticism. "[T]he lives I witnessed," Updike claims, "have staved off real death. All my novels end with a false death, partial death." He insists, moreover, that there is neither violence nor an impending sense of major historical catastrophes in the American climate he re-creates: "In general, the North American continent in this century has been a place where catastrophe was held off." Critics who read his "undercutting any apocalypticism"[43] as merely a sign of callowness, seem attuned only to Updike's American voice and deaf to his Barthian one. As Barth's subjective points of awakening are not related to historical apocalypses, so Updike sees no need to stage catastrophic endings in his fiction. If anything, Updike intends the over-peaceful climate and ambiguous endings of his fiction to awaken the readers to a missing element in their recklessly relaxed existence.[44]

"Short Easter"[45] is the telling title of a story in which Updike presents, through Barthian lenses, an ironic biography of the Great American Sleeper. The protagonist, introduced only by his last name—Fogel—is a middle-aged, middle-class American, whose anxieties are restricted to the well-being of his autonomous inflated selfhood. Fogel's trivial concerns are cynically illustrated by the daily exchange of "deliberate affront" and "pure intimidation" between his stately Mercedes, and the other cars on the highway (97). His moments of dread are, likewise, caused "absent-minded[ly]" by "the intimidating Sunday newspaper" and the noise of "doves thrashing into the air." An unusually shortened Easter Day, caused by "the advent of Daylight Saving Time clipping an hour off," generates a sudden fear in Fogel that an impending apocalypse is beckoning in the visible horizon. He experiences a moment of almost Lutheran angst, a sense that life is pointless, and that in it "all work . . . was also a Sisyphean matter of recycling, of pushing inert and thankless matter back and forth" (103).

An Emersonian dreamer, Fogel portrays himself as master of his universe. During an afternoon nap on that Easter Day, "he presided over the busy lit stage of his subconscious as prompter and playwright, audience and *deus ex machina* as well as hero" (105). Yet the very dream debunks his illusions of Emersonian autonomy and mastery, for it shows his parents hovering authoritatively above him, speaking "urgently to each other, in a language he did not know."

An urge to recapture his threatened giantism awakens Fogel from the dream:

> Fogel became heavy in every cell, so dense that he fell through into wake-fulness, though the dream world tried to cling to his warm body, amid the unnatural ache of resurrection—the weight, the atrocious weight, of coming again to life! (105)

The discourse Updike expects his readers not to know is that of Barthian confession which conflates apocalypse, resurrection, and awakening into a single moment of prophetic crisis. Read through a Barthian prism, Fogel's awakening is as empty as a sign without a signifier. Unlike Barth's broken subject Fogel does not awaken to the terrifying experience of Barth's prophetic subject. Neither does he awaken to a confident Emersonian feeling of being alone with the gods at the center of creation. At the point of crisis—awakening in chilling terror—Barth's subject resorts to self-questioning and ad-mission of nothingness, leading to a NO to autonomous selfhood and a YES to God. Updike's American subject, by contrast, experi-ences a moment of terror and uncertainty without real awakening to his creaturely proportions: "Everything seemed still in place, yet something was immensely missing" (106). Fogel's chronicles are cut short at midpoint, suggesting future reiteration of "absent-minded" moments of dread.

V

Critics are inclined to mistake the protagonists' failed awakening for a failure on Updike's part to make a clear statement or to under-take a serious act of self-examination. In other words, they criticize him for the very failure he exposes in American selfhood, both indi-vidual and collective. Updike's most sustained and recent expose of Emersonian delusion is *In the Beauty of the Lilies*, where any chance of awakening is precluded by what one contemporary theologian has called "living in the reel world."[46]

The repression of the Barthian voice by the Emersonian or Holly-woodian voice is staged partly by Updike's fictional history, and partly by his rendering of Hollywood's "unreality." Historically, the story begins with a lapsed minister, whose faith in God fails, and with it his powers of judgment and self-criticism. The story of the following three generations moves from a son who ignores God, to a granddaughter who exchanges God for a movie-camera, down to a great-grandson, whose anguish at the absence of both a divine and a maternal guide drives him into the arms of a false prophet.

By situating a major part of his novel in the realm of the movie industry, Updike is able to introduce the dual role of the cinema in the years after Auschwitz and Hiroshima. On the one hand the movies bring home the sense of chaos, crisis, and catastrophe:

> The motion pictures . . . embraced the chaos that sensible men and women in their ordinary lives plotted to avoid . . . The cinema wished to leave nothing hidden, to throw nakedness up on the screen, and grief and fistfights and explosion and violence. (137–38)

On the other hand, the cinema serves as an anaesthetic by providing both illusions and excessive self-confidence:

> Death and oblivion were down there waiting for the movie to be over. Not so, these movies tried to say. Life was not serious; it was an illusion, a story, distracting and disturbing but at bottom painless and merciful. (138)

One would expect, Updike seems to intimate, that the camera which exposes sordid reality should turn the moment of catastrophe to a point of awakening. Yet the very horrors which serve Barth to describe self-negation, drive Hollywood and its creators to fantasies of smiling self-reliance.[47]

Essie/Alma, the protagonist/actress in the novel, inhabits the angst-ridden world of America. As a child she is exposed both to the scary "newsreel . . . [which] showed running soldiers and explosions . . . and that stupid Hitler with his tiny moustache," and to reassuring Mickey Mouse cartoons (228–30). On the threshold of her career as a movie star, Essie adopts a new name (299). In the guise of this new persona—her Alma self—she provides the admiring American spectators with generous doses of desired illusions:

> As the Alma character was borne off by the inevitable censorious rectitude of the script, audiences felt that something precious in them was being carried away, in this land of promise where yearning never stops short at a particular satisfaction but keeps moving on into the territory beyond. (313)

Here, as in "Short Easter," potentially apocalyptic moments are voided of religious significance. Neither character nor audience are borne away to a spiritual beyond. Still less do the name and figure of Alma carry Christian associations as they do for example in Melville and Spencer. The epigraph and title Updike chose for his own novel specifically talk of Christ as prophet and savior:

> In the beauty of the lilies Christ was born across the sea / With a glory in his bosom that transfigures you and me / As he dies to make men holy, let us die to make men free / While God is marching on.[48]

A Barthian reader might expect an Alma figure to imitate Christ, by inspiring her audience, in moments of dread, to say No to the self and Yes to the glory of God. Updike's Alma parodies both American versions of prophetic performance and the relaxed society consuming them with pleasure. She answers the audience's expectations by becoming, as Brooke Allen suggests, a "midcentury substitute for the deity, a screen goddess, whose image is worshipped throughout the country."[49] As such, she continues to escape from reality to illusion carrying her audience to further sleep of ignorance:

> Essie had wondered why anything in real life should be excluded from the stage, but then, when she became Alma, she saw that this clarity makes a refuge for the actors and audience both, lifting them up from fumbling reality into a reality keener and more efficient but not less true. (315)

Alma's son, Clark, does look for a way to the Barthian moment of crisis, but takes a wrong and tragic road. Feeling the catastrophe of his remote, uncaring, self-inflated mother and her admiring audience, he is drawn to a community of seekers who crave a transcendent being whose voice will fill their existential void. Far from following the path of Barth's pilgrim theology, they gather around a false prophet who provides affirming and consoling answers, instead of directing them to further self-questioning. Jesse, the Koresh-like false prophet, abuses the young people's moment of crisis and directs them, like an Emersonian or Fascist prophet, to violence and destruction. When Clark awakens from the delusions of the false prophet he succeeds in preventing the apocalypse of mass massacre, but is unable to save himself.

Living only in the "reel" world, Alma arrives on the scene at Lower Branch, Colorado, more to be interviewed by television reporters than to grieve for her son. More committed to the aesthetic illusions she serves than to the reality beyond the scene, Alma is incapable of feeling the full horror of her son's death. There is no hint of terror, grief, or repentance as the moment of crisis is missed by a popular version of Emerson's cult of illusions. Awakening is repressed by an illusion that saves the mother and television audience from the pain of penetrating reality. According to Updike, cinematic aesthetics are postulated in such a way as to avoid dread and anxiety. They lull the audience by showing that

> familiar stars, who suffered and died on the screen . . . returned a month or two later differently costumed but unchanged. . . . [They] led up there a life that was always renewed, movie to movie, without permanent harm. (138–39)

By diametrical and tragic contrast, those who die on screen in Colorado do not rise in reality. Still, the mother avoids real life and returns in total oblivion to her soporific reel life. In *In The Beauty of the Lilies*, as in his pervious texts, Updike's dual narratives and stammering voice imply that American ideology is founded on an ontological self-reliance which precludes the possibility of awakening, and, more alarmingly, one which invites violence.

A few years before *In the Beauty of the Lilies*, Updike observed in *Self-Consciousness* that awakening is within our power: "The frangibility and provisionality of the self is well within our modern competence to perceive" (230). Yet such a perception is too painful and too humiliating to take seriously. Moreover, it is far from the desires of American readers, who have inherited a by now anachronistic and tragically inappropriate trust in the American Sublime and in the "giant that destroys itself."

What his readers are able but not willing to do for themselves, Updike performs with a vengeance, in an act of writing tantamount to the public confession of a medieval penitent. He confesses to the readers his repugnant plight of "deformity and shame"—physical flaws, presented as means of subduing his giant. His lifelong skin disease, minutely described, is seen as a humiliating punishment for a sin which "had to do with self-love" (74). Likewise, his stammer gains ontological stature, as an indication of self-diminishment: "Stuttering, perhaps, is a kind of recoil at your own voice, an expression of alarm and shame at sounding like yourself, at *being* yourself, at taking up space and air" (90).[50]

For Gore Vidal, as for other critics, this "splendid coda (to date) of Updike's physical apparatus" fails to convey "some self-mocking play on his self-consciousness," let alone genuine self-examination.[51] Yet a more attentive reader may notice that, precisely in *Self-Consciousness*, Updike keeps his "voice in the lower half of its register" (90), offering an almost inaudible confession. One sin acknowledged is pursuit of pleasure, evident in his fiction-writing: "It is an addiction, an illusory release, a presumptuous taming of reality, a way of expressing lightly the unbearable. . . . Writing, in making the world light . . . approaches blasphemy" (238).

From his early poems collected in *Midpoint* (1969), to his recent memoirs, Updike has criticized not only his marketable writing but also his Emersonian self, responsible for such writing. His strategy in these early and recent confessional texts differs mainly in the proportion of self-diminishment. In *Midpoint*, the voice of the prophet/poet blatantly emulates that of the first person singular of *Song of Myself*, with an intensity verging on an Emersonian precursor:

> Of nothing but me, me
> —all wrong, all wrong—
> as I cringe in the face of glory
> I sing, lacking another song
> the night sky, with a little luck,
> was a camera back, the constellations
> faint silver salts, and I the crux
> of radii, the tip of two huge cones,
> called Heaven and Earth
> that took their slant and spin from me alone. (7)

Yet, unlike Whitman, Updike introduces an implicit critical voice through assertions such as "I was that O, that white-hot nothing." Furthermore, he does not wish to identify with the giant American self, but rather "to seem a creature, to subdue / my giant solipsism to a common scale" (7). Because of the ambivalent voice, the poem remains stuck precisely at *midpoint*, between the inflated tone and the diminishing intention.

Twenty years later, the deflation in the confessional text is almost non-ambiguous, and the Whitmanesque voice is whittled away to resemble a disciple of St. Augustine. The speaker ruthlessly exposes the weaknesses of both body and soul, with the extreme shame and mortification that have caused critics to recoil to cynical critique. Vidal curiously enough uses a trope of Puritan exhibitionism, when he describes Updike situated in a "City on a Hill, where he can now . . . enjoy the solace of Religion," and indulge in self-centered writing.[52] One reason for Vidal's and even Bloom's misreading of Updike might be their refusal to take seriously his Barthian intertext, which obviously is very far from the American cultural context. More misleading, however, is the conviction—so predominant in American culture from Emerson to our own time of narcissistic autobiographies—that "confession" is the genre par excellence for constructing the American self.

Foucault draws the fine line between different ways of writing the self. He distinguishes between Stoic (autobiographical) notebooks, Christian confessions, and the contemporary "Californian cult of self," in which psychoanalysis plays a central role in self-exposure.[53] Current cultural criticism in America tends to ignore Foucault's distinctions. Instead, they use indiscriminately—as synonymous genres—confession and autobiography, also defined as chronicling "the journey from *there* to *here*." The title of a recent special issue of *The New York Times Magazine*—"True Confessions: The Age of the Literary Memoirs"—is a telling example.[54] I tend to agree with Foucault that there is a clear distinction between autobiography and confession, since there is no confession without self-examination. By radical contrast, the contemporary "Californian cult of self," notably its Hollywood variant, is self-invention and self-idolization.

Updike's fictional characters do not make the effort of self-invention, nor do they achieve self-criticism. Rather, the imagery of self is produced and consumed by the cinema or the travel industry.[55] In *Self-Consciousness*, by contrast, where Updike speaks in his own voice, there is no contrapuntal rendering of Emerson's cult of self and Luther's examination of self. The style is more explicitly self-diminishing, and the giant-self is all but dissolved. From the outset Updike presents his Lutheran upbringing as an alternative to the "unthinkable truth" of American egotheism (40). His assertion, at the end of *Self-Consciousness*, that "a loud and evident God would be a bully," and that God is a "Thou," totally distinct from the human "I," resounds with Barth's critique of liberal theology and with his concept of God as *totaliter aliter*. Far from an Emersonian self-deifying self, Updike's "impalpable self cries out to Him and wonders if it detects an answer" (241). His Lutheran heritage offers "a Yes, a blessing" which he accepts, "offering in return . . . my art, my poor little art."[56]

Whether veiled by irony in the fiction, or explicitly expressed in the nonfiction, the professed intention of Updike's confessional voice in his recent texts is not merely to arrive at midpoint between two rival prophetic voices. Resorting to confessional rather than exhibitionist writing, Updike aims to subdue his giant to the less than common posture of the penitent, and attain a moment of Barthian awakening to reduced selfhood.

3

Vision Without Prophets: Violence Without Fission of Subjectivity in Flannery O'Connor

> I have found that violence is strangely capable of returning my characters to reality and preparing them to accept their moment of grace.
>
> The Devil's greatest wile, Baudelaire has said, is to convince us that he does not exist.
>
> —Flannery O'Connor, *Mystery and Manners*

I

What distinguishes Flannery O'Connor from the other writers examined in this book, even from John Updike, is the explicitly theological reading her rhetoric invites. Many critics of O'Connor have focused on her professed theological/metaphysical concerns. O'Connor herself directs the reader to the relevance of religious faith to her art:

> I see from the standpoint of Christian orthodoxy. This means that for me the meaning of life is centered in our Redemption by Christ and what I see in the world I see in its relation to it.[1]

O'Connor's readers, however, do not pay overt attention to the correlation between religious rhetoric and the remarkably grotesque and violent subject construction inherent in her narratives. For the most part O'Connor's critics examine the ideological tradition in her text and intertext. "In the view of most critics," Emily Miller-Budick has recently noted, "O'Connor's writings comprise an obvious, sometimes even simplistic rendering of the contours of the divine presence in the world. They verify the truth of Christian history and dogma."[2] The dialectical tension in O'Connor's writings between her theological perspective and the growing secularism in the contemporary ideological situation has prompted readings which range from the more common emphasis on her religious faith, to existential interpretations. Richard Giannone, for example, notes O'Connor's intertextual recourse to the tradition of the self-alienated desert Fathers, and claims that her "response to the realities . . . in her cherished South found expression in a subliminal narrative of desert adventure and self-denial."[3]

More pertinent to my analysis of identity crises in contemporary American fiction are readings which relate O'Connor's concerns not only to theological, metaphysical, or ontological questions but also to the problematics of subject construction and deconstruction. For example, observing that in O'Connor's works "man is essentially a homeless creature who must make his own 'place'," Paul Nisly addresses her complex structural strategies of producing characterization and genre. Noting the recurrent doublings and divisions of O'Connor's character construction, Nisly remarks that Gothic fiction features similar strategies. Her characters, "like many split persons in Gothic fiction . . . find no satisfaction or completion in [their] double[s]."[4] Also useful for the following analysis of O'Connor's double and divided subject constructions is Claire Katz-Kahane's reading. Katz-Kahane implies that the problematics of subjectivity are more central to O'Connor's aesthetics and fictional concerns than are the problematics of theology: "[A]t the center of [O'Connor's] work is a psychological demand which overshadows her religious intent, shaping plot, image and character as well as her distinctive narrative voice." In Katz-Kahane's psychoanalytic reading, the genesis of duality is traced neither to a generic tradition nor to prophetic rhetoric or ethics, but to Oedipal cleavages. Splitting and doubling are linked partly with castration anxieties and partly with "the author's psyche, split into the punishing parent and the rebellious child."[5]

According to Emily Miller-Budick, American romance features recurrent "doubling and redoubling." Miller-Budick traces this feature not to a sacred fission of subjectivity but to secular, male chauvinist self-repetition. What Miller-Budick sees as "an egocentric pattern of self-replication. . . . of male self-conception," and Katz-Kahane sees as Freudian splitting of the psyche, leave unexplained the sacred shatterings suffered by O'Connor's prophetic subjectivity.[6]

No modern American prose writer quite so explicitly declares prophecy to be his or her vocation. As a Catholic Southern writer,

O'Connor's gaze "touches that realm which is the concern of prophets" (*Mystery*, 45). "Prophecy is a matter of seeing, not saying," she claims, "and is certainly the most terrible vocation. My prophet will be . . . burnt by his own visions."[7] Neither Katz-Kahane nor Miller-Budick relate to the psychology and theology of grace framing O'Connor's constructions of violently split and shattered selfhood.

Closer to my own reading is John Updike's description of O'Connor's storytelling as "the pinpoint tunnel to Jesus at the end of all perspectives." Updike suggests that O'Connor constructs "diminished" human figures drifting through "a suffering, apparently Godless world."[8] I agree that viewed from O'Connor's grotesquely realistic perspective there remains nothing sublime about prophetic experience. Where Updike merely diminishes the American sublime, O'Connor demolishes it. In her parables of cultivated blindness there are no giants to subdue. Whereas Melville's, Whitman's, and Emerson's satanic and Promethean giants draw their inspiration from Greek and Judeo-Christian myth and tragedy, O'Connor's reluctant heirs of the tradition draw their inspiration from comics. They are ridiculous, not sublime—victims of voluntary ignorance, not of apocalyptic dragons or fallen angels.[9]

In Melville's nineteenth-century apocalyptic romance, a titanic hero with a "crucifixion in his face" chases "Job's whale" round the world. Like Job, Ahab puts God on trial, while like Jonah, Ishmael probes the belly of the whale.[10] In O'Connor's twentieth-century grotesque prophetic realism no chaos-monster is challenged to battle and no visible powers of evil inspire titanic ravings against injustice. In *Wise Blood* the belly of Jonah's whale is diminished to a darkened cinema theater; in *The Violent Bear It Away* Jonah silently struggles to silence the whale.[11]

II

There is nothing sublime about O'Connor's not merely diminished but grotesquely deformed prophets, especially not in her first novel, *Wise Blood*. The novel tells the story of Hazel Motes, a would-be prophet from a country town in Tennessee, who comes in the aftermath of World War II to the big city, to preach a new church— "the church of truth without Jesus Christ Crucified" (28). Up to the

War, Motes knew that like his grandfather, he was going to preach of the Fall, of Christ's sacrifice and of Redemption:

> He knew by the time he was twelve years old that he was going to be a preacher. . . . He meant to tell anyone in the army that he was from Eastrod, Tennessee, and that he meant to get back there, that he was going to be a preacher of the gospel and that he wasn't going to have his soul damned by the government or any other foreign place it sent him to. (11)

The War, however, does damn his soul, not by tempting him with earthly sins but by making him a nihilist converted "to nothing instead of to evil" (11). In the desolate city Motes encounters two false prophets—a fake-blind fake-preacher called Hawks (58), and Hoover Shoats, who preaches salvation through happiness and sweetness (85–86). Motes even has a disciple—Enoch Emery, a "pimpled boy" who works in the city zoo, and spends his free time watching horror movies, reading comics, and eating candy. Enoch steals a shrunken stuffed mummy from a museum near the zoo, offering it to Motes as an ersatz Jesus. Two women try unsuccessfully to seduce Motes—a mock-innocent young girl, supposedly Hawks's daughter, who refers to Motes as "king of the beasts" (87) and Motes's elderly landlady—Mrs. Flood—who fancies less the preacher himself than his monthly government allowance. Unable and unwilling to relate to other people or see beyond his own illusions, Motes blinds himself with quicklime and dies in a drainage ditch.

No giant begets or destroys itself in O'Connor's stories.[12] The worst violence her protagonists inflict on themselves is self-blinding, but even this act of self-mutilation is emptied of the protesting significance of Oedipus's response to awakening and injustice. Neither are they Samsons whose blindness restores their power of prophetic insight and action.

O'Connor's characters do not baptize themselves, do not confess their allegiance to any God or devil. They do not upbraid God for saying nothing or for lying and deceiving. They do not sell their souls to a satanic mysterious stranger who sermonizes about negativity and nothingness. Neither absence of good nor proliferation of evil interests them. They substitute (horror) movies and comics for newspapers (history), and even when they do read the papers they do not read them as evidence of divine injustice or diabolic captivity.

Unlike Updike, O'Connor allows no crack in the sustained sordidness of her scene; no monumental colossi even in figurative frame. In *Wise Blood* the devils and fallen angels of *The Apocalypse of Enoch* are replaced by midget mummies reduced to museum pieces, idols of a vanished titanic civilization. Even the museums of high culture and the mummies of vanished cults are too exalted frames for O'Connor's scenes of idiocy-worship. The latest form of titanic infidelity is celebrated by O'Connor's idiots at zoos and at cinemas, ogling live gorillas and their celluloid images—King Kong or street shows of anonymous "Jungle Monarch" (*Wise Blood*, 90).

The grotesque dwarfs who mutilate themselves in O'Connor's stories can be read as variations on Updike's theme of subduing the Emersonian giant in himself and his readers. But O'Connor's ruthlessly witty point is that by now there remain no giants to subdue; there are only false prophets preaching by rote that there is no God, no text in sky, no birth, no death, no Fall, no Judgment:

> No truth behind all truths is what I and this church preach. . . . You needn't look at the sky because it's not going to open and show no place behind it. . . . If there was any Fall look [in yourself], if there was any Redemption, look there, and if you expect any Judgment, look there, because they all three will have to be in your time and your body and where in your time and your body can they be? (*Wise Blood*, 84)

But belief in nothing (15) also means that there is no judge to heroically defy. O'Connor reduces (absent) apocalyptic giants to a shrunken mummy in a museum stuffed with sawdust and squashed by a giant stone (50).

In *Moby Dick* Melville reduced the idols of nineteenth-century Neo-Paganism to a black baby idol—Yojo. But there was nothing shrunken about his brown, red, and black pagan harpooners—Queequeg, Tashtego, and Dagoo. By contrast (possibly with Yojo and Queequeg in mind) O'Connor reduces the idols of the Nietzschean and Emersonian church of American titanism to a squashed museum piece no one worships and no one misses. Yojo in church has been replaced by King Kong at the zoo and in the cinema. Emerson's heirs being everywhere and Whitman's grand animals being purchasable for peanuts (82), these stereotype idols of popular taste hardly merit an assault. Rather, O'Connor attacks the producers and consumers of these sawdust dolls. Whatever the ideology peddled by the media, the subjects produced by it are as hollow-eyed as their idol, not by fate but by choice.

O'Connor claims that the culture industry has taken over the task of producing an American self emptied of desire or ability to read beyond the material and materialist scene of history:

> The trash put out by the mass media industries is causing the American imagination to rot and . . . this is as dangerous for the life of the nation as any of the external threats to our security. Fed continuously on a diet of fantasy which is not recognized as such, the American will eventually find his life ordered on the basis of unreality that can destroy the moral fiber of the nation.[13]

O'Connor's characters blame the war for blunting their sensibility to the significance of cultural signs. The war did something to their insides in the figurative sense, leaving them free of inner light. Outwardly regarded, newspaper images of Auschwitz and Hiroshima cry out for anguished and anxious responses. But no such response is aroused in the stone souls of O'Connor's newspaper readers (*Wise Blood*, 10). However, it is not political history but ideology that O'Connor holds responsible for endemic insensitivity. She exposes, through what Shoates peddles as "prophets for peanuts" (*Wise Blood*, 82) a gospel of repressing unpleasant insights and pursuing happiness (*Wise Blood*, 78–79). Happy are they whose eyes are hollow, is the gospel of false prophets in *Wise Blood* which can be seen as O'Connor's version of Eliot's "The Hollow Men."[14] While he blames the war, she blames Emersonian ideology. The scene of ruins accounts for the hollowness in Eliot, the sin of refusing to see accounts for the hollowness in O'Connor. Nothing is hollow in *Wise Blood* but the eyes of the mannequin fashioned by artists (81) and self-blinded prophets of hear no evil, see no evil—human shame, guilt, outrage, and injustice. Hollow eyes make for hollow men: That is O'Connor's message in a (pea)nutshell. Hitler's war does not wake up her characters but confirms them in their quest for the sweetness of sleep. Mrs. Flood, the greedy landlady in *Wise Blood*, proclaims it in a transparent parable: "If she had been blind, she would have sat by the radio all day, eating cake and ice-cream, and soaking her feet" (112). Enoch—the thief of the one-eyed mummy—solves the problem of unbearable, "unpleasant" visions by eating candy bars (89) and cakes and reading comic strips: "It was Enoch's favorite part [of the paper]. He read it every evening like an office. While he ate the cake . . . he read and felt himself surge with kindness and courage and strength" (99).

In *Simulacra and Simulation*,[15] Baudrillard complains against the demonic images peddled by today's culture industry. In *Wise Blood* O'Connor suggests that films and museum simulacra flourish when historical reality becomes too painful to bear, or see, or hear.[16] Free of old-fashioned puritan terror, American audiences welcome demonic or beastly simulacra, which is all their digestive powers can take, spoiled by an excess of cultural candy and ice-cream.[17] Mrs. Flood's gospel could reduce even the dragon of the Apocalypse to a piece of cake with the aid of blindness and media simulacra. Outside and inside she is clean of old-fashioned American eyes for the devil and ears to hear the crucifying call of conscience. Like the happy, once-born souls William James describes in *The Varieties of Religious Experience*,[18] Mrs. Flood dismisses as morbid Hazel Motes's obsession with inner uncleanliness. Indeed she dismisses all religious "Sinsations" (31) as sick and insane and takes pride in not suffering from a morbid theological streak.

III

After *Wise Blood* O'Connor wrote no more stories that overtly taunt her readers with horrifying visions which they refuse watching.[19] No more does she plague her reader with traces of St. John's beast or with fiery trials. Instead, she invents visions without prophets to perceive them and retellings of familiar Bible stories without religiously competent implied readers to interpret them.

Even her retelling of the *akedah* story, which Miller-Budick rightly recognizes as the scriptural setting for *The Violent Bear It Away*,[20] does not invite any traditional interpretative response. There is no hint of either Abraham's anguish as Jewish midrash presents it or the night of faith's agony as Kierkegaard describes it.[21] Kierkegaard's Abraham knows he is making a leap from the ethical to the religious, and the knowledge is terrible. By radical contrast, no moral judgment is made by a distant father who murders his son by proxy in *The Violent Bear It Away* (243).

The novel tells the story of a young boy, Francis Marion Tarwater, raised in the backwoods by his great-uncle—a self-professed prophet. Upon the death of the old man Tarwater leaves for the city where Rayber, his schoolteacher uncle, lives with his retarded son Bishop. Tarwater drowns his cousin in a lake, while Rayber does not come to his son's rescue. On his way back to the backwoods Tarwater is sexually violated by the driver who gives him a ride.

Miller-Budick reads the message in O'Connor's retold akedian tale as a call to *responsibility*.[22] My own reading maintains that O'Connor exposes the absence of ethical and religious visionary *response*. The terrible thing about O'Connor's apocalyptic scenes, I find, is that their corresponding insight remains repressed. Even violence evokes no prophetic response. In what follows I assume that O'Connor's parables are about the consequences of being cleansed and hollowed of Christian prophetic insight.[23]

My working hypothesis is that O'Connor's attacks against sightless "sinsationalism" assault the "imperial self"—as Anderson calls it—or "gigantic self"—in Bloom's phrasing.[24] Bloom emphasizes the disparity between O'Connor's Christian characters and the paradigm of the sublime ego which he finds both in the gnostic element of the American Religion, and in the Romantic tradition. Bloom calls attention to "something of a gap between O'Connor as lay theologue and O'Connor as a storyteller . . . [whose] fictive universe [is] essentially Gnostic."[25] In a separate remark, without attempting to link the two aspects, Bloom makes a valuable observation regarding O'Connor's use of violence. The violence predominant in O'Connor's narratives, Bloom suggests, aims to upset the *readers'* imperial ego, luring them towards a religious experience:

> It is not her incessant violence that is troublesome but rather her passionate endorsement of that violence as the only way to startle her secular readers into a spiritual awareness. As a visionary writer, she is determined to take us by force, to bear us away so that we may be open to the possibility of grace."[26]

Bloom refers here, of course, to the title and epigraph O'Connor chose for her novel: "From the days of John the Baptist until now, the kingdom of heaven suffereth violence, and the violent bear it away" (Matthew 11:12). While many readers allude to the deployment of violence by O'Connor as part of an aesthetic of violence for its own sake, Bloom sees it as a strategy modeled on the rigorously Christian meaning of violence in St. Matthew.[27]

Bloom's recent studies of the relation between American literature and theology are helpful to my study in three ways. First, he insists on the emphasis in American culture on "imagined religion"—the link between aesthetics and theology.[28] Secondly, he sees as central to American fictional religion the paradigm of gnostic individualism, in which the genesis of the subject is intimately connected with its relation to the godhead. Thirdly, Bloom's model of subjectivity is Promethean, sublime, and so—and here I take issue with him—he refuses to accept as model (what for him is) an heretical option of American religious subjectivity which is bent on shattering the sublime ego rather than celebrating it. Bloom narrows down the gnostic heresy to instances of heroic rebellion. He chooses to disregard the theory of good and evil central to the Valentinian system of Gnosticism on the one hand and the Manichaean on the other. O'Connor would be interested precisely in the way in which both systems present blindness, intoxication, and sleep as the work of the Devil, while the Redeemer's function is a terrifying awakening of the fallen subject.[29]

With regard to O'Connor, Bloom argues that she is unaware of the heretical aspect of her narratives, that they "are more equivocal than she evidently intended" and deploy, implicitly, practices which she explicitly repudiates. So conceived, her fictional writings portray individuals less modeled by O'Connor's professed religious orthodoxy, than by the tradition of Emersonian/gnostic Sublime which her nonfiction texts reject. Young Tarwater, the prophet-to-be in O'Connor's novel *The Violent Bear It Away*, is seen by Bloom as a "Gnostic version of Huckleberry Finn," who "values his own freedom above anything and anyone, even his call as a prophet."[30] "As a reader of herself," Bloom bluntly concludes, "I cannot rank O'Connor very high."[31] He dismisses, as ideological flaws, the violent deflation of self in O'Connor, just as he rejects Updike's humbling spirituality. Catholic O'Connor suffers from "spiritual tendentiousness" just as Lutheran Updike suffers from "churchwardenly mewing."[32]

My analysis will try to trace and explain on the one hand, the failure of the gnostic Sublime in O'Connor's narratives, and on the other, the fundamentalist Christian rhetoric of violence deployed to produce it. Like Bloom's, my reading argues that O'Connor deliberately deploys strategies of apocalyptic violence to produce in the reader a shattering openness to the experience of self-under-Judgment. However, my reading will argue that the shattering and psychologically violent breakdown of the Huck Finn-like individuals is O'Connor's deliberate strategy for carrying the reader to the threshold of death and Judgment. In Updike's writing, and perhaps even more strongly in O'Connor's writing, apocalyptic moments of sub-

ject shattering are not moments of violence for its own sake, but moments of apocalypse in the Christian sense, when catastrophe
awakens sinners to the sacred light of divine Judgment.[33]

O'Connor describes her candidates for violent awakening as monsters:

> When I sit down to write, a monstrous reader looms up who sits down
> beside me and continually mutters, "I don't get it, I don't see it, I don't
> want it". . . . I know I must never let him affect my vision, must never let
> him gain control over my thinking . . . ; yet I feel I must make him see
> what I have to show, even if my means of making him see have to be
> extreme.[34]

O'Connor portrays two opposite types of the monstrous reader,
whose response is invited by two opposite grotesque characters in
the text. One type of character/reader, she notes, embodies a Catholicism so radically dualistic that it prompts him "to be more of a
Manichean than the Church permits . . . separating nature and
grace as much as possible" (*Mystery*, 147). The opposite type is so
secure in his egotistic sublime, that "he recognizes spirit in himself
but . . . fails to recognize a being outside himself . . . and consequently he has become his own ultimate concern," indifferent to
divine Judgment (*Mystery*, 159).

O'Connor's hollow-eyed readers are protected by delusions of
grandeur and self-sufficiency from being shattered. Unlike Barth's
awakened sinners, they never experience what he describes as "this
dynamic force which so powerfully and irresistibly drives me to recognize the closed circle in which I live" (*Romans*, 198). For Barth,
titanism and prophetic insight are mutually exclusive. For both
Barth and O'Connor, grace means the discovery that man is not his
own God.[35] Barth, we saw, says that "a god who stood at the end of
some human way . . . would not be God", and that "a drowning man
cannot pull himself out by his own hair."[36] O'Connor formulates the
same gospel of grace by endorsing the belief "that man has fallen
and that he is only perfectible by God's grace, not by his own unaided efforts."[37]

Between Bloom's poetics of sublime prophetism and Barth's rhetoric of crisis, O'Connor's contrapuntal rhetoric produces complex
texts which at once construct and deconstruct—put under Judgment—Promethean selfhood. Bloom may be right in locating in
O'Connor's fiction the Emersonian "gigantic" subject, but he ig-

nores the Barthian double by whom that subject is shadowed and shattered. Under the deflating, fierce gaze of grace or Judgment Day, Bloom fails to notice, sublime heights not only are not scaled by the individual, they are inaccessible to sinners who resist awakening.

Both Barth and O'Connor deny that titanic individuals are illuminated, or inspired by divine intuition. For both theological writers titanism spells blindness, while illumination requires and produces the symbolic death of the titanic (sinful) self. Barth marks this state of awakening precisely as the point where we are able

> to see the darkness in which we stand. . . . [T]he tenacity of men is invisibly, yet most effectually, disturbed and shattered and dissolved; . . . [and] the competence of God, of the spirit of Eternity, can enter within our horizon. (*Romans*, 354, 239)

According to Barth, the breaking-in of the divine into the human is not a moment of aesthetic inspiration but rather of ethical Judgment, reducing merely human efforts to nothing. When God breaks down titanic selfhood, it is "the Judgement . . . which gives the attack its real power" (*Romans*, 194).

IV

Neither God nor titanic Devil animate O'Connor's characters. By deliberate opposition to nineteenth-century American Romantic glorifications of Promethean devils, O'Connor creates devil figures whose function is not to inspire resistance to injustice but, on the contrary, to encourage blindness to injustice. Contrasting her strategies with those of Melville and Poe, she confesses that her secular role model is Joel Chandler Harris's Br'er Rabbit (*Mystery*, 55–56).

In a letter to John Hawkes, O'Connor explicitly contrasts the titanic paradigm of the Romantic satanic school of giantism with her own paradigm whose task is to inspire humility:

> You haven't convinced me that I write with the Devil's will or belong in the romantic tradition. . . . I think the reason we can't agree on this is because there is a difference in our two devils. My Devil has a name, a history and a definite plan. His name is Lucifer, he's a fallen angel, his sin is pride, and his aim is the destruction of the divine plan. Now I judge that your Devil is co-equal to God, not his creature; that pride is his virtue, not his sin; and that his aim is not to destroy the Divine plan because

there isn't any Divine plan to destroy. My devil is objective and yours is subjective. (*Habit,* 456)

In the violence-free subject construction of secular romance, O'Connor, much like Updike and Barth, finds the failure of contemporary catastrophes to arouse moral horror and outrage. Satanic titanism cannot be treated with tenderness. Christian tenderness without the source of Christian mercy, namely justice and Judgment, can only end in Auschwitz: "When tenderness is detached from the source of tenderness . . . it ends in forced-labor camps and in the fumes of the gas chamber."[38] Like Barth, O'Connor sees Romantic titanism as a precursor of national socialism and its crimes. In America, she warns, the road to the gas chambers is paved not with titanism but with the tender sentimentalism of a vaporized Christianity without a cross, for whose origins she holds Emerson responsible. (*Mystery,* 161).

How can a writer break down contemporary American readers' resistance to reading the history of the Holocaust and to imagining the stench of incinerated corpses? Only through the mystery of diabolical evil and violent divine Judgment can the individual "do the work" of cracking thick skulls:

> Our age not only does not have a very sharp eye for the almost imperceptible intrusions of grace, it no longer has much feeling for the nature of the violences which precede and follow them. The Devil's greatest wile, Baudelaire has said, is to convince us that he does not exist. . . . I suppose the reasons for the use of so much violence in modern fiction will differ with each writer who uses it, but in my own stories I have found that violence is strangely capable of returning my characters to reality and preparing them to accept their moment of grace. Their heads are so hard that almost nothing else will do the work. (*Mystery,* 112)

O'Connor seems to agree with Baudelaire. Jonathan Culler's commentary on Baudelaire's poetics sheds light on the wiles of O'Connor's own diabolic procedures. Most pertinent for my purpose, Culler writes that Baudelaire's most significant practice is in making the imagination the "enemy of reality."[39] O'Connor does not say in so many words that the devil is manifest in "reality dismembered or torn to shreds by the power of the imagination." Rather, she says that the value-free fragmented world represents the masked face of the devil: "[The novelist] may find that . . . he has only reflected our broken condition and, through it, the face of the devil we are possessed by" (*Mystery*, 168).

The connection between hollow apocalyptic violence and the work of demonic art is drawn by David Jasper. In "Apocalypse Then and Now" and in "Living in the Reel World: The Bible in Film" he examines the question of why film, art, and literature continue to present us with apocalyptic fictions stripped of sacred insight. Jasper agrees with Baudrillard that the very media of film and television cater to a life which has lost the ability to read the image as an awful insight into the real world.[40] The cinema, Jasper writes,

> has . . . employed the strong images of apocalypse, sometimes in a disturbing intertextuality with the Biblical text. . . . James Cameron's *Terminator II: Judgment Day* (1991), partly because of its popular appeal, manages to capture a feeling for apocalypse. . . . It is, however, a film which has failed to grasp the deep pessimism of its own culture . . . and ultimately does not appreciate the dark demons of its own images with their totalitarian implications. One of the most frightening aspects of *Terminator II* is its almost wilful lack of self-perception in a violent world. . . . What bothers me, however, is that so much of our postmodern literature, perhaps with much more honesty and less kitsch than the Hollywood epic . . . takes up the language of apocalypse, but without any sense of rebirth or restoration.[41]

Jasper notes our age's sharp eye for the "death of the subject." But we do not see the most dreadful of traps the Devil sets. Only in the hands of this Catholic ironic writer can the Devil's wiles lure the reader through disintegration to apocalyptic "revision of vision," as Jasper aptly calls it. O'Connor makes a similar observation figuratively in representing the culture industry as a "Sinsational carnival" (*Wise Blood*, 31) which produces no sensations at all. She describes film goers as so many Jonahs who, watching human monsters shove girls into incinerators, remain unmoved as stones (*Wise Blood*, 71). The sin of carnival culture is that the subjects it produces are sensationless blocks and stones, and worse than senseless things (*Wise Blood*, 10).

For such Devil's disciples violent loss of vision is its own reward. The presence of the Devil, therefore, is found precisely in his seeming absence (*Mystery*, 189). No wonder then that astute readers like Bloom and Updike, alert to the relevance of religion to American aesthetics, are disappointed by Flannery O'Connor's fictional world. Where is the added dimension, each wonders in his own way.[42] It is *not* there. Bloom does not find traces of his sublime American religion of self-destructive titans. Updike does not find his shattering Christian-American religion of Fall and Judgment. My reading claims that the traces of O'Connor's "added dimension" are precisely in the *not*. The not sublime, the not sinister, the not manifest presence of grace is, precisely, the Devil's doing. His work is to make the evil that *does* exist seem as if it does *not*. Her avowed targets are modern readers who declare that there is nothing beyond the text: "If you must look for anyone in him [the devilish author], Reader, look for yourself."[43]

O'Connor fears that her diabolical wiles and masquerades may defeat her prophetic intention to force the Devil to name himself and to help the Devil's possessed victims face the split between the Devil's share in their subjectivity and the possible share of grace. She knows that the violence of her Devil is manifest while her own redemptive purpose is not. The result is that her art may seem more like a work of Medusa turning her readers to stone, than a tribute to Moses pulverizing the icons of the blind (*Mystery*, 149, 59). O'Connor's fears are not ungrounded. Even an approving reader such as Miller-Budick complains that O'Connor uses excessive violence, signifying no religious gains. In *Engendering Romance* Miller-Budick responds to O'Connor's grotesque violence as follows:

> Yet there is something too grotesque, too violent, too painful, in O'Connor's fiction for us not to feel uneasy with such unifying, even celebratory readings. It seems immoral, even anti-Christian, to make rape and murder instruments of the divine will, even, if the stories are to be read symbolically and allegorically—as transparent representations of the processes of grace—leaving the odd possibility that we are intended to conform our own lives to the configurations recorded in them. Does a story like *The Violent Bear It Away* mean for us to understand that only through acts of violence, which pierce the secularist complacency of a godless world, can we achieve our own salvation or effect it for others? Could such a meaning in any way correspond to a religious vision?[44]

In view of O'Connor's explicit declaration of dependence on violence as one of her instruments of literary grace, and in view of her conception of grace as a ruthless breaking down of the imperial ego, whose walls require cruel battering (*Mystery*, 112–13), the answer to Miller-Budick's question might be, Yes! Grace requires grotesque strategies for its operation.

O'Connor's aesthetics of grace deploy a strategy of triple violence.

On the literal level of story and history the violence is physical; on the moral or psychological level the violence is spiritual; on the anagogic level the violence is theological.[45] Behind physical violations inflicted by characters on other characters is the psychical and moral violation of the victims and the perpetrators' innocent ignorance of evil. Deepest of all is the satanic violation of the twice-born soul, called into being by the other forms of violence.[46]

This triple strategy produces a split-level text modeled after the pattern of Medieval allegory and accessible only to readers who believe that there are more layers to texts and their historical contexts than meet the literalist eye. Reading anagogically, according to O'Connor, does not confine vision, as New Americanists would claim, but on the contrary, extends the range of vision. To resist political injustice to disenfranchised groups a reader should believe in the absolute existence of evil, in the absolute wrong that one must never inflict on others, and in the diabolical incarnate represented by each and every fallen human subject.[47] Beyond the violence inflicted by one social group on another, according to O'Connor, and enabling such violence to be perpetrated with a clear conscience, is the Devil, whose reality must be believed in order to be resisted. Beyond the relative rights and wrongs of politically defined injustice is the satanic evil which preaches that right is what is right for me and wrong is what is wrong for me. Or as Emerson says, "the only right is what is after my constitution, the only wrong what is against it."[48]

The Devils incarnate in O'Connor's stories who function as agents of aborted grace are those who stitch together with threads of oblivion the tear of guilt in the subject's soul. The Holy Ghost incarnate in or inspiring the crazy freak-like prophets (*Mystery*, 118) in her stories restores the split structures of text and psyche that the Devil is bent on veiling and thus destroying. Prophetic figures create salutary splits with a voice harsh and clear. Satanic voices destroy the divided discourse of moral conflict, simply by silencing the prophetic voice or rather seducing their dupes to turn a deaf ear to it.[49] Prophetic denunciations and warnings construct subjects torn between natural instincts and spiritual or supernatural prohibitions. Incarnate Devils destroy the prophetically split structure by the violence of bearing spiritual insight away.[50] O'Connor's texts, like Emerson's, address readers with two pairs of eyes (*Mystery*, 180). Unlike Emerson she represents the act of putting out the spiritual eyes with which we see "the soul's mumps and measles,"[51] as an act of violence far more destructive than putting out physical eyes. As agent of physical and moral pain the Devil remains an agent of divine grace, since stupid self-stupefied subjects require rude awakenings. But as putting the awakened spiritual pair of eyes to sleep, satanic violence destroys the work of grace.

O'Connor's prophetic figures deploy violence hoping that its victims will bear it and let it bear fruit in Judgment and rebirth. Her satanic figures bear the effects of violent awakening away, and thus bury in advance any chance of rebirth.

Prophetic grace helps one read one's own self as a freak, split into two images that emerge when the eyes of faith are opened. One image is that of a fallen freak, the other, of a grace-afflicted realist of distant Judgment brought near.[52] Satan's victims of course see themselves as heroes rather than freaks. Mrs. Shortley in "The Displaced Person" sees herself as a knight of righteousness, Tarwater in *The Violent Bear It Away* sees himself as a new Moses.[53] Such inflation however, as O'Connor represents it is yet another work of the Devil, who inflates us in order to be sure that we never regain our insight. Inflated with her own clear conscience, Mrs. Shortley remains blind to the suffering she allows others to inflict on the Displaced Person. Inflated by his rationalist and scientific pretensions, Rayber, in *The Violent Bear It Away*, explains away the existence of satanic crime.

Violent grace invades innocent self-ignorance and violates narcissistic psychic integrity. Satanic violence induces its victims to pretend that the tear does not exist by putting a veil over the accusing face of Mosaic and Pauline Judgment. O'Connor's world is rent with echoes of Holocaust and Hiroshima history, with hints of racism and anti-Semitism. These echoes and hints are faint because readers' eyes and ears are perversely shut. When splits of American subjects are stitched together by Emerson's "vaporization of religion," (*Mystery*, 161) and Whitman's assurances that evil does not really exist, O'Connor can only hold a mirror up to the sinister face of their painkilling ideologies.

V

O'Connor's antidote to American illusionism and dream-culture is keeping the two competing voices audible, and beyond them the eternal war between angels who know themselves to be freaks and devils who resist such self-knowledge. Speaking of Levinas's "strategy of violence" in "At This Very Moment in This Work Here I

Am,"[54] Derrida uses the twin metaphors of text as texture and writing and reading as violent tearing of textual textures. His reading of Levinasian violence can be used to illuminate O'Connor's violent artistic practices and the split-level texts they construct. Derrida stops short of showing how Levinas uses textual violence as strategy of violently deconstructing the subjectivity of the reader and thus giving birth to a prophetic subject. My own interpretation of O'Connor's violence of grace examines how Satan stitches together torn subjectivities to avert any chance of prophetic rebirth.

O'Connor's "freaks" suffer from subjectivities torn by awakening grace but held together by their own refusal to accept the gift. While one act of violence violates their self-enclosed, self-sufficient circle of selfhood, a counter-act of defensive violence strives to eliminate the self-shattering voices and visions. When these invasive agents of grace refuse to disappear, their violated victims adopt the next best way to make the invaders vanish. They "vaporize" the accusing stranger by reducing him to an unreal or insignificant nonentity.[55] Thus in *The Violent Bear It Away* and in "The Displaced Person" subjectivities restore their redemptively shattered self-enclosure by resorting to defense mechanisms that de-realize the agents of their violated simplicity. In "The Displaced Person" Mrs. McIntyre, whose enclosed circle has suffered religious violence, reduces the priest's talk to the droning blabber of an idiotic old man and the atrocities of the Holocaust to a mere dream ("Displaced," 226, 231). In *The Violent Bear It Away*, Rayber considers sin, Judgment, the Fall, Jesus, and the Devil as nothing and calls their spokesman, old Tarwater, a senile lunatic (pp. 186–87, 193).

Satan's task is to help along the reality-destroying work of dismissal. In *The Violent Bear It Away* the satanic stranger tells young Tarwater that "there ain't no such thing as a devil. I can tell you that from my own self-experience. I know that for a fact. It ain't Jesus or the devil. It's Jesus or *you*" (146). O'Connor's modern readers are like her characters: their moral sense and Christ-haunted if not Christ-fearing imaginations (*Mystery*, 44) have been atrophied by Emersonian gospels of reducing all evil to mere shadows and subjective charades.[56] Readers, O'Connor half-jokingly said, distort the very title of *The Violent Bear It Away*, calling it *The Violets Bloom Away*, or worse still, *The Bear That Ran Away With It*.[57]

The pattern of subjectivity attacked by grace and defended by acts of destroying the attacker's moral reality can be illustrated by the "conflict between . . . two sets of eyes" (*Mystery*, 180), in *The Violent*

Bear It Away and in "The Displaced Person." In both texts the characters' prophetic eye opens on unbearable evils. Diabolic blinkers give him or her a lift, or bear the unbearable reality away.[58] Nothing forces Rayber, Mrs. Shortley, or Mrs. McIntyre to sacrifice their old sinful selves and thus be reborn on the frontier of Judgment. For them Jonah is not a type of Christ, Isaac is not a type of Christ, and the *akedah* is not a type of the Crucifixion,[59] to which a believer must respond by acts of spiritual baptism.[60] To Paul (Romans 6), as to Barth commenting on Paul, and to O'Connor, objective sacraments of sacrifice (such as bread and wine)[61] signify and produce subjective correlatives in the believer who participates in the Sacramental rite. There is no grace without believers, O'Connor claims, and no Sacramental text without readers (*Mystery*, 109, 112, 161). The subjective correlatives that prophetic dramas must produce in readers are souls shriven with guilt and humility, not Promethean selves bloated and blinded with pride. Without a participating spectator whose soul is shattered with repentance, the murder of a victim is mere killing and represents neither *akedah* nor crucifixion. Thus Mrs. McIntyre—the "logical practical" protagonist of "The Displaced Person"—assures herself that "there are no ovens . . . and no camps and no Christ Our Lord" ("Displaced," 231). Both the women spectators in "The Displaced Person" and the men spectators in *The Violent Bear It Away* hollow their selves of subjective correlatives to the violence they suffer, or inflict, or perceive from a defensive distance.

Inflated by his pride of knowledge, the schoolteacher, Rayber, resists knowing himself as a fallen sinner or moral freak. The same goes for the "logical practical" moral freaks in "The Displaced Person." In the story, the priest tears open the eye of Christian conscience while Mrs. McIntyre stitches the torn texture of her cognitively enclosed circle ("Displaced," 224). How? She insists that the priest is nothing but a droning chatterer, that the Holocaust is nothing but a dream, and that she is as righteous as ever. Mrs. McIntyre's acts of self-blinding as self-healing are more effective than those of Rayber and Tarwater. They, at least, were faced with an actual devil to un-name himself ("there ain't no such thing as a devil." *The Violent*, 146). Mrs. McIntyre *sees* concretely neither Devils nor Jesuses. She cannot be excused as being possessed by a Devil. The Devil O'Connor read about in "cases of possession in the 19th century," never extinguished the identity of the victim he possessed (*Habit*, 360). The victim always preserves her name, and the Devil, his. The task of the priest or prophet as a "realist of distances" (*Mystery*, 179), O'Connor insists, is to make the Devil name himself in order to give the victim the freedom to resist him (*Habit*, 360). In O'Connor, the gift of grace leaves characters and readers free to see or not to see the face of the Devil incarnate who confronts them and tempts them not to see. O'Connor makes Mrs. McIntyre free to hear or not to hear the voice of the priest, the crunch of the Displaced Person's bones under the tractor ("Displaced," p. 234). The silence that prevails is her fault, not the author's.

In O'Connor's stories, as in Church belief, grace gives the self the power to see, to name, to resist a very real Devil as well as the sinner's own temptation to make the reality of the Devil disappear. Resisting the Devil requires, first, a recognition that his share in me is real, and secondly repentance. It should be recalled that Catholic priests perform the sacrament of Confession which is part of the rite of Penance. In "The Displaced Person" neither Confession nor Penance is elicited by the priest from Mrs. McIntyre. She resists grace by *not* recognizing anything wrong in herself and hence by repenting nothing. "I am not responsible for the world's misery" she retorts to the priest, and "squints furiously" at him when he tells her "about Purgatory" ("Displaced," 223–24).

To put it another way, in O'Connor resisting the Devil requires prophetic vision which recognizes the self as split between an old sinful self (to "kill" or "bury") and a newborn self, candidate for redemption. In *The Violent Bear It Away*, the sinful failure of O'Connor's characters and modern, disbelieving readers to accept her gift of prophetic self-knowledge is represented by scenes of baptism hollowed of baptismal significance and subjective correlatives.

To conclude, let me briefly illustrate these hollow rites that frame *The Violent Bear It Away*. The novel begins on the day the old prophet—Tarwater—dies, and young Tarwater gets too drunk to give him a Christian burial. Orphaned at birth, young Tarwater was first raised by Rayber—his schoolteacher uncle in the city—until his great-uncle kidnapped him and brought him to Powderhead to baptize him and raise him as a prophet. Tarwater's great-uncle tells him repeatedly of his prophetic mission to baptize Rayber's "dim-witted" son, Bishop, who lives with his father in the city. It is this baptismal mission that young Tarwater is expected to continue after the death of his great-uncle. Young Tarwater humbly hopes that when called he would say "Here I am, Lord, ready!" (128). But working against prophetic submissiveness is his Promethean yearning to be as sublimely heroic as "Moses who struck water from a rock, or . . . Joshua or Daniel" (128). That such self-worship is hardly the humility required and produced by baptism follows from a stranger's voice which invades Tarwater's inner ear the day his great-uncle dies. The voice presses him not to bury the old man but to burn him (138). Jeering at prophetic rhetoric and baptismal rites, the strange voice eliminates in advance any hint that burning old Tarwater symbolizes baptismally burying one's old self.[62] The voice inflates Tarwater with delusions of intellectual genius and with pyromaniacal desires. Young Tarwater sets his great-uncle's house on fire and catches a lift to the city with a salesman named Meek, whose real name, O'Connor claims, is the Devil (*Habit*, 359, 367).

Entrenched in his self-contained self-inflation, Tarwater remains inviolate to Rayber's efforts to initiate him into modern life (177). Rayber himself, being insulated and self-enclosed, turns a deaf inner ear to his nephew's freakish prophetic delusions and baptismal intentions.[63] Rayber watches from a distance, with perverse insensitivity, the silent spectacle of his son being drowned by Tarwater. A Freudian reader might interpret Rayber's failure to intervene as the work of his own repressed wish to drown his son. Rejecting Freudian readings,[64] O'Connor would prefer a Christian reading which would recognize the sinister de-meaning of literal murder voided of shattering, subjective awakening to guilt.

On his way home to the backwoods, having "baptized" his cousin by drowning him, Tarwater undergoes violation in a state of sleep and insensitivity, sedated by yet another stranger who gives him a ride.[65]

Violence without the shattering of enclosed selfhood also frames a baptism by fire that Tarwater performs after the "baptism" by water. Tarwater's fiery baptism relates intertextually to Captain Ahab's baptism by fire in *Moby Dick*, and by that token to its Satanic precursors—Teufelsdrockh's in Carlyle's *Sartor Resartus* and, further back, the gnostic reversal of baptism by water into a fiery rebirth. O'Connor juxtaposes the two kinds of baptism:

> Water, it seems to me, is a symbol of the kind of purification that God gives irrespective of our efforts or worthiness, and fire is the kind of purification we bring on ourselves—as in Purgatory. It is our evil which is naturally burnt away when it comes anywhere near God. (*Habit*, 387)

Like the Christian spectacle so the Promethean one is hollowed of prophetic subjective correlatives.[66] Here O'Connor takes a Promethean Romantic trope of fiery rebirth, and once again leads the reader into temptation to expect a fiery baptism that leaves him happily in hell. However, by fusing the fire with the lake, and by implicitly fusing gnostic baptism by fire with Christian baptism by water, O'Connor ironically makes fiery baptism itself a step in the traditional Christian journey to redemption, associating it with Purgatory rather than with hell. In other words, fiery baptism is associated with souls in progress towards purification rather than with souls condemned to be imprisoned in their sins eternally.

On the *anagogic* level the ritual scenes revolve around a baptism coded in two opposite symbolic systems. On the *psychological* level this double-coded baptism represents two alternative models of subject construction—Bloom's closed imperial and titanic prophetic subject, and Barth's almost anachronistic prophet, whose old self is baptismally "dissolved" and "drowned" on the frontier of Judgment.[67] In *The Violent Bear It Away,* Tarwater seems on the threshold of a similar ritual of dissolution: "[T]he boy's white face . . . drained but expectant, lingered a moment at the threshold . . . as if waiting for an invitation to enter" (206).

Why does Tarwater linger? Apparently he must undergo a violent ordeal and a shattering self-dislocation and self-division before an invitation can reach him. Violent awakening, such as the "violation in the woods,"[68] is a necessary but not sufficient condition for recognizing violence as a vehicle leading to the frontier of baptismal rebirth. Furthermore, which rebirth does the door invite American readers to enter? Does trial by fire in this story precede renewal by water as Purgatory precedes Paradise in Dante's paradigm? O'Connor leaves the paradigms void of symbolic keys, which in any case only the Church can offer and only believers can accept. The mystery-drama is enacted as a silent spectacle whose repressed layers of mystery O'Connor expects hostile readers to ignore (*Mystery*, 41–42).

Rather than purifying himself by water, Tarwater chooses purgation by fire:

> He kicked the leaves together and set them on fire. Then he tore off a pine branch and set it on fire and began to fire all the bushes around the spot until the fire was eating greedily at the evil ground, burning every spot the stranger could have touched. (261–62)

Readers no more learn what the final revelation may be than know to what end the Devil offers a lift. But religiously literate readers can guess that ritual paradigms of prophetic rebirth have been hollowed of sacramental grace violations. In O'Connor as in Barth, baptismal apocalypse means an ever-present moment of threshold experience, where the shattered subject opens to a crisis of Judgment to which he can submit but which he may also refuse. In a remarkably explicit passage in *The Violent Bear It Away*, O'Connor distinguishes between apocalypse in the sense of final catastrophe, and apocalypse as the crisis of deconstructed selfhood. Religiously experienced, sacred violence requires that its victims remain awake while their subjectivity is violated. On at least two occasions in *The Violent Bear It Away* sacred paradigms are not emptied out of subjective correlative violation. First, old Tarwater envisages his prophetic calling as both outer catastrophe and inner "Krisis":

> The old man, who said he was a prophet . . . had set out to the city to proclaim the destruction awaiting a world that had abandoned its Saviour. He proclaimed from the midst of his fury that the world would see the sun burst in blood and fire and while he raged and waited, it rose every morning, calm and contained in itself. . . . It rose and set and he despaired of the Lord's listening. Then one morning he saw to his joy a finger of fire coming out of it and before he could turn . . . the finger had touched him and the destruction he had been waiting for had fallen in his own brain and his own body. His blood had been burned dry and not the blood of the world. . . . That was not the last time the Lord had corrected the old man with fire. (126)

The transmissibility of such moments is then suggested by a reenactment young Tarwater experiences of a version of his mentor's apocalyptic crisis. Where the old man felt that destruction had fallen in his own brain, Tarwater feels "like one condemned, waiting at the spot of execution" (177). For both, revelation is a personal crisis as well as a historical catastrophe. The moment of violent shattering and burning of self produces in young Tarwater a new prophetic sight and insight: "His scorched eyes no longer looked hollow or as if they were meant only to guide him forward. They looked as if, touched with a coal like the lips of the prophet, they would never be used for ordinary sights again" (262). Molded to "the fate that awaited him," Tarwater sets back to the "dark city, where the children of God lay sleeping" (267). "My prophet," O'Connor writes, "will be inarticulate and burnt by his own visions. He'll have to explode somewhere" (*Habit*, 373).

4

Footsteps and Echoes: Jewish Figures of Prophetic Diachrony in Grace Paley's Family Tales

Speaking to us—are the dead not freed from death, resuscitated in their very death? Only the living would ask for more existence.

—Emmanuel Levinas, *Proper Names*

I said to them: " . . . You said that after the second catastrophe no one was left alive in the town. So you are yourselves no longer alive!" They smiled, then, as the dead smile when they see that we think they are no longer alive.

—S. Y. Agnon, *The Fire and the Wood: The Sign*

"You," he said, "you have no ideas, what are you? . . . Let me tell you, a dead man tells you this, at least I had a life, at least I understood something!"

—Cynthia Ozick, "Envy; or Yiddish in America"

I

Silence and deafness after Auschwitz are not allowed by Paley's characters. But neither does Paley find a living language in which to voice her response to Holocaust history,[1] except perhaps in her story "Dreamer in a Dead Language,"[2] where she permits the father of Faith—her narrator—to tell his grandchildren about their murdered relatives with grim, unreadable wit:

Let's think up a good joke. . . . There's an old Jew. He's in Germany. It's maybe '39, '40. He comes around to the tourist office. He looks at the globe. . . . He says. . . . Where you suggest, Herr Agent, I should go? . . . He points to America. Oh, says the agency man, sorry, no, they got finished up their quota. . . . A few more places . . . the answer is always, port is closed. . . . So finally the poor Jew, he's thinking he can't go anywhere

on the globe, ... He pushes the globe away, disgusted. But he got hope.
He says, So this one is used up, Herr Agent. Listen—you got another
one? (271)

Why tell the terrible tale of the free world's refusal of asylum to Hitler's prospective victims as a black joke? Why tell Old World tales
altogether? And are the two questions connected?

Only by juxtaposing the New World's aversion to oldness with to-
talitarian history does Paley quietly protest against Anglo-Saxon
codes of disregarding the call of others. Cultures of newness which
culminated in historical catastrophes for Jews cast their shadows on
the New World cult of newness and non-listening represented by
American dreamers in living, contemporary languages. In
"Dreamer in a Dead Language" the avant-garde poetics of old-re-
pressing newness is counterpointed with Nazi and Soviet politics of
exterminating old people and old books. The battle of the books
fought by furious arguers is foregrounded by the Kulturkampf in
Germany, and by the exclusion of Faith's old relatives from a place
of asylum. There is no place for Jewish grandfathers on the multicultural globe of the free world: "So finally the poor Jew, he's thinking
he can't go anywhere on the globe" (271).

Framed by Holocaust history, excluding grandparents from a
place on the globe cannot be read as a figurative plea for multicultural tolerance. The question is not merely linguistic or heteroglossic. The question is not only who has and who does not have a right
to speak in the contemporary conversation. It is also who has and
who does not have a right to exist.[3] A story which begins with a question, Why listen to the old? and continues with, Why is there no
place for grandfathers on the globe? is an attack against the aesthetics and politics of silencing the old physically. "Dreamer in a Dead
Language" voices Paley's protest against the injustices practiced by
xenophobic cultures. Against the background of xenophobic deafness to the cry of old people, Paley's practice of xenophiliac listening carries ethical connotations that she herself traces to biblical
and Talmudic sources, and to a type of prophetic discourse.

Responding to the politics of Hitler's and Stalin's murderous anti-
Semitism requires a prophetic ethics. Read through Levinas' concept of prophetic ethics, the point of the joke Paley's Jewish grandfather tells his grandchildren is messianic: listening itself is the
caress of consolation that rescues victims of tragic insulation from
living with doors and windows closed.[4] Where is this other place—

globe or universe—where the hope of opening closed doors remains? For Faith's father(s), as for Levinas' prophetic people,
elsewhere is in the extraterritorial space of the Book: "we are here
living mostly People of the Book," says Faith's father, "Book means
mostly to you Bible, Talmud etc., probably. To me, and to my generation, idealists all, book means BOOKS . . ." (275).

As we have seen, for Levinas the message par excellence of prophetic ethics and its Talmudic interpretations is, "thou shalt love
[the stranger] as thyself; for ye were strangers in the land of Egypt"
(Leviticus 19:34).[5] It seems to me that this message, albeit more subdued, is communicated by Paley in her unique art of listening. In
chapter 1 I analyzed elements of Paley's dialogic staging of the contradictions she finds between Promethean models of prophetic selfhood and the Jewish models that her parents and grandparents
brought with them from the Old World. Aesthetically regarded, the
stylistic and thematic elements found in Paley's writing, such as
dialogism, diachrony, feminism, sympathy towards elders, and acceptance of or non-allergy towards strangers, seem unrelated com-
ponents of her narrative style.[6] Read through the lenses of competing prophetic models in her cultural conditioning, these elements
turn out to be connected. Her younger-generation characters
preach and practice Emersonian newness and anxiety of influence.
Like Bloom's Emersonian poets, Paley's protagonists cultivate newness and seek release from the prison-house of relation.[7] Like Levinas's Amos, Samuel, and Isaiah, by contrast, her Old World, older
Jewish speakers preach and practice care, responsibility, and respect
for precursors and strangers. Paley's narrator is split between the
ethical responsibility she practices and the Promethean newness she
perceives and accepts in others.

Here I will not comment on the breakthroughs in narrative identity, the use of "Yiddish accents," or the feminism, which critics of
Paley have explored.[8] Rather, I will concentrate on analyzing her art
of prophetic listening with the help of Levinas's model. On the level
of ethical and prophetic depths, Levinas shows, Jewish listening is
not only hearing stories told by other tellers. It is also doing whatever authoritative voices command.

No Promethean would allow precursors to tell him or her how to
write a story or let them criticize the way he or she chose to write it.
Yet in Paley's "A Conversation With My Father," Faith and her
father argue about how to write a story.[9] Faith's failure to produce a
satisfactory result may be due to the double bind produced by con-

flicting imperatives of her father's Jewish telling and her own Promethean way. Listening is a strategy of breaking down self-enclosed or self-cultivating narrative identities. Listening itself reverses the Promethean gnostic model of allergy to antecedents, as Levinas calls it, or the anxiety of influence as Bloom calls it.[10] An heir of the prophetic tradition that Bloom calls the gigantic, or Promethean sublime, would not listen to the commandments of her parents, least of all if they tell her not to argue with her father.

Arguing with precursors to the point of erasing them is exactly what Bloom's Emerson instructs sublime poets to do. But when Paley stages scenes of listening or scenes of instruction, she constructs generational relations in which the later generation is told not to argue with the earlier, and obeys. In scenes of telling and listening, Paley's model features the generosity toward influence which Bloom claims went out with the Enlightenment.[11] Perhaps it went out from the New World. In Paley's multicultural dialogues it is excluded by the official ideologies of the younger generation. So multiculturalism cannot solve the problem of traditional Jewish alienation. All other voices in the contemporary conversation aim at replacing old canons by new ones. The Jewish voice is ideologically alien since in it the old claim the right to consideration and respect precisely because they are old. Faith and her author are able to live with both competing commands—do, and do not do, as your old precursor tells you. This double bind does not paralyze Paley's powers of creativity, but nurtures them. Yet more than multicultural polyvocality produces the splits in Paley's stories and characters. A further split is the incompatibility between the ethical imperative: "don't argue with your father," and the Promethean declaration: "what is yours is mine, my father."[12]

In chapter 1 I showed that gnostic Promethean allegory requires stealing, subverting, and suppressing paternal precursor paradigms. Likewise, what Foucault describes as a "California Cult of Self" in the American "technology of the self" requires discontinuing all bonds with the past and its burdens.[13] The anti-Promethean elements in Jewish prophetism were defined with Levinas's help as anchored in a religious and moral devotion to the traditions of a past so remote as to be virtually inaccessible. By contrast with their Promethean contemporaries and like Levinas, Paley's Jewish characters treat the past with a respect Levinas would call an ethics of diachrony.[14]

This chapter will focus on showing that in Paley's scenes of gener-

ational instruction, listening and telling have the same ethical prophetic depths as in Levinas's accounts of the master/pupil relation
between prophetic call (telling) and prophetic response (listening).

For Paley, as for Levinas, ethical prophetic experience requires
treating the precursor and the stranger as one's absolute master, not
with rage and murderous aggression but with compassion and availability. For such a reversal of xenophobia into xenophilia, the Promethean subject must be released from tragic self-enclosure.

I have chosen for purposes of illustration stories where names link
the aesthetics of diachronic listening to prophetic ethics, as Levinas
describes them. While her politics of feminism require that she practice civil disobedience, the prophetic aesthetics of Paley's characters
permit her to indulge her Jewish daughterly respect, responsibility,
and loving-kindness.

"Is there any way for . . . parents and children . . . to speak to
one another?" Miller-Budick asks, as she studies instances of intergenerational disagreement in Paley's fiction.[15] Miller-Budick insight-
fully points to painful moments where offspring disregard the suffering, despair, and estrangement of their parents and of older people
in general.[16] She seems to see these instances as part of the conflict
between Paley's/Faith's feminist agenda and the patriarchal law
(particularly in Jewish tradition). "Anxiety of influence," Miller-
Budick maintains, "seems to take an especially nasty turn when it is
cross-gendered."[17] Like Miller-Budick, I think that Paley's narrator-
daughter is split ideologically and morally, but I find that more than
cross-gendered conflicts account for very painful situations created
by these conflicts. My chapter explores a conflict between two cultural codes, namely the ethical, religious code of Faith's lapsed Jewish heritage and, as opposed to this, the secular political code of
Faith's contemporary alignments.

As we shall see, only Faith's politics of identity can be described
with reference to a Bloom-like anxiety of influence. The antithetical
anxiety, from which the older generation suffers, is precisely that of
being abandoned by the refusal of bonding on the part of over-anx-
ious offspring. My reading of Paley's ethical strategies is indebted to
Bloom's insistence that nothing can be less Jewish than an aversion
to and repression of one's ancestral heritage.

II

To situate Paley's stories on a map of Jewish critical conversations
concerning what is Jewish literature,[18] what is Jewish-American litera-

ture, or whether Jewish-American literature is possible, let me re-hearse a conversation in *Commentary* between Harold Bloom and Cynthia Ozick.[19] It should be remarked in advance that Ozick agrees with Bloom on two points. One point of agreement is that there can be no major American-Jewish poets. If they are major they are not Jewish in theme or rhetoric; if they are Jewish in theme and rhetoric they are authentic but minor. The other point of agreement is that whatever else may make Jewish-American writing Jewish—and that is a moot point—there can be no American-Jewish writing which, as Jewish, does not bear the brand of its biblical heritage. Unlike non-Jewish debtors to the scriptural tradition, Jewish debtors display no anxiety of influence, no hostility against precursors, no strong personal claim. On this matter Bloom and Ozick make almost identical observations.[20] For Ozick it involves no revision of her earlier positions since she draws very clear lines between pagan, Emersonian, prophetic pretensions and the Hebraic, scriptural, prophetic tradition.

While Bloom does not draw any distinction between the prophetic visionary imagination of Jeremiah and Blake in either *The Anxiety of Influence* or *Poetry and Repression,* he does draw a distinction of this kind in his *Commentary* essay, published a year before *The Anxiety of Influence.* Here Bloom enlarges his visionary American company to embrace a clear contrast between Jewish and non-Jewish prophetic rhetoric. Only the latter is a rhetoric of rebellion against a precursor, or father as Jews would call him. The former is a rhetoric of lamentation for a lost father or rejoicing at being found by a father, and only thus finding the self.[21] Here Bloom does not present Jeremiah versus the city, but rather the Jeremiah of Lamentations, mourning for a city that has vanished.[22]

It is not moral seriousness alone that bears the mark of Jewishness, Bloom observes, since high moral seriousness marks Twain as well as Scholom Aleichem, Melville as well as Malamud—to name some of the writers Bloom and Ozick both admire. Moral seriousness unites Jew and non-Jew. What divides them is first the strong personal stance present in the latter and absent in the former, and secondly, the strong devotional or liturgical ties to the past that bind only the former. According to Bloom, a Protestant vision displaces the personal accent of Luther's individual-God relation onto a relation between the poetic personality of ephebe and the poetic power of precursor. Nothing can be less Jewish than such an obsession with personality and with the repression of a precursor:

Clearly there is a peculiar problem of poetic influence at work among American-Jewish poets. . . . All post-Enlightenment poetry in English tends to be a displaced Protestantism anyway, so that the faith in a Person easily enough is displaced into an initial devotion to the god-like precursor poet. This, to understate it, is hardly a very Jewish process. . . . However far from Jewish tradition they may be, something recalcitrant in the spirit of young Jewish poets prevents them from so initially whole-hearted surrender to a Gentile precursor, and indeed makes them nervous about the process itself.[23]

Displaced Judaism turns to a more traditional kind of devotion, a devotion which is not only aesthetic but also theological. Bloom doesn't go to Ozick's lengths of claiming that only observant, Hebrew-literate writers can be authentically inspired by the tradition of the Scriptures—Halacha and Aggadah (the Law and the Midrash). Rather, he translates his definition of authentically devotional Jewish writing into the language of his essentially Freudian model. A devotional Jewish visionary must be found by a father before and as precondition of finding his poetic self and poetic voice. By diametrical opposition, for an Emersonian visionary poet, being found by a father before finding a poetic self and voice is an obstruction devoutly to be displaced. Being children of *both* American prophetic traditions, American-Jewish writers walk a tightrope of inescapable incongruity[24] between the burden of Jewish themes and their Emersonian rhetoric. If anything characterizes their anguish of dual identity, Bloom maintains, it is the irresolvable incongruity of their fictional way out of the dilemma.

Like Levinas and Bloom, Ozick distinguishes the figure of the Jew as a figure of displaced alien, from the stranger who constitutes the preferred persona of modern and postmodern writers. Displacement of the Jew among gentiles, or Hebrew among English writings, or Judaism with which Yiddish and Hebrew are saturated among pagan and Christian ideologies, is a displacement that cannot be bridged by translation. Bloom is right that translation is like the marriage of strangers, Ozick observes in "A Translator's Monologue" and in "S. Y. Agnon and the First Religion."[25] But Bloom is wrong to assume that translation can provide release and poetic redemption for both the translator (ephebe) and the translated (precursor). Translation might be a scene of rebirth where one becomes the other. But the rebirth of the translated poem spells the death of the original.[26] The same destructive effect follows upon translation, or marriage of strangers in the opposite direction, Ozick claims in "S. Y. Agnon and the First Religion." She reads Agnon's *Edo and Enam* as a parable of the deadly marriage occurring when pagan originals are translated into Hebrew. The newborn language and culture are destroyed from within by the precursor they hoped to master by translation.[27]

It is not surprising, therefore, that Ozick is more pessimistic than Bloom about the possibility of Jewish-American hyphenation. Promethean American or Apollonian-American prophetic inspiration is one thing. Jewish, Hebrew, scriptural, prophetic inspiration is very much another, she insists at length in *Metaphor and Memory*. In "Judaism & Harold Bloom" Ozick rebukes Bloom for replacing Jewish commitment and continuity with gnostic rupture and discontinuity.[28] Bloom retaliates by charging Ozick with practicing ruptures but professing self-deceptively not to. In the introduction to a collection of essays on Ozick, Bloom sharpens the differences between his vision of Jewish-American writing and Ozick's. She denies "consciousness of rupture between normative Hebraism and her own vision," he says. This "denial of rupture must be honored as the given of her fiction, even as the fierce Catholicism of Flannery O'Connor must be accepted as the ground from which everything rises and converges in the author of *The Violent Bear it Away*."[29] But as a writer, Bloom insists, Ozick's Jewishness is no more relevant than Auden's gentleness is relevant to his writing.[30] Ozick, Bloom claims, misreads herself; her writing is less liturgical and more revisionary than she admits. At best her stories are structured by an "agonistic element" in which two rival languages and codes struggle endlessly. He cites Ozick's confession: "I had written 'Usurpation' in the language of a civilization that cannot imagine its thesis."[31] In other words, he argues, she confesses to an incongruity of form and burden which Bloom no longer regards as distinctly Jewish but as a mark of agon between a younger and an older generation, whether Jew, Gentile, or Buddhist. Against the grain of his earlier elegy for Jewish literature Bloom claims that there is only one model of influence anxiety, and it is neither Jewish nor gentile. Indeed the whole religious issue is irrelevant, to his mind.[32]

Besides dismissing the distinction Ozick draws between Jewish and gentile anxieties of influence, Bloom also questions her differentiation between the idolatrous Gnosticism of aesthetic religion and the idol-breaking wisdom of Hebraic tradition. He does not refer in so many words to Ozick's offensive description of modernist poets as

Terach's tribe, or to her flattering description of Jewish liturgical or devotional writers as Abraham's tribe.[33] But he does cite her own denunciation of the paganizing, aestheticizing Hebrew poet, Shaul Tchernikhovsky, feasting naked with idols until "the taciturn little Canaanite idols call him, in the language of the spheres, kike."[34]

Bloom retorts that Jewish fiction qua fiction is just as idolatrous as pagan fiction, qua fiction:

> Fictions remain stubbornly archaic and idolatrous, to the scandal of Eliot and Auden as pious Christians, and of Ozick as pious Jew, but very much to the delight of Eliot and Auden as poets and dramatists, and of Ozick as story-writer and novelist.[35]

What Bloom says about the narrative strategies Ozick uses to reconcile her "ambivalences" as she works both sides of the generational divide, applies with less ambiguity to Paley's narrative strategies of ambivalence.[36] It applies to Paley because she too constructs a "dialogue between generations."[37] It applies to Paley with less ambiguity because, unlike Ozick, Paley makes no liturgical or devotional claims for the Jewish or choral voice in her stories. Neither are the generational conflicts in her stories staged as agons between secular and sacred ideological positions.[38] What remains as the *distinctly Jewish* element in both women writers, I argue against Bloom, is precisely that of intergenerational dialogue.

I agree with what Ozick has to say in her critique of Bloom concerning a significant difference between a seemingly similar anxiety of indebtedness shared by all writers. Non-Jewish writers show no pity and no generosity towards their precursors, Ozick observes, citing as evidence the following comment from *Anxiety of Influence*: "If the imagination's gift comes necessarily from the perversity of the spirit, then the living labyrinth of literature is built on the ruin of every impulse most generous in us." According to Bloom, Ozick continues, "all of us are disconsolate latecomers; . . . we are envious and frustrated inheritors." Our obsessive concern is how to "steal the fire that the great ones before us, our fortunate Promethean precursors, have already used up for their own imaginings." The answer is rupture, discontinuity, undoing the work of the giants who walked the earth before us.[39]

Ozick denies that this applies to all writers or that religion is irrelevant to whether influence is experienced with generosity or with aggressive envy. "The notion of 'undoing' the precursor's strength," she maintains, "has no validity in normative Judaism." Her distinction between Modernism and Jewish liturgy is worth quoting at length:

> Jewish liturgy . . . affirms *recapturing without revision* the precursor's stance and strength. . . . "Torah" includes the meaning of *tradition* and *transmittal* together. . . . In Jewish thought there *are* no latecomers. . . . Modernism, perforce, concerns itself with the problem of "belatedness." Modernism and belatedness induce worry about being condemned to repeat, and therefore anxiously look to break the bond with the old. . . . In the Jewish view, it is only through such recapture and emulation of the precursor's stance, unrevised, that life can be nourished, that the gift of the Creator can be received, praised, and fulfilled.[40]

The point here is that there are two ways to tell a dialogue-of-generations story. One is the gentle, grateful diachrony for the sake of survival and continuity. The other is hostile, resentful, envious discontinuity for the sake of self-inflation and self-destruction.

Bloom blithely ignores the distinction Ozick draws between Jewish anxiety to continue the life of the precursor and gentile desire to discontinue that life. For gentiles the inherited life of ancestors is a curse, for Jews it is a gift. Ignoring this distinction, Bloom cites as evidence of Ozick's own Promethean anxieties a dialogue of generations in her story "Envy; Or Yiddish in America." He ignores the diametrically opposed sense of influence and heritage dividing the old poet who wants to be translated and the young woman who refuses to translate him, or as she calls it be vampirized, cannibalized, and dybbuked by him.[41] The old Jewish poet perceives intergenerational indebtedness as a gift of continuing life beyond the grave, received and bestowed in the same spirit of Jewish hope. The young de-Judaized, Nietzschefied translator rejects his historicizing proposal as murderous. She accuses him of proposing a cannibal burial of the living by the dead. Here is what Bloom cites, letting the venomous voice of the paganized young translator have a say and dismissing the appealing pathos of the old poet's voice as "hysterical":

> "You," he said, "you have no ideas, what are you? . . . You were never born, you were never created!" he yelled. "Let me tell you, a dead man tells you this, at least I had a life, at least I understood something!"
>
> "Die," she told him. "Die now, all you old men, what are you waiting for? Hanging on my neck . . . hurry up and die."[42]

Paley and Ozick would call the pathetic appeal of the old Jewish poet historical rather than hysterical. The young translator parrots hysterically cliches of Emerson's and Nietzsche's aversion of history.[43] The poet expresses satirically the nihilism and destructiveness, rather than creativity, of that drive to discontinuity:

> "Go get a memory operation! You have no right to it, you have no right to an uncle, a grandfather! No one ever came before you, you were never born! A vacuum!". . . .
> "You dead old socialists. Boring! You bore me to death . . . you despise, you bore, you envy, you eat people up with your disgusting old age—cannibals, all you care about is your own youth, you're finished, give somebody else a turn!"[44]

Bloom concludes that "as a dialogue between the generations it hurts magnificently. . . . Ozick herself is on both sides and on neither, *as a storyteller.*"[45] Ozick's essays, however, tell us she is on the side of hope, generosity, pity, and continuity.

A strikingly similar intergenerational dialogue, with a similar satiric dig at the Promethean position of the younger generation, occurs in Paley's "A Conversation with My Father." In both stories the grieving older generation laments the failure of the younger to inherit and continue the values of family life. But the response of the younger generation in Paley is gentler than its counterpart in Ozick. The difference is similar to that between a violent religious quarrel and a gentle secular conversation. Both writers agree that to end the process of transmittal or translation is to end life. In Ozick's "Envy; Or Yiddish in America," the young translator ends the old poet's life by refusing to continue it through translation; in the story told by Paley's narrator in "A Conversation with My Father," the son refuses to continue the life of the mother by leaving her lonely and heirless. Ironically the paganized son in Faith's story has been bred by the paganized mother who cuts off in advance the stalk from which life could flower.[46] By another turn of the ironic screw, the son is less anxious about continuing maternal company than she is—"what about you too mom?" he asks. The inner story, told in two different ways by Faith the daughter-narrator—before and after the father interferes—parallels the frame situation of diachrony. Diachronic family devotion in Paley's stories encapsulates a larger embeddedness in history, which links the narrative identity of her characters to their historical or group identity.[47]

III

In an interview with Joan Lidoff, Paley foregrounds the dialectical tension at the center of her writing: "I think it's two events or two characters . . . or two ideas or whatever, bumping into each other, and what you hear, that's the story."[48] Paley anchors this dialectical tension in rival models of selfhood and of historical identity. These she finds in (old) ethical prophetic codes and in (new) American cultural ones that she inherited, and which are as radically divided against one another as the different languages—"the street language [English] and the home language with its Russian and Yiddish accents"—to which she is heir.[49] She sets up arguments between gnostic Promethean rebels against history and Jewish (biblical and Talmudic) adherents to history. The orientation, which rejects the free interpretation of traditional narratives, is practiced by individuals who project an Emersonian self, shut off from others and obsessed with themselves. The counterpointed self Paley offers is open both to past history and to the voices of others: "I became interested in having things more open at the end . . . sort of open to something else . . ."[50]

Like Levinas and Ozick, Paley makes diachrony and historicality the core of Jewish prophetic ethics. In "Dreamer in a Dead Language" the "anachronism"[51] of Jewish diachrony is criticized by Faith's father. Explaining why Faith's mother is reluctant to leave her Jewish old-age home he says:

Your mother likes it. She thinks she's in a nice quiet kibbutz. . . . She organized the women. They have a history club, Don't Forget the Past. That's the real name if you can believe it. (277)

Like Faith's mother, Paley's narrator apparently belongs to a "history club," since she consistently makes family history the locus of the narrative identity she creates.[52] What Paley has to tell should be understood "historically rather than psychologically."[53] One function of telling a story is to write imaginary history, which Paley claims is "totally invented and yet could happen every day, and probably has happened . . . ,"[54] and in which exclusions made by real history can be corrected or forgotten, superseded or resurrected. Imaginary history, as Fredric Jameson has shown in "Max Weber as Storyteller," can reconcile in textual play the conflict of codes which leads, in historical reality, to replacement.[55] The narrative, he claims, can supersede "the naive linearity" of realistic historical representation, introducing instead the "phenomenon of what is currently termed 'intertextuality' in which the text under study must be seen in a relationship of tension . . . to some older text without which the first cannot properly be understood."[56]

More than intertextuality underlies Paley's strategies of diachronic subject-construction. Faith's dialogues with her father involve ethical conflicts between competing attitudes to time and narrative, and competing models of narrative identities.[57] "A Conversation with my Father" is but one example of New American versus Old Jewish in the father-daughter dialogues.[58] Behind their aesthetic argument concerning plot structure in literature there is a deeper disagreement about the ethical faiths and philosophies of history to which father and daughter both implicitly adhere. In "Dreamer in a Dead Language" Faith and her father argue about the meaning of Old and New (or prophetic and Promethean). While they argue, the distance between father and daughter is opened only to be narrowed again: "She moved away from her father—but not more than half an inch" (277). Ironically, the daughter who has consciously assimilated to the culture of the New World is closer in her practice to the ethos of Jewish historicality than her father, who is still burdened with Old World cultural baggage. It is Faith who advocates the ethical art of diachronic stretching, to borrow an expression Ricoeur uses,[59] while her father is the one who resists being released from the self-enclosed and therefore, according to Levinas, tragic self. Old and New, Jewish and Promethean positions exchange roles in the discourse of the story. But the plot structure of the story is postulated on an open, diachronic subjectivity built into the father-daughter relationship within a Jewish family from before the story begins. Whatever their ideologies, no matter how mutually exclusive the content of what they say, their act of saying and the contact it presupposes indicate that their author created a father and daughter dialogically and diachronically bound to one another at the very core of their subjectivity.

Paley's imaginary history does not aim at exclusion. The fictional text reflects a "simultaneity of the mutually exclusive,"[60] ethically as well as aesthetically. Paley's opposing voices speak "from their own latitude and longitude, and from their own time in history," thus keeping the story open on both thematic and narrative levels, and narrative subjectivities open on an ethical level. The text, nonetheless, preserves the one linearity Paley subscribes to—that of "generational discussion . . . not in the Freudian sense but in an historical sense."[61] Unlike emplotment, which she renounces as being "too much of a line,"[62] the generational line suggests what Ricoeur calls, in *Time and Narrative*, "a principle of coexistence and of interaction."[63] A central aspect of this coexistence is the transmission of tradition which is "not the inert transmission of some already dead deposit of material but the living transmission of an innovation always capable of being reactivated."[64] Ricoeur examines the affinity between historical events and those framed by the narrative and finds shared lines of longitude and latitude:

> Corresponding to the perpetuation of societal existence is the connection between generations that intertwines life and death, and provides the living not only with contemporaries but also with predecessors and successors.[65]

For Paley, the vertical line of historical perspective in the fictional narrative, which allows for the Old World, Old Testament tradition to be transmitted and reactivated, intersects with the horizontal line of multivocal societal or political perspective in the relations between the storyteller, her characters, and her listeners.

Silencing the exchanges of conflicting voices and languages, by rejection of the generational line, can cause a "cultural dead end," as Hana Wirth-Nesher has shown in the case of Henry Roth, who "is cut away from the mother tongue, whose proficiency in the newly acquired language exceeds that of the mother tongue, but who cannot transfer his emotional involvement to that acquired language."[66] Paley, by contrast, refuses to be "cut off from the truth of our tongue."[67] She avoids the schizophrenic or paralytic effects by treating the cultural crisis historically and not psychologically. Thus, the languages bumping against each other in her cultural heritage serve "to remind me of the person I really was . . . the comfortable daughter of hounded wanderers, resting for a generation between languages."[68]

One could claim that in the sphere of empirical history the Americanized daughter has superseded the displaced father—the "ghetto Jew" with "a kind of deference to Anglosaxonism"[69]—just as one language has superseded the others, and American cultural codes have displaced the Jewish ones. Yet the process of telling the imaginary history of relations among relatives who never question their mutual bonding, allows Paley to store the historically displaced elements—such as her father and his tradition—in her memory, like the storytellers of primitive tribes who "say that the store of memory is in the belly and can be released through the throat."[70] The stories she retells issue from that vertical line of "some continuous narrative that moves through history, that your parents speak to you about, that your grandparents spoke to your parents about."[71] In Paley, as in Levinas, ancestral memories are not alien to one's identity, but rather its very essence.

Upholding the generational line is represented in Paley's stories as going against the grain of Promethean responses to history. According to Bloom, in the American Sublime tradition history is an insult and injury of imitation and destructive influence. His tracing of this tradition to Emerson might find support in Emerson's appeal, in "Nature," to be detached from the vertical generational line: "Why should not we have a poetry and philosophy of insight and not of tradition, and a religion by revelation to us and not the history of theirs?"[72] In *The Anxiety of Influence* Bloom himself negates the line of longitude linking the artist with "cultural history, the dead poets, the embarrassment of a tradition grown too wealthy to need anything more."[73]

Bloom's prophetic model represses the family into the self. He cites Kierkegaard's maxim: "He who is willing to work gives birth to his own father."[74] By contrast, Paley constructs creative subjects who are open to and fruitfully invaded by family members. Her family is not only biological but cultural:

> Isaac Babel! When I read him . . . I said, 'Wow! He had the same Mommy and Daddy I had!'. . . . The other writers don't so much influence you as have the same historical life that you have, that you come from, the same language structures.[75]

The rivalry between the two mutually exclusive responses to what Bloom calls "belatedness" is presented in Paley's "Zagrowsky Tells," where the elderly Jewish storyteller finds his generational discourse pitted against the multicultural American one, used by his wife and his interlocutor, Faith.[76] Zagrowsky refuses to see the past as "only a piece of paper in the yard." Every occurrence in reality seems "[t]o remind us. That's the purpose of all things" (353, 359). Aware of the dichotomy between his old Jewish approach to history and the New American one, he mocks the younger listener of his tale: "An American girl has some nerve to mention history" (358). His wife,

by contrast, is accused of having abandoned her place in the generational line. She "says, Ai, ai. She doesn't say oi anymore. She got
herself assimilated into ai . . ." (353–54). Contemporary American
language, he complains, has replaced his wife's traditional one to
such an extent that concern with the wrongs of racial discrimination
supersedes the nightmares of Holocaust history. He resents her solidarity with those he accuses of directly or indirectly practicing violent injustices against his people: "We? We? My two sisters were
being fried up for Hitler's supper in 1944 and you say we?" (354)

Like Ricoeur, Paley sees generational relations as a "we relation"
in an imaginary community which exchanges codes across time.[77] In
"Zagrowsky Tells," language and social commitment seem interchangeable when the elderly narrator accuses his wife not only of
supplanting one language with another but also of replacing one
community with another. Her attempt to partake of the responsibility for racial discrimination in American society seems to Zagrowsky
a betrayal. To his wife's "Yes Iz, I say: *We*," he responds: "Don't think
this will make you an American . . . that you included yourself with
Robert E. Lee. Naturally that was a joke, only what is there to laugh"
(354).[78]

When Paley's consciously Jewish characters say "we," they refer
to a community-identity defined by diachronic bonds. But a "we"
structure also characterizes Paley's own narrative voice which is a
composite of diverse, often conflicting voices. Like her fictional storyteller, Paley castigates members of her society for the predomi-
nance of a self-centered, congested "I" that refuses to open up to
social dialogue:[79]

> We're individualists! and we say "I and the universe, I and the moun-
> tains," I and almost anything. Whatever it is, it's "it and I." But there are
> cultures after all, which said "we." They said "we." And the fact that we
> can't imagine the word "we" as sometimes a word meaning all humanity
> . . . is also a failure of the imagination, as far as I can see.[80]

By contrast, Paley's political aesthetics constructs a listening/telling
subject open to absorb the voices of others: "You tend to find your
own voice if you really listen to lots of voices."[81] Like Cavell, Paley is
not oblivious to the dangers of Promethean reduction of the individual subject:

> What happens to [the alienated subjects] is that they are supposed to
> fulfil themselves and develop themselves, and not one of us, really, can
> . . . develop ourselves, our single self, without being hurtful to others.[82]

Her art, by contrast, requires listening, openness, and exposure: "Listen!," she calls out in the introduction to her *Collected Stories*, "I *have* to tell you something!" (ix, Paley's italics). Thus viewed, the act of telling and listening constitutes "an imposed task," a commitment and a responsibility which involves the suffering of interferences and incursions. Presented as "the act of bringing justice into the world a little bit," it is predominantly ethical and not merely aesthetic.[83]

In Paley's fiction as in Levinas's philosophy, sociological and ethnic[84] identities are transcended by the diachrony of prophetic being-for-the-other. In both, the ethics of gratuitous, generous giving of the self to the other, without losing the self, undermines the "reign of identity."[85] In the "extraterritorial"[86] space of liturgical telling and listening, political/ethnic identities are irrelevant. Reading "Zagrowsky Tells" is enhanced by recalling that according to Levinas "the extravagant generosity" towards another creates "a living duality between politics and religion."[87] Paley does not say in so many words, as Levinas does in *In the Time of the Nations*, that the "Jewish Bible I quote is not the originality of an ethnic particularism."[88] Instead, she stages "the living duality" of politics and ethics, by exposing the irrelevance of ethnic particularism to the understanding of Zagrowsky's strange charity.

Historically and politically, Jews and blacks are trapped by identity politics in ethnic and class strife. Jewish ethnic identity does not suffice to transcend ethnic war towards ethical peace among strangers.[89] Faith is Jewish ethnically, but not open ethically to hearing the message of her father's gratuitous generosity. Jewish family commitments alone do not suffice as grounds for creation of ethical selfhood. The daughter has not been told what to do and why, liturgically, and so what the historical scene tells her empirically makes no sense to her. Here again, lack of diachronic pre-formation precludes ethical, graceful inspiration and performance. How does the living duality of politics and ethical devotion rescue the prophetic remnant?

IV

For a conceptual structure of the relation between language, ethical responsibility, and open subjectivity, there seems no stronger paradigm than Emmanuel Levinas's philosophy of the self-for-other.

Levinas's relevance derives from his prophetic ethics which assaults the Promethean, "imperial" ego. Levinas distinguishes between a sovereign and autonomous subject—a self-enclosed "dominant me . . . who would be master of the world"—and a heteronomous, prophetic subject that "divests the ego of its imperialism" by becoming exposed and indebted to the other in an asymmetrical relationship.[90] "To communicate," Levinas claims,

> is indeed to open oneself, but the openness . . . is complete not in opening to . . . the recognition of the other, but in becoming a responsibility for him [sic] . . . where the for-the-other proper to disclosure . . . turns into for-the-other proper to responsibility.[91]

Levinas's responsible subject is accountable for the other to the point of "vulnerability, exposure to outrage, to wounding, passivity . . . trauma of accusation suffered by a hostage to the point of persecution."[92] Passivity in this sense does not mean self-annihilation but "relaxation of virility without cowardice," the "holding back" of narcissistic vanity. Submissive exposure offers an alternative discourse to that of masterly "egoisms struggling with one another, each against all, in the multiplicity of allergic egoisms which are at war with one another."[93]

Submissive exposure is achieved by human contacts that Levinas calls "Saying" as distinct from "Said": "It is the *Saying* that always opens up a passage," he writes in *Proper Names*. By "Saying" he means the "Gift and sacrifice," of self to stranger. "Saying," unlike the "Said," is always readable as "an awakening of Self by the Other, of me by the Stranger, of me by the stateless person."[94] Saying maintains and at the same time bridges the rupture between sayer and listener, intensifying the uniqueness of each. In listening to the stranger's appeal, Levinas maintains, my uniqueness as myself, instead of being alienated, is intensified.[95]

In Paley's fiction as in Levinas's philosophy, the relatedness of Saying, beyond the rivalries and ruptures of what is Said, sustains human contact and calls for mutual responsiveness and responsibility. For Paley's irrevocably bonded speakers as for Levinas's the contact they maintain seems "even more important than the content it communicated . . . the voice as important as the message."[96] Like saying, hearing is a demonstration of contact and commitment. As scriptural prophets respond to the prophetic call "Here I am! Send me" (Isaiah 6:8), so too, do Jewish mandated subjects. As "hostages"[97] of others before whom and for whom they are responsible, mandated subjects are "called to leave . . . the concept of the ego . . . to respond with responsibility: *me*, that is, *here I am for the others.*" Insofar as the subject is open to the sign of the Other through attentive listening, he is "potentially a prophet."[98] In diametrical opposition to Promethean selfhood, the self produced by prophetic hearing bows to the authority of the past. Respect for anteriority requires learning "lessons from everyone else and from the whole of the past . . . the whole thing integrating itself as tradition."[99]

Like Levinas, Paley treats Jewish materials in relation to their gentile cultural milieu in various ways. Sometimes she practices polyglossia and heteroglossia of cultural and linguistic contact and mutual translation. To interpret her heteroglossic strategies requires consulting Bakhtinian models of textual linguistic and cultural dialogism.[100] But sometimes, especially in her expressly Jewish-tradition-oriented stories, Paley practices diachrony in addition to dialogism. While her dialogism allows conflict-free conversations between Jewish and Emersonian discourses, diachrony requires laying bare the radical contradictions between the old Jewish image of "prophetic" selfhood and the new Emersonian image of poetic selfhood.

In stories that foreground the discord between scriptural and Promethean possessions, the structure of the narrative is modeled on diachronic patterns of continuity, while only the discourse of the speaker supports Promethean rupture. Story and setting represent Jewish family ethics as being outside the contemporary American field of discourse, in principle and in advance. The mutual exclusiveness of Jew and Promethean does not follow from what they say but from where they say it and due to given family structures. My reading focuses on diachrony and its accretions: exteriority, heteronomy, Here I am!, femininity, and oldness or anteriority. All these features are foregrounded by Levinas in texts where he pits new philosophical ideologies of self against old scriptural images.[101]

Levinas retrieves from Kierkegaard's Protestant protest[102] a structure of self which is diachronic and affiliated to an anterior other at the very core of its identity. Likewise, Paley retrieves from Emerson's Romantic protest a structure of self which is family-affiliated, and pre-verbally bound, from its inception, to anterior others. As Miller-Budick has shown, dialogic structures can leave the violent, egotistic sublime of the speakers and their groups intact. "You kept me down three hundred years, you can stay down," a "big colored fellow" says to white Mrs. Zagrowsky in the subway.[103] Cultural contact is always dialogic, but dialogues as such are not necessarily violence-free by any means. In history and in Paley's stories Black-Jew dialogues are rife with verbal violence and behind it with the violence of clashing group-ideologies.

By contrast, diachronic family dynamics in Paley's Jewish family romances are free of verbal as well as egotistic violence. Whatever the characters' ideology may be, Paley upholds in advance, by the very premises on which the story is structured, the rights of parents and of children. Like Levinas, though not in so many words, Paley experiences her Jewish legacy as a "divine comedy of transcendence" without violence.[104] Or more accurately, as a human comedy of exotopic[105] heteronomous bonding with others without an aggressive anxiety of influence, without parricidal malice towards precursors.

Like Levinas, Paley presents *old* Jewish diachrony as an antidote for and the antipode to *new* romantic ideologies. Like Levinas she holds that dialogism can, but need not, contribute to construction of an ethical, as opposed to an egotistically sublime, selfhood. But like Levinas she believes dialogism can be potentially ethical or Other-oriented only if it is molded in advance on diachronic models. In her stories, self-begotten poetic orphans can talk to one another; but in poetic Promethean principle, they cannot recognize any debt to or responsibility for precursors or successors, parents or offspring. By contrast, characters constructed and functioning as offspring, display an otherwise-unexplained concern for others. Emersonian characters pursue the new by forsaking the old. Jewish characters just as committed to the new by their American ideology are strangely caring for the old. Both the dialogic and diachronic way to subdue the giantism of the Emersonian American self are very old. But the attribute of ethical oldness is built into the very essence of diachrony. Oldness, pastness, anteriority are excluded in principle from Emerson's gospel.[106]

In Paley's Jewish stories, romantic Emersonian newness and Bloomian anxiety of influence (by debt to the old and the anterior) are put into question in advance by the diachronic family relations which structure the speakers' subjectivity of Jewish selfhood (as opposed to American selfhood).

V

Where diachronic bonding fails, so too will the prophetic potential of Paley's story. A living-community lifeline can be sustained only by shared dreaming in a *living* language. No such living Jewish language is available for Paley's Jewish "listeners." In *The Political Unconscious: Narrative as a Socially Symbolic Act*, Jameson observes that Marxist and historicist criticism have reduced to the status of dead languages the once life-giving myths, liturgies, and sacred traditions which formed the "locus of group-identity."[107] In "Dreamer in a Dead Language" and also in "Faith in the Afternoon," Paley's laconic allusions to the language of Jewish scriptures and liturgy trace, for individuals who have already lost the "locus of group-identity," a hollow space where a community once existed. The loss is due partly to assimilation and partly to mass extermination. These allusive traces of a dead cultural-religious language may be read as Paley's aesthetic solution to the problem facing American-Jewish writers.

How, lacking a living community of senders and receivers, does one communicate at all in "a dead language?" How does one remember the lost religious community in a language to which the keys are lost? Paley's solution might be called a narrative oxymoron, telling and listening in a language at once living and dead. Traditional remains are "resurrected" only to be emptied of any living traditional meaning, by living listeners who lack the literacy with which to respond. Resurrected remnants remain dead for all cultural-religious purposes of keeping a continuous group identity alive. Thus Paley's allusions are at once living and dead. Living as Yiddish and Hebrew words in the mouth of living speakers; names of the dead carved on benches in an old-age home,[108] signs without context, or significance, or literate reception,[109] or "Listening," as Paley calls it. The scriptural figures are there, but deprived of any living, life-sustaining function.

Thus, in "Samuel,"[110] a story whose very title alludes to the biblical scene of call and response—"Here I am!" (I Samuel 3:8)—Paley's plot subverts the biblical paradigm. By telling the story not so much without an elaborate biblical intertext as without the ethical weave of diachronic responsiveness, Paley empties the prophetic name—Samuel—of any scriptural ethical meaning.

In "Samuel" Paley tells the story of a boy killed in a subway accident. Her interest in the tale, Paley says in an interview, is focused on "what it is mostly to the mother. What that loss is."[111] Naming the boy Samuel, Paley alludes to the biblical story of Hannah who pledged her firstborn child to God (I Samuel 1:27).[112] Framed by her biblical precursor, the ethical ambiguities in Paley's portrait of modern maternity emerge.[113] Scripturally slanted, maternity requires that Hannah offer Samuel up with resignation, and that she take consolation both in the ethical sign borne by her firstborn, and in the promise of continuity through the other children with which God blesses her. Paley's protagonist, unlike her intertextual prototype, is deprived of any consoling vision of continuity. On the contrary, she responds to her loss within the narrow and despairing horizon of atomistically isolated individuality: "But immediately she saw that this baby wasn't Samuel. She and her husband together have had other children, but never again will a boy exactly like Samuel be known" (198). More than the loss of a child is involved in Paley's presentation of the bereaved mother. Intertextually, there is also the loss of "maternal" or "prophetic" availability. It seems that for Paley, as for Levinas, maternity serves as metaphor for the prophetic, ethical response, or "signification [which] signifies . . . in nourishing clothing, lodging in maternal relations."[114]

Conspicuous in its absence in Paley's depiction of Samuel's narcissistic mother, is the Levinasian prophetic-maternal subject as responsible, exposed "hostage," indebted to the other:

> It is . . . maternity, gestation of the other in the same. . . . the groaning of the wounded entrails by those it will bear or has borne. In maternity what signifies is a responsibility for others, to the point of substitution for others and suffering. . . . [In maternity] the ego repudiates the past present; bent under the charge of an immemorial weight, the inflexible ego, an undeclinable guarantee against any cancellation, supports the other it confronts because it would have committed itself to that weight, or in reminiscence would have assumed, as ancient and essential, commitments it would have taken on unbeknownst to itself.[115]

Levinas stresses that unlike the commitment or engagement freely undertaken endorsed by existentialists, in maternal commitment the subject does not choose but is rather chosen. Levinas writes:

> the effort is made to reduce all commitment to freedom. Such a reduction refuses the irreducible anarchy of responsibility for another. Maternity, vulnerability, responsibility, proximity, contact—sensibility can slip toward touching, palpation, openness upon . . . , consciousness of . . . , pure knowing, taking images from the "intact being," informing itself about the palpable quiddity of things. . . . Subjectivity of flesh and blood in matter—the signifyingness of sensibility, the one-for-the-other itself—is the preoriginal signifyingness that gives sense, because it gives.

Not because, as preoriginal, it would be more originary than the origin, but because the diachrony of sensibility, which cannot be assembled in a representational present, refers to an irrecuperable pre-ontological past, that of maternity.[116]

Vulnerability, responsibility, proximity, contact, palpitating sensibility, touching, and above all giving are missing from Paley's portrait of Samuel's mother.

A similar strategy of counterpointing a Promethean self-enclosed character in the text with an exposed scriptural prophetic model in the intertext is practiced by Paley in "Zagrowsky Tells." Again Paley sets up an ironic contrast between the biblical paradigm and its twentieth-century parody. The intertextually-uninformed reader will not understand why Cissy, the narrator's daughter, insists on naming the colored boy she bore to an African American gardener, Emanuel. Possibly a reader more in touch with scriptures than Paley's implied target for criticism would recognize a reference to the paradigmatic, consolatory prophecy of the Judeo-Christian tradition: "Therefore the Lord himself shall give you a sign; Behold, a virgin will conceive, and bear a son, and shall call his name Immanuel" (Isaiah 7:14).[117]

As we have seen, Levinas regards Saying, or the very giving of signs, as pregnant with ethical significance. Be the content of the said what it may, Saying itself signifies giving:

Signification is the ethical deliverance of the self through substitution for the other. . . . There is deliverance into self of an ego awakened from its imperialist dream . . . awakened to itself, a patience as a subjection to everything.[118]

In "Zagrowsky Tells," however, the ideology of Me-ism that dominates what is said submerges the intertextual ethics of Saying. Emanuel, conspicuously unlike his scriptural namesake, is self-engrossed and "jumps up and down yelling Me, me me" (349).

But beyond the link to the boy's biblical namesake, why the implied reference to Esau in Zagrowsky's laconic remark—"he's from Isaac's other son, get it?" (359) On the political/historical register Zagrowsky's explanation remains unclear. The reader can "get it" more clearly on the register of Levinas's prophetic ethics. Since politically his previous behavior has been biased,[119] Zagrowsky must reverse his position before mutual alienation between African

American and Jew can be reversed into a kinship bond. Only the reference to Esau fills the gap created by this strange reversal: "Thou shalt not abhor the Edomite, for he is thy brother; thou shalt not abhor an Egyptian, because thou wast a stranger in his land" (Deut. 23:8). This is the text to which Levinas appeals when making the welcome of strangers the core of his prophetic ethics. Relating to the story of Esau the Edomite and Jacob—two warring brothers who still avoid bloodshed—Levinas recalls the Halachic commandment: "love the stranger!"[120] From this tale the Talmud draws the corollary that the Jewish people are to treat as fraternal neighbors the nation of Edom whom Esau fathered. In Paley's story, Zagrowsky meets the call of his grandson Emanuel by overcoming his racist, xenophobic attitude, transcending identity politics, and adopting the child precisely because he is a stranger. In answer to the question why he adopts the stranger, the alien child, he states: "To remind us." Remind us that we should love the stranger as ourselves; that we should open up our Promethean self-enclosed selves and listen to the call of the Other, especially of the stranger. Framed by this biblical prophetic intertext, Zagrowsky's act seems less unreadable than it appears to Faith and her friends. To their scripturally illiterate new-American minds, totally divorced from historical/traditional perspectives, the boy does not fit into Zagrowsky's life. However, seen through Jewish ethical lenses, Emanuel "fits like a golden present from . . . Egypt. . . . He is Isaac's other son, get it?" (359).[121]

"Zagrowsky Tells" ends with a communal feminine bonding among Faith and her friends after hearing Emanuel's story. While they are seen "gabbing in a little clutch," Emanuel ultimately establishes his identity in the silent sign: "This is the first time he doesn't answer me. He's writing his name on the sidewalk EMANUEL. Emanuel in big capital letters" (364).

VI

In her interview with Joan Lidoff, Paley confesses that for a while she was possessed by narcissism and consequently suffered from writer's block. Only by exposing herself to other voices, "reach[ing] out to the world" and escaping self-enclosure, did she find her own voice:

Until I was able to . . . hear other people's voices, that I'd be hearing all my life, you know I was just talking me-me-me. While I was doing that I couldn't write these stories. And when I was able to get into other voices consciously . . . and become the story hearer . . . I just suddenly wrote them.[122]

In the story "Debts," the retelling of stories attentively heard is presented as the ethically imposed task of a mandated self: "I did owe something to my own family and the families of my friends. That is to tell their stories . . . in order, you might say, to save a few lives" (133). The act of telling is a responsibility not to be taken lightly: "There is a long time in me between knowing and telling" (132).

Their preexisting intergenerational bonds endow family tellers and listeners with a narrative identity anchored in inescapable and unquestioned diachronic indebtedness. In "A Conversation With My Father" Paley stages an irreconcilable argument between two ideological voices—the traditional prophetic voice of the old father, that advocates diachronic relations and venerates precursors (232), and the newness-cultivating, self-enclosed, Promethean voice of the daughter, that insists on change and progress (237). The son in the tale Faith tells her father mirrors her own deafness to the (older) Other, as he bars his mother from his ever-changing, newness-seeking life in the present "funny world" (236–37). Seen through Faith's Promethean-prophetic lenses, freedom from the prison-house of relations releases both son and mother to become "a hundred different things in this world as time goes on" (237). By radical contrast, read through the father's scriptural-prophetic lenses, the generational breach is neither funny nor beneficial, and the very genre in which it is told changes.

Framed by Levinas's ideas concerning "Judaism and the Feminine,"[123] my reading of the father's tragedy does not see death as the tragic element. Rather, from a Jewish Old Testament perspective, tragedy consists in cutting off intergenerational continuities. Here, a Jewish father urges upon his daughter the role of reaching "beyond death"[124] to an eternity of endless listening. According to Levinas, tragic heroes such as Hamlet and Macbeth are obsessed with self and therefore with their own being or nonbeing.[125] Prophetic personalities, however, are far more concerned with the death of the Other than with the death of the self. By listening to them and saying "Here I am!" living listeners are making the dead continue to reverberate. In *Existence and Existents* Levinas argues that "the hero is overwhelmed by himself. Therein lies what is tragic in him . . . we are not going to find in the subject the means for its salvation."[126] He claims that it is the feminine "caress of consolation" which can free the Promethean ego from the bondage of tragic existence, simply by listening and responding to human others: "Woman does not simply come to someone deprived of companionship to keep him company. She answers to a solitude inside this privation."[127]

In an essay on Roger Laporte and Maurice Blanchot, Levinas discusses Blanchot's argument that properly-listened-to language as such, by stretching between bygone past-self and unborn future-self, gives death an open-endedness it does not have in well wrought tragic plots with beginnings, middles, and ends. In prophetic listening the dead lie endlessly dying:

> Perhaps for Blanchot himself [the domain of literature] represents the after-death or the impossible death. . . . In their own time the dying will never cease dying. . . . This voice that approaches in becoming more distant, like an echo or a rhythm, hovers at the edge of silence and forgetfulness. . . . Is language a listening that perceives or a contact that brings close?[128]

By listening, Paley's story hearers safeguard their families against death as forgetfulness. Their commitment to continuity might be their way of rescuing relics of an otherwise forgotten biblical heritage.

VII

In Paley's stories, scenes of prophetic (Jewish) listening are often staged at the seashore. To her Romantic American listeners the seashore might carry Whitmanesque, mystic, sublime, self-destructive yearnings. But to her fictional characters, as they listen to remembered and overheard conversations, the ocean inspires no such Promethean yearnings. Paley's listening characters make no anxious claims to firstness, originality, inventiveness, and divine creativity that require stealing the precursors' fire if not displacing them altogether. Born listening, a child all ears,[129] Paley's listener is contentedly belated, related to a sea of family speakers by whose remembered conversations her creative life is nurtured. To a reader whose ear is attuned to intertextual absences, the absence of Whitman's poems of poetic death and rebirth is intriguing. In Paley's Jewish, as tacitly opposed to Promethean, oceanic scenes, the inspired speaker is not alone but facing a densely populated "cosmos." Her self-transcending stance is ethical and realistic and humbly historical, not sublime or metaphysical. The plain familiar historical fact is that her parents took her to the seashore, as Jewish families did in summer in the days of old-fashioned bourgeois family bonding. Faith follows in their footsteps and takes her sons Tonto and Richard to the beach, playfully inviting them, as parents do, to bury her in the sand ("Dreamer in a Dead Language," 282–83). No metaphysical connotation is evoked by the Jewish mother's appeal to her sons to give her a proper burial. To a Jewish ear, sand has affirmative, prophetic, and liturgical connotations. In the prayer said at end of the Sabbath, (*Havdalah*) the believer blesses the Lord who "makes the distinction / between sacred and unhallowed," and who "our sins . . . will forgive / our seed and our wealth / will . . . increase like sand / and like the stars of the night."[130]

Sand and sea do not evoke associations of death, dissolution, and *unio mystica* in Paley's scenes of listening any more than they do in Jewish liturgy. Her narrator's care for her parents and her offspring, her passion for continuity, are liturgical in so many acts, if not in so many words. Whitman's oceanic sublime is defiant and destructive, leaving the poet alone, with his parental inspiration "untouch'd, untold, altogether unreach'd, / withdrawn far," and with his maternal seductress whispering "through the night . . . the low and delicious word death. . . . laving me softly all over, / Death, death, death, death, death."[131] By cultural contrast, Paley's oceanic realism is affectionate, devoted, fecund and, if we recall the *Havdalah* prayer, forgiving.

The forgiveness is for her precursors, for knowing very well what to demand of her and for molding her in their ethical image. Forgiving her children for burdening her with anxiety of continuity, Paley implicitly reverses Whitman's defiant "What is yours is mine my father,"[132] and displaces it with her inherited, forgiving inter-debtedness. What is hers, in every act of listening and liturgical speaking, is her father's and her mother's and her grandparents', her husband's and her friends', no matter how derelict, how self-centered. For Paley's as for Levinas's listeners, listening is gratuitous, whether the per-

son heard and responded to deserves it or not. For the Jewish listener, listening without forgiving is not really listening.

In a story transparently called "Listening,"[133] two speakers insist
that to listen is to forgive. The linkage becomes more transparent if
read through the prism of Ozick's definition of fictional liturgy in
"America Towards Yavne," and in "Metaphor and Memory."[134] Even
more illuminating here is Levinas's linkage of prophetic liturgical
ethics with forgiving. In *Totality and Infinity* Levinas argues that the
prophetic openness to the other means patience and forgiveness:

> The supreme ordeal of the will is not death, but suffering. In patience,
> at the limit of its abdication, the will does not sink into absurdity. . . .
> [Patience] is produced only in a world where I die *as a result of someone
> and for someone.* . . . in patience, where the will is transported to a life
> *against someone and for someone,* death no longer touches the will. . . . The
> plane of the inner life is that of apology."[135]

In *Fragments of Redemption,* Susan Handelman argues that Levinas
describes this movement of apologetic self-giving with the "Greek
word liturgy, whose original signification, he notes, includes gratuitous investment with no strings attached—liturgy with no religious
connotations but as 'absolutely patient action.' "[136]

In Paley's stories the voice of liturgical ethics requires nothing devotional, only "absolutely patient action." Her liturgical strategy
consists in acts of listening to vulnerable Others, whether dead ancestors, self-centered, derelict husbands, or friends in need. Perhaps
the function of literary liturgy is to allay the American element in
Jewish-American writing, to soothe if not silence the rumble of Promethean anxieties. This seems to follow from Paley's story "Listening," where interlocutors half-listen to one another, while rebuking
one another for not listening. Here, listening can actually feed Promethean fury. Thus Cassie, Faith's lesbian friend, accuses her of fail-
ing to tell her tale, leaving her "out of everybody's life" (386).
"From now on," Cassie threatens, "I'll watch you like a hawk. I do
not forgive you" (386).

Unlike Levinas's implied liturgical-prophetic listener, whose
being is for others, Faith's friends and even Faith herself hunger to
be avidly listened to and glorified in tales revolving around their
own personal litanies of grievances. Often, Faith does not listen gen-
erously but from a distance of embittered criticism. The listeners/
speakers fail to forgive one another and listen gratuitously to one

another in a liturgical mode of listening. In their contemporary New American conversation, liturgical listening is missing. Paley misses it; in her interview with O'Sullivan Paley confesses that "in 'Listening' . . . I realized I hadn't listened. . . . So it was really a self-criticism."[137]

VIII

Miller-Budick elegantly entitles her chapter on Paley "The Graceful Art of Conversation: Grace Paley."[138] In her concluding remarks Miller-Budick uses the term "grace" in reference to Paley's strategy of confronting catastrophe by weaving names of author and female protagonists together. According to Miller-Budick, Paley's protagonist "is always aspiring, through hope, to grace—and on through the chain of displacements, from grace through hope to faith restored."[139] My own reading would refrain from using "grace" to describe the responses of Paley's characters to past catastrophes, or as Paley calls them, the "little disturbances" of their lives.[140] Both the Christian psychology of Grace and the Jewish ethics of *Hessed*—mercy and generosity—are fueled by strong religious emotion and framed by institutional patterns of prayer and sacrament. Paley's style may be graceful in the secular aesthetic sense and register; but can it be regarded as full of grace in the sacred, religious sense? Hardly, I would suggest.

"Grace" (unless used in a strictly aesthetic sense) carries eschatological connotations of individual and communal regeneration and resurrection, which are absent in Paley's tales, including those featuring traces of Jewish-prophetic traditions. A crisis of forgotten faith and hope shadows the younger generations who display loud indifference to questions of religious despair and hope, ruin and resurrection, annihilation and survival.[141] Both Christian and Jewish experiences of grace require as their precondition mourning and repentance for sins of the past. In Lamentations, the ruins of Jerusalem are mourned as visited upon the Jewish people for their sins. Likewise in Isaiah, prophecies of hope, consolation, and regeneration are preceded by denunciations of sin and impending penal catastrophe. As shown above, in the *Havdalah* prayer recited every Sabbath after sundown, the Jewish believer binds together tears for past sins with hope for forgiven fecundity: "Our sins He will forgive / Our seed and our wealth / Will he increase like sand / . . . .

As for my sins, pass over them / Like the yesterday that has passed /
. . . . I am worn out with my sighing / I float in tears each night."[142]

In Christian rituals of psychic and spiritual rebirth, effective grace
presupposes confession of and mourning for the sinful self. In Levinas, opening towards the stranger requires questioning and transcendence of the self-obsessed self.[143] In Ozick, Jewish *Hessed* is
expressed in liturgical acts of generosity, mercy, and kindness. Thus,
the biblical Ruth, says Ozick, "sees into the nature of the Covenant,
and the life of the story streams in. Out of this stalk mercy and redemption unfold."[144] In Bloom, Jewish writing—if it is Jewish—is
framed in tones of lamentation and mourning for the ruins of the
Temple and for the annihilation of European Jewry.[145] By marked
contrast, Paley's gracefully witty tales of friendship may express a
quest for happy forgetfulness, but hardly a contrition triggered by
obsessive memories of crime and punishment.

In her introduction to "A Conversation with my Father," Paley
describes her parents as "hounded wanderers, resting for a generation between languages."[146] Literally, this refers to Yiddish and English; but metaphorically, as introducing a story about two ways to
tell a tale of family estrangement, this refers to an existential condition of being caught between two codes and two Midrashim related
to the one master story in which they are encoded. The story about
which the parent—Judaism—and the offspring—Christianity and
Gnosticism—have been carrying on an age-old conversation is the
story of the Temple's destruction, exile, and the hope for salvation.
The original Jewish version, told by all the Hebrew prophets, is a tale
of *penal* estrangement, whose ethical message is "thou shalt love
[the stranger] as thyself; for ye were strangers in the land of Egypt"
(Leviticus 19:34), and whose eschatological promise is one of redemptive reconciliation and release from estrangement. The other,
Gnostic (and openly anti-Jewish) Midrash on estrangement is of
redemptive estrangement, told by an alien messenger, who exposes
reconciliation as the ruse of a devil-god, and the anxiety of estrangement as a saving awakening. Retold by the Gnostics, the message of
the stranger is to insist on one's strangeness, to rebel against strangers who lure and welcome one to their prison-house of lies.[147]

As Ruth, Faith's friend, senses in "Midrash on Happiness," Faith's
Midrash contradicts itself or talks in two competing voices. On the
one hand, Faith dreams of happy independence or rupture, on the
other hand, of happy continuity, happy avoidance of intergenerational estrangement. To illustrate the difficulty that Jewish-American

poets have in speaking the American-Gnostic language of anxiety and influence, Bloom cites Charles Reznikoff's poem:

> My grandfathers were living streams
> in the channel of a broad river;
> but I am a stream that must find its way
> among blocking rock.[148]

Unlike Reznikoff, whose union with "the speech of strangers" drives him to seek his lost tradition, Paley's second- and third-generation Jewish-American characters speak English without a sense of loss and without seeking to resurrect any "dead language." What is missing from her perhaps too "graceful conversations" is the pain pervading Bloom's bilingual poets.[149] Bloom cites Irving Feldman's poem on the quest for "vanished bones / of the broken temple," and a poem by John Hollander, occasioned by *Tisha B'av,* mingling "the Lamentation of Jeremiah with the prophecy of ruin for New York as the Newer Jerusalem":

> In place of black skullcaps, read what was
> wailed at a wall
> In the most ruined of cities. Only the City
> is missing.[150]

Much more than the city of Jewish words is missing in Paley's strategy of "resting for a moment between two languages." For me what is most painfully missing is precisely the anguish and agony of loss which Bloom reads Jewish poets as expressing and evoking in their readers. The effects of Feldman's and Hollander's lamentations and of Ginsberg's *Kaddish,* Bloom writes, are not "*imaginative* suffering for the reader, but . . . akin to the agony we sustain when we are compelled to watch the hysteria of strangers."[151] In Paley's fiction, except for fragmented, muted references to names of prayers or biblical figures, no living remnant of lost linguistic, religious traditions provokes Faith or the reader, if not to search, then at least to weep for lost traditions. Where no anguish is expressed by speakers, at home in a no-longer-strange new language, no agony of watching "the hysteria of strangers" is inflicted on the reader. At most a subdued sadness haunts one of Paley's/Faith's story hearers—Ruth. In "The Expensive Moment" Ruth allows herself an exceptional moment of sadness.[152] In "Midrash on Happiness" she is quietly hounded by a sense of something missing from Faith's American dream of violent pursuits of libertarian happiness at all costs.[153]

Like her parents, Faith is caught between two languages; by day, the language of rebellious avant-garde; by night, an old scriptural language which reads newfangled dreams as old-fashioned nightmares. In "The Story Hearer," awakening in horror, Faith seeks alleviation for her Jewish anxiety of abandonment by reaching for the Old Testament.

Characteristically, she reaches for the wrong text. The right one, given that her friend Ruth is the one to express anxiety, would have been the biblical romance of Ruth, a sad story of death, loss, and exile with a happy ending of a welcome stranger raising up the seed, just as Faith wishes her estranged lover would raise up her seed. But she faintly remembers another story of estrangement redeemed by miraculous fertility—the story of Abraham, Sarah, and Isaac—told significantly not for its akedian violence but for its romance of bonding and continuity (345).

Perhaps Bloom's omission of Paley from the group of *Jewish* writers he studies stems from the absence of the religious dimension he seeks. My own feeling is that prophetic Jewish elements are present in Paley only as absent, missing, or missed. Paley's readers are guided to recognize that only the younger generation can hold the promise of resurrection in the Jewish sense of survival, continuity, fecundity, and stretching across the distance of time and death. We are made to miss in Paley's youthful characters notes of creative liturgical lamentation chanted for the razing of the city of Judaism.[154] Only old mothers shed tears, and their sorrow is almost silent. Their silence does not reverberate, as it does in Levinas, with language as contact and continuity. Rather, the young go off, leaving their future and their parents' past cut off from one another, thus allowing no hope for continuity. This is true not only of the apostate drug-addict mother and son, who forsake the Jewish fold in "A Conversation with my Father." This is also true of Ruth's runaway daughter and of the mother who mourns in vain for the derelict offspring who will not remember her mother.[155] Names are often significant in Paley's stories—but precisely as hollowed of any graceful meaning. Ruth is not a figure of grace as she is in the scriptural romance. Neither is Samuel in Paley's "Samuel" the son of a providence-serving, mourning mother, but of one who mourns for herself alone.

Ironically, Jewish children in Paley's stories are not expected to mourn. On the contrary, they are raised to pursue the American dream of liberty, equality, and the pursuit of happiness—their own, of course: "Faith really is an American and she was raised up like everyone else to the true assumption of happiness."[156] Ironically mournful American-Jewish parents encourage their offspring to be happy, thus excluding, in advance, the *Hessed* of creative lamentation. In prophetic ethics, without graves there can be no cradle of rebirth, and Paley's essentially secular stories tell of no uncanny contact with resurrected ghosts found in Levinas and Ozick. There is no grieving for sins of the past, collective or personal. Without repentance, lamentation, forgiving, and listening, what remains of prophetic grace? This is the question my chapter has explored, and my answer is that what remains is only the trace of its loss.

5

James Baldwin's Schizophrenic Alienation: Between Marcion and Marx

> I am not at home here and never will be. That means that I will never, never, never, as long as I live, be at home anywhere in the world.
>
> —James Baldwin, *A Rap on Race*

I

Harold Bloom hails James Baldwin as heir to the Judeo-Christian prophetic tradition. Bloom reads texts such as *The Fire Next Time, Go Tell It on the Mountain* and *No Name in the Street* for scriptural allusions that mark not only Baldwin's "evangelical heritage," but even more significantly his "authentic descent from Jeremiah." According to Bloom, Baldwin shares with Jeremiah not only lamentations for a destroyed city or ferocious exhortations against its destroyers, but mostly a split between the call to protest against social injustices and an acute sense of self-estrangement. Like his scriptural precursor, the African-American writer is "a visionary of a certain involuntary isolation," and a "rhetorician of his own psychic anguish."[1] Yet in recounting Baldwin's tale of self-estrangement Bloom reduces his anguish of isolation and alienation to ethnic and sexual categories:

> Unlike Emerson . . . Baldwin speaks, not for a displaced Yankee majority, but for a sexual minority within a racial minority, indeed for an aesthetic minority among black homosexuals. . . . [H]e is a minority of one, a solitary voice breaking forth against himself (and all others) from within himself.[2]

In a similar vein, Bloom's reading reduces the dimension of Baldwin's prophetic experience and expression to moral aesthetics: "[Baldwin] is post-Christian, and persuades us that his prophetic stance is not so much religious as aesthetic."[3]

120

In chapter 1 I suggested that Bloom's preferred prophetic models are solipsistic visionaries whose origins he traces to the heresies of the gnostic religion.[4] Here I argue that Bloom introduces Baldwin as such a solipsistic visionary whose prophetic authority is most strikingly revealed in subversive denials of institutional Christianity and its God.[5] And yet Bloom denies Baldwin's prophetic language the transcendent dimension which he grants the prophetic paradigms of his American Religion.

One may claim, as Bloom does, that in Jewish-American prophetic ethics the religious dimension is repressed.[6] But in African-American writings in general and in Baldwin's in particular, a distinctly transcendent religious dimension furnishes an asylum from the predicaments of oppressed minorities, whether racial, ethnic, or sexual.

It seems to me that Bloom misreads Baldwin's strategies of self-estrangement and his model of prophetic selfhood. Baldwin addresses a distinct concept of alienated selfhood, different from both the imperial self of Yankee majority that Bloom's Emersonian selfhood elevates, and the circumscribed sexual and ethnic self to which he limits Baldwin. Bloom's reading raises a basic question: Can traditional models of Judeo-Christian prophetic selfhood be useful to African-American writers? My argument is that neither Levinas's model of "hostage" subjectivity nor Barth's model of condemned subjectivity can furnish oppressed groups with appropriate frames for self-fashioning.

Though Bloom denies Baldwin a transcendent religious dimension, his model of prophetic subjectivity is valuable for my study of Baldwin's strategies of subject construction because it transcends the sociopolitical frames of reference guiding a large majority of African-American studies. These studies, as Henry Louis Gates claims, have centered, over the past generation, on issues of collective and individual identity.[7] The debates have focused extensively on the sociopolitical aspects of what Du Bois in 1903 termed the problem of the color line. Gates predicts that future studies will foreground "the problem of ethnic differences, as these conspire with complex differences in color, gender and class."[8] My own concern is less with sociopolitical considerations than with the religious and prophetic strategies of estrangement of African-American writers.

Theories of African-American alienation deploy frames and categories based on historical and/or sociological models. Whether modeled on Marx or Goffman, for example, alienation theories refer to marginal groups excluded from the institutional centers of self-definition.[9] In this historical/sociological context, alienation implies "the view that human reality is totally self-enclosed, having no transcendent domain to which to relate. Hence . . . man is totally historical," and is held responsible for his temporal existence.[10] To the best of my knowledge, the Judeo-Christian sense of alienation, as well as its subversion by the gnostic narrative of redeeming estrangement, remain to be invoked as a tool for exploring the structure and dynamics of black religious alienation.

Ever since Paul and Augustine made a virtue of the Christian pilgrimage to alien worlds, the adventures of alienation as a key concept occupy a central position in the history of Christian theology and its heretical fringes. In the Judeo-Christian tradition exile was a punishment for disobedience—breaking the covenant with God. Thus Paul connects alienation with infidelity: "That at that time ye were without Christ, being aliens from the commonwealth of Israel, and strangers from the covenants of promise, having no hope, and without God in the world" (Ephesians 2:12). Paul and Augustine, and later the Gnostics who adopted and distorted their paradigm, translated the experience of alienation into a double-edged model. Spiritual elites were initiated into alienation as liberation from the prison-house of worldly existence, while pagan sinners and other unregenerate human beings continued to suffer alienation as a penalty for their lack of faith.[11]

In slaveholding America, the penal aspect of alienation was advocated by the slaveholders as a convenient ideology for encouraging slaves to accept captivity as penalty for sins against God and man. It would take two centuries of consciousness-raising for African-Americans to adapt to subversive purposes the redeeming side of the alienation experience. In modern and postmodern African-American writing, alienation is often seen not as punishment but as the privilege of the awakened captive, who recognizes the deceitfulness not only of his human captor but of the entire historical world.[12]

Baldwin is not only aware of the manifold and antithetical uses of the concept of alienation, but embraces it, playing on the complexity to suit his artistic purposes. Baldwin's sense of alienation is marked both by heretical Christianity and by Marxist theorizing.[13] The anguish he feels is both for himself and for others, as emerges in an interview with Richard Goldstein: "You see, I am not a member of anything. . . . I'm a maverick, you know. But that doesn't mean I don't feel very strongly for my brothers and sisters."[14]

His diverse, even diametrically opposed, responses to alienation find expression in his conversations with Margaret Mead. Mead is surprised by Baldwin's pessimistic, almost fatalistic view of White-Black history as a scene of irremediable evil. She reminds him that whether as an American or as a Marxist, he is committed to the optimistic belief that human beings have the power and the obligation to remake history. Baldwin concedes both positions. On the one hand, he voices a Marxist call for change within the existing "power structure," in order to abolish alienation, "to get out of the hands of the people who have the means of production and the money, to get it out of their hands and into the hands of the people at various local levels so that they can control their own lives."[15] On the other hand, he relapses with a gnostic-like pessimism into a reading of history as a scene of radical, almost ontological alienation, from which there can be no liberation within the temporal world. Home is nowhere—neither in America, nor in France, certainly not in Africa:

> I am not at home here and never will be. That means that I will never, never, never, as long as I live, be at home anywhere in the world. . . . No power under heaven or under the sea or beneath hell will ever allow me to take my place in this particular pantheon. (*A Rap on Race*, 238–39)

History is a major cause of this almost predestinated homelessness— "the knowledge that white people wrote history and in a sense wrote [me] out of it. Not in a sense; in fact" (*A Rap on Race*, 117).

Baldwin affirms his responsibility to the African American and homosexual communities, and hopes for change: "The sexual question and the racial question have always been intertwined. If Americans can mature on the level of racism, then they have to mature on the level of sexuality."[16] But the alienation he suffers, as an isolated individual and artist, verges on a sense of metaphysical exile from historical temporal existence as a whole: "There is nothing to be done about it. . . . We are nonexistent."[17]

However, my reading focuses not on the multicultural, sociohistorical dimensions of Baldwin's alienation narratives, but on their gnostic metaphysical dimension. My claim is that, resorting to gnostic strategies of subversion, African-American writers undermined the white man's reading of black history which justified slavery as a penalty for their sins.

Although it is true that Christian ideology played a sinister role in domesticating and defending slavery in America, African-American reading of scriptures surreptitiously conveyed a meaning diametrically opposed to that purveyed by white Christian discourse. Their subversive reading was facilitated by an ideological ambiguity to which the Christian scriptures lend themselves. Official Christian ideology features two opposed elements: resignation to masters, and resistance to the world, the flesh, and the devil. The gospel of obedience generated a narrative of master-servant relations, promoted by white masters. But as an oppressed group, African-American slaves found it hard to accept a religious framework which underscored the demand to obey the master: "The preacher came and he'd just say, 'Serve your masters. Don't steal your master's turkey. . . . Do whatsomever your master tell you to do.' Same old thing all the time."[18] In preaching submissiveness to their African slaves, white American clergy harnessed the Judeo-Christian ethos of obedience to the father, whether divine or human. This ethos linked the call to obedience with the notion of slavery as penalty for sin, as well as with the blackness of evil, and the guilt of transgression. As Sollors has shown, the most frequently used biblical source in this context is Noah's curse on Ham (Genesis 9:20–27).[19] From Talmudic sources of the second century to biblical studies of the twentieth century, Judeo-Christian readings of this text combined the African's skin color with slavery, sin, and guilt. But as we shall see, African-American readings invert the master's sermon and reverse its figurative encoding.

To put it generally, the counter-gospel of resistance secretly generated narratives of rebellious defiance, casting the masters in the role of the devil and their slaves as the heroic antagonists. More specifically, Baldwin invokes the Ham tradition and inverts its implied moral lesson. The color black is not a penalty for freely chosen sin, but a fate built in to an evil creation (created by an evil god, the gnostics would say):

> I realized that the Bible had been written by white men. I knew that, according to many Christians, I was a descendent of Ham, who had been cursed, and that I was therefore predestined to be a slave. This had nothing to do with anything I was, or contained, or could become; my fate was sealed forever, from the beginning of time.[20]

Baldwin is not the only one to use the double-edgedness of a dominant discourse to imply one meaning for white readers and an opposite meaning for blacks. In his discussion of Richard Wright, Sartre suggests that divided readerships generate double-edged discourses as a matter of general modern fictional practice. Depending on his or her implied audience—black or white, captor or captive—the African-American writer will either pretend to tell a tale of submissive homecoming, or secretly intend by the same narrative to endorse an experience of rebellious alienation. Sartre shows that Wright's fiction addresses at least two audiences, and that this duality is part of the difficulty facing any African-American writer. Wright's discourse

> contains what Baudelaire would have called a double, simultaneous postulation; each word refers to two contexts. . . . Had he spoken to the whites alone he might have turned out to be . . . more abusive; to the negroes alone . . . more elegiac. In the first case his work might have come close to satire; in the second, to prophetic lamentation. *Jeremiah spoke only to the Jews.* But Wright, a writer for a split public, has been able to maintain and go beyond this split. He has made it the pretext for a work of art.[21]

The very duality that poses a problem suggests its own aesthetic solution. Incorporating the split into his narrative strategies, Baldwin exploits a potentially ambiguous pronoun "we" to infect the reader with the anguish of a double and divided elusive persona. Whereas Wright, according to Sartre, is obstructed as a writer by the split, Baldwin shares the obstruction with his reader: "I couldn't talk about 'them' and 'us'. So I had to use 'we' and let the reader figure out who 'we' is" (*Conversations*, 275). When he defines the addressee more clearly, Baldwin underscores the duality: "we—and now I mean the relatively conscious whites and the relatively conscious blacks" (*Conversations*, 379). Besides baffling them with an ambiguous "we," Baldwin tricks his dual audience by letting the ideology of his text tacitly abuse the *orthodox* reading of the narrative:

> If we . . . do not falter in our duty now, we may be able . . . to end the racial nightmare, and achieve our country, and change the history of the world. If we do not now dare everything, the fulfillment of that prophecy, recreated from the Bible in song by a slave, is upon us: 'God gave Noah the rainbow sign, No more water, the fire next time!' (*The Price of the Ticket*, 379)

To an orthodox white Christian reader, the allusion to God's covenant with Noah suggests the traditional assurance that his obedience will be rewarded with infinite fertility and earthly domestication:

> Whoso sheddeth man's blood, by man shall be his blood shed: for in the
> image of God made he man. And you, be ye fruitful, and multiply: . . . .
> And I will establish my covenant with you; neither shall there any more
> be a flood to destroy the earth. (Genesis 9: 6–11)

But to an African-American reader Baldwin's text calls attention to
significant absences: no call for atonement of sin, no promise of
rooted existence, and no threat of exile. Into the gaps Baldwin insin-
uates the figures of Ham and Christ—by orthodox light the disobe-
dient black son, and the divine, white suffering servant—and inverts
their positions. Implicit in Baldwin's laconic inversion "no more
water, the fire next time," is a radical reversal of moral values—
suffering won't save; only rebellion can redeem. It is moreover significant that Baldwin resorts to, and radically inverts, God's promise
to Noah and his sons, one of whom is to commit the sin of disobedience and become the archetypal slave.

Baldwin's revisionary prophecy illustrates the dual African-American interpretation of the obedient servant paradigm in Judeo-Christian rhetoric. As a young preacher of a black church congregation,
he says, "I felt that I was committing a crime in talking about the
gentle Jesus, in telling them to reconcile to their misery on earth in
order to gain the crown of eternal life" (*The Price of the Ticket*, 348).
Baldwin goes on to shift the responsibility for sin and suffering from
the oppressed African-American community to their white oppressors. If anyone is to blame for captivity and alienation it cannot be
the captive but only the captor.

Transposing the guilt and responsibility to the deceiving oppressors, rather than placing them on the oppressed servants, Baldwin
reinterprets the traditional prophetic narrative of obedience and
loyalty.[22] Whatever prophetic discourse of guilt and responsibility he
resorts to, his self-definition practices irony rather than authenticity.
In his conversations with Margaret Mead, Baldwin professes his adherence to the New England prophetic tradition: "Maybe I am an
Old New England, Old Testament prophet. We were talking about
guilt, before, and responsibility." However, he revises his heritage
into a diatribe against the guilt and responsibility of white society.[23]

II

Surprisingly, the African-American use of aesthetic and theological reversal has not been related to the long tradition of gnostic re-

bellion; not even by Bloom. In his studies of the gnostic tradition in (white) American poetry, Bloom shows how American writers inverted their precursors to produce an aesthetics of rebellion. Since Bloom foregrounds Gnosticism in his ground-breaking studies of American aesthetics and religion, it is strange that he never seeks among African-American writers likely candidates for resurrecting the gnostic tradition. No African-American author can write a jeremiad of redemptive co-optation. Instead, more than one have translated traditional alienation narratives in the spirit of the gnostic challenge to orthodox Christian aesthetics and ideology.[24] My analysis of Baldwin aims at amplifying Bloom's models of American Gnosticism to include features which Bloom's confinement to a white corpus neglects.

In constructing his model of American gnostic subjectivity, Bloom centers predominantly on the issue of sublime individual autonomy, and the doubling of the inspired self by an angel or demon:

> American religion, for its two centuries of existence, seems to me irretrievably Gnostic. It is a knowing, by and of an uncreated self, or self-within-the-self, and the knowledge leads to freedom, a dangerous and doom-eager freedom: from nature, time, history, community, other selves.[25]

Bloom's gnostic subjects are Promethean romantics—in the spirit of Emerson, Blake, and Byron—who reject precursors in order to re-create their sublime subjectivity within human time. Whatever anxieties they may be subject to resound more with Freud's Oedipal anxieties of paternal rivalry than with gnostic cosmic dread and metaphysical paranoia.[26]

In structuring his gnostic model on the idea of liberated sublime subjectivity, Bloom exploits only limited aspects of the vast and rich texture of gnostic mythology and ideology. He completely ignores the dark aspect of the tradition, a sphere which generates harrowing existential anxieties for the alienated subject: anxieties of evil and lying creators—masters of the earthly existence; of the subject's sense of a split self in search of true identity; of loneliness, estrangement, and "dispersal" (exile); and of the demonized nature of history. Bloom thus disregards ontological pessimism, central to Gnosticism. He also neglects alienation narratives featuring metaphysical rebellion against the entire cosmos as a vast space of diabolical deceit. The elements excluded by Bloom furnish guidelines for relating an African-American deconstruction of elusive prophetic subjectivity to the gnostic heresy.[27]

My discussion of the aesthetics and ideology of Gnosticism is heavily indebted to Hans Jonas's trailblazing study *The Gnostic Religion*, and to Elaine Pagels's *The Gnostic Gospels*. In his study, Jonas compares ancient Gnostic and modern existential systems of thought. Central to the analogy he draws between the cultural climate in the Eastern empire of the first Christian centuries, and the modern Western world, is the collapse of the existing world view, generating a sense of extreme alienation, of homelessness and cosmic dread. Existentialism and Gnosticism thus share "a certain dualism, an estrangement between man and the world," which engenders a nihilistic approach to existing reality.[28] Influenced by notions of slavery in a new world order, Jonas contends, the gnostic religion speaks of masters-creators who lie and distort in order "to rule and coerce." Imprisoned by forces over which they have no control, individuals— alienated and forlorn—engage in a desperate search to be liberated from their servitude. This is paradoxically gained through intensified alienation: "The world (not the alienation from it) must be overcome; and a world degraded to a power system can only be overcome through power."[29] Despite the difference between the gnostic revolt and "modern man's power relation to world causality," Jonas claims that "an ontological similarity lies in the formal fact that the countering of power with power is the sole relation to the totality of nature left for man in both cases."[30] Gnostic metaphysical revolt, not unlike its existential counterpart, is the last resort of an alienated self in search of its true identity.

More relevant to the modern phase of the philosophy of alienation and metaphysical rebellion is the description of the modern individual offered by Camus in the *Myth of Sisyphus* and in *The Rebel*.[31] In the former, Camus defines modern skepticism as alienation without sin, while in the latter he traces the history of modern nihilism and despair to the metaphysical rebellion of second-century gnostic heresy. In *The Rebel* (published in the same year as Jonas's study of Gnosticism and Existentialism), Camus introduces metaphysical rebellion as man's "protest against evil . . . against his condition and against the whole of creation."[32] Drawing a parallel between the slave's revolt against his master and the metaphysical rebel's protest against human condition in general, Camus claims that "in both cases we find an assessment of values in the name of which the rebel refuses to accept the condition in which he finds himself."[33]

Baldwin's reliance on Camus has come under fire. In an uncomplimentary reference to Baldwin, Ralph Ellison comments that this alienated writer would gain more from reading the American writers, Melville and Hemingway, than the French Existentialists, Sartre and Camus. The Existential connection is particularly pertinent here, since Baldwin (like Richard Wright and Ellison), was exposed to existentialism during his residence in Paris.[34] Baldwin does not draw a connection between the modern French and American traditions of metaphysical rebellion, and the gnostic traditions to which, in diverse ways, they both pay tribute. In recommending Melville to Baldwin, Ellison neglects to remark that Melville preceded Camus in linking the Existential and gnostic version of metaphysical rebellion. Yet one might imagine Ellison as remarking that Baldwin "the non-existentialist" might have been a gnostic rebel in disguise, had he studied the great American tradition.[35] My reading of Baldwin proposes that he was indeed a gnostic rebel even without appealing to his white American precursors.

Baldwin's knowledge of the scriptures furnished ample weapons for waging a campaign of aesthetic-metaphysical rebellion, similar in its intention and effect to the poetics of rebellion practiced by Jonas's gnostic heretics. To characterize Baldwin's rhetoric of aesthetic rebellion, it is helpful to recall briefly Jonas's illuminating description of gnostic allegory. Gnostic tractates depict a cosmos governed by wicked arrogant archons, whose "luxury is deception . . . and [who] steered the people who had followed them into great trouble by leading them astray with many deceptions."[36] In order to free herself from the illusions and "empty fictions" of the oppressing archons, the exiled and estranged elusive subject must look for guilty agents in the external sphere, rather than within her own subjectivity: "Who carried me into my captivity away from my place and my abode. . . . Who brought me to the guilty ones, the sons of the vain dwelling?"[37] The answer is: the evil god, the lying creator and author of scriptures. If the author of Bible history is a liar, so too are his ethical judgments. Therefore, his villains become the gnostic heretics' heroes. Their subversive reading of scriptures, which Jonas calls Gnostic allegory, exalts scriptural outcasts such as Cain, Korah, and Judas. "In the construction of a complete series of such countertypes stretching through the ages," Jonas explains, "a rebel's view of history as a whole is consciously opposed to the official one."[38]

III

Trained in oppression, branded with the blackness of evil, and deprived of adequate language to narrate their plight, African-American artists, like gnostic alienated subjects, deliberately invert existing discourse. "Language," Baldwin asserts, "is meant to define the other—and, in this case, the other is refusing to be defined by a language that has never been able to recognize him" (*The Price of the Ticket*, 649).

In Baldwin's secularized version of the gnostic narrative, the villainous demiurge is replaced by a no less villainous white capitalist, colonialist Christian. But the sin of the lord is the same: deceit on a grand cosmic scale. Like the demiurge's universe, so American culture and history "is based on a lie. . . . So one is trapped in a kind of Sunday purgatory, and the only way out of that is to confront what you are afraid of" (*Conversations*, 280). The difference between himself and his white interlocutor (as representative members), he claims, is "that you, historically, generically, have betrayed me so often and lied to me so long that no number of facts according to you will ever convince me" (*A Rap on Race*, 251). Baldwin asserts that "the failure and the betrayal are in the record book forever, and sum up, and condemn, forever, those descendants of barbarous Europe who arbitrarily and arrogantly reserve the right to call themselves Americans" (*The Price of the Ticket*, 454).

What further strategies, enabling self-expression in an alien language, might a gnostic poetics provide? According to Pagels, gnostic strategy was not only a matter of inverting traditional stories and reversing their values. On the contrary, they often rejected tradition entirely, and recommended free imaginative creation. The Gnostics, she claims,

> argued that only one's own experience offers the ultimate criterion of truth, taking precedence over all secondhand testimony and all tradition—even gnostic tradition! They celebrated every form of creative invention as evidence that a person has become spiritually alive.[39]

On the one hand, as a preacher and son of a preacher, Baldwin naturally turned to the technique of inverting traditional readings of the scriptures.[40] However, he discovered that the official language resists subversion, and even when abusing it African-American writers are "in some kind of collision . . . with the assumptions of . . . what we will call the master language" (*A Rap on Race*, 39). They have to invent a new discourse out of the raw material of the available language, without resorting to the total rejection of tradition described by Pagels.

Baldwin does not claim so much to invent a new language, as to invert and force "the language to pay attention to you in order to exist in it" (*The Price of the Ticket*, 473). He finds creative energy for the inversion of the language in black church discourse and the cadences of black music:

> The English language as such was not designed to carry those spirits and patterns. I had to find a way to bend it the way a blues singer bends a note. . . . When I realized that music rather than American literature was really my language, I was no longer afraid. And then I could write.[41]

Bending and inverting the master language, Baldwin created a system of words eagerly adopted, as Toni Morrison affirms, by "every dissident, every revolutionary, every practicing artist." Morrison regards the newly formed language as Baldwin's most important legacy to African-American self-fashioning, and her praise is worth quoting at length:

> You gave me a language to dwell in. . . . You made American English honest—genuinely international. . . . You stripped it of ease and false comfort and fake innocence and evasion and hypocrisy. And in place of deviousness was clarity. In place of soft plump lies was a lean, targeted power. In place of intellectual disingenuousness and what you called "exasperating egocentricity," you gave us undecorated truth. . . . You went into that forbidden territory and decolonized it, "robbed it of its jewel of naivete" and un-gated it for black people so that in your wake we could enter it, occupy it, restructure it in order to accommodate our complicated passion . . . all the while refusing "to be defined by a language that has never been able to recognize [us]."[42]

The discourse which African-American artists invent by inverting or "decolonizing" the existing language serves to reconstruct an identity untainted by official narratives of history. "History," Baldwin ironically notes, "is now meant as an enormous cloak to cover past crimes and errors and present danger and despair. In short it is a

useless concept. Except that it can be used as a stick to beat people
without history like myself over the head" (*Conversations,* 192). His
biography furnishes evidence that African-Americans are stigma-
tized from birth by official (white) historical narratives: "How can I
claim history as the past if two grown men committed a heinous
crime on a black boy because he's black. . . . I was ten and nearly
died because of history written in the color of my skin" (*A Rap on
Race,* 206). Like the gnostic heretics who demonized historical existence created by the deceiving demiurge, so Baldwin expresses the
sense of betrayal and alienation felt by African-Americans in historical time:

> Their apprehension of this history cannot fail to reveal to them that they
> have been robbed, maligned, and rejected: to bow before that history
> is to accept that history's arrogant and unjust judgement. This is why,
> ultimately, all attempts at dialogue between the subdued and subduer,
> between those placed within history and those dispersed outside, break
> down. . . . The subdued and the subduer do not speak the same lan-
> guage. (*The Price of the Ticket,* 473–74)

The Gnostics perceive historical time as the abode of estrangement,
servitude, oblivion, and exile from one's true home: "In this world
[of darkness]," laments the terror-stricken, exiled Gnostic, "I lived
for a thousand myriad years, and no one knew that I was there."[43]
With no friend to recognize her, the gnostic victim is vulnerable to
the deceits of the demiurgic world and to her own false identity, created by the demiurge. Only an alarming call from beyond time and
history can awaken her to her true self, to its alienation in history,
and to its true home beyond history.

African-Americans, Baldwin claims, can trust nothing and no one
within their temporal abode. They "have been betrayed so often,"
he tells Studs Terkel in an interview, "that they don't believe the
country really means what it says, and there is nothing in the record
to indicate that the country means what it says" (*Conversations,* 13).
This total mistrust generates, as it does in gnostic allegory, a sense
of total alienation from historical and temporal existence: "*Home!*
The very word begins to have a despairing and diabolical ring" (*The
Price of the Ticket,* 355). Unlike Bloom's white, Promethean-gnostic
poets, Baldwin does not invent a personal (hi)story for himself, by
emptying himself through incorporation of his historical heritage,
or by repressing his cultural past. Rather, like Jonas's gnostic here-

tics, Baldwin dismisses all history, particularly his own, as a domain of demonic captivity from which a counter-alienation offers the only release.

Radical alienation cannot be performed by kenosis or repression or any practice on history, within history. The historical world must be totally shattered. As Bultmann remarks, gnostic liberation "cannot be conceived as a real event in this world at all . . . it must be an eschatological event, a breach, a dissolution or a separation of the real Self from the body and soul."[44]

Are African-American writers at liberty to break down their historical selves and those of their characters and readers, in search of elusive prophetic selves elsewhere? Translated into sociopolitical terms, making this breach indeed requires betraying one's historical group. Such betrayal presented no problem to Bloom's white gnostic rebels, but Baldwin and his fellow African-American writers cannot simply pride themselves in adopting a posture of heroic betrayal. They know that exiling themselves will rightly be seen by other African-Americans as a moral crime, not a gnostic virtue. Baldwin's self-exile to France was criticized by many African-Americans, who expected him to be their public spokesman.[45] To a typical disparaging question: "Brother Baldwin, how do you see yourself as a black man here in the 'sunny hills of southern France'?" Baldwin's only possible reply is: "The world's judgment is something I have to live with" (*Conversations*, 153).

IV

Among the rich variety of gnostic allegories furnished by Jonas, the most appropriate for capturing Baldwin's betrayal anxieties would be the Gospel of Marcion. Marcion's alien God and the strangers he comes to confirm in their estrangement, would encourage Baldwin to live with the world's judgment, while assured of sanctuary in his alien Father's mansions.[46] Yet only one voice of Baldwin lives with a forsaken world from a metaphysical distance. The other, more audible voice, speaks as a Marxist engaged in humanity's struggle to right the wrongs of history within history. Baldwin's Marcion-like anxieties of history and betrayal are counterpointed by his Marxist faith in man's historical responsibility, and his capacity to change and refashion it:

If history were the past, history wouldn't matter. History is the present. You and me are history. We carry our history. We act in our history. . . . And if one is to change history—and we have to change history—we have to change ourselves because we are history. (*A Rap on Race*, 188)

Thus viewed, he is not only a Marcionite, who despairs of history as the devil's domain, but also a Marxist, who professes his wish to re-shape history according to the needs of the time: "I am responsible for this particular place and this particular time. . . . It is in that sense, I think, that one transforms the world and makes history something one can live with" (*A Rap on Race*, 217). Moreover, he is committed not merely to his present time and existing community, but also to future generations: "I mean that I am determined, something in me is determined, to do everything in my power to break the assumptions which can kill (my grand-nephew's generation)" (*A Rap on Race*, 135).

In his dialogue with Margaret Mead, Baldwin repeatedly claims responsibility for historical wrongs, and tries, unsuccessfully, to have her accept that responsibility too:

I'm saying that at a certain point in one's own life . . . one has to accept the history which created you. And if you don't accept it, you cannot atone. . . . I was born, and so are we all, carrying one's history on one's brow, whether you liked it or not. (*A Rap on Race*, 178–80)

Mead's baffled and irritated responses to Baldwin's inconsistencies are shared by many readers who find Baldwin's art of splits and dualities hard to comprehend. It is mainly the Marxist Baldwin, who wants to change history, that arouses the interest of scholars and critics. They interpret the inconsistencies of style and subject-matter as effects of the notorious double consciousness with which African-American writers see themselves as being afflicted. My reading of Baldwin builds on these illuminating explorations of double consciousness. They deploy sociopolitical and multicultural categories, and concentrate on the dilemmas experienced by African-American subjects, living under post-colonial and postmodern conditions.[47] Taking the findings of these studies as my point of departure, I proceed to explore the dimensions beyond history and sociology. I refer to dimensions to which writers such as Ellison, Walker, and Baldwin direct their readers, in calling for the breakdown of hyphenated, visible selfhood. The fading of historical subjectivity does not denote reducing the subject to nothing, but rather producing a vanishing, estranged self, elsewhere.

Baldwin's prose offers two parallel sets of dualities, each of which overtly specifies only one dimension. The first duality involves two kinds of estrangement, one of which can be overcome in historical time, while the other is radical and absolute. The second duality offers two responses to history—the Marxist, which requires wrestling in order to capture and change history's assumptions, and the gnostic which requires a complete escape from history.

In a Marxist context, alienation denotes the estrangement of the individual from objects produced by him. This kind of estrangement can be overcome within historical time, through change initiated by the individual. In a Marcionite context alienation also relates to history, but in a negative sense. The conditions of history are evil to the extent that only further alienation from it can offer possible redemption. In *Just Above My Head*, Baldwin points to and even articulates the double divisions of history and alienation. The two dimensions of estrangement are personified in two of the protagonists: "Guy and Arthur may be equally lonely, but guy [sic] is far more isolated. Arthur is far more a stranger to Guy than Guy can be for Arthur."[48] The nature of Guy's alienation is alluded to by his gnostic-like twofold selfhood—an inner, extra mundane self seeking self-knowledge and held captive within a physical, mundane self:

> There is a look in Guy's eyes. . . . There is an anguish in those eyes, at the bottom of those eyes, like something living, and determined to live, in the depth of a dungeon, having been hurled there: which knows, and wants to know that it knows, what happened; something which refuses reconciliation. (479)

The estrangement of Guy's trapped inner self, like that of the gnostic spark, "sinking within all the worlds," is absolute.[49]

The different kinds of alienation—radical and controlled—generate "unutterably different," even dichotomous, modes of dealing with history. "Who, then" asks the narrator, "to use Guy's term, is trapped?" (481).

> To overhaul a history, or to attempt to redeem it—which effort may or may not justify it—is not at all the same thing as the descent one must make in order to excavate a history. To be forced to excavate a history is, also, to repudiate the concept of history, and the vocabulary in which history is written; for the written history is, and must be, merely the vo-

cabulary of power, and power is history's most seductively attired false
witness. . . . Perhaps, after all, we have no idea of what history is.
(480–81)

Two rival modes of subjectivity occupy the competing registers of
historical alienation in Baldwin's texts. The Marxist register is occupied by a self divided according to Sartre's categories of self-for-self
(*pour soi*) and self-for-others (*pour autrui*). The Marcionite register is
occupied by a self divided according to gnostic categories of true
(transcendent) self, and false (historical) self. Baldwin's familiar
ethnic self is framed in existentialist categories—a *pour autrui*.[50] This
self is inconsistently constructed and labeled by others as "Uncle
Tom," "Angry Young Man," "a spokesman for The Negro" and "a
minority of one." Baldwin's response to such a confusing array of
labels is ruefully humorous: "It makes one's head spin, the number
of labels that have been attached to me."[51] On a more serious note,
he realizes that he cannot allow himself to be coopted by such label-
ing, including presumably that of the spokesman: "It seems to me,
in the first place, that if one's to live at all, one's certainly got to get
rid of the labels" (*Conversations*, 55).[52] Getting rid of labels marks a
move to a gnostic register, the dualities of which only compound the
paradoxes of his multi-divided self.

V

No sociological hyphenation and no history-based category can articulate Baldwin's complex, often contradictory self. My suggestion
is that he stages in narratives of alienation the inner splits which no
available language can articulate. Just as in gnostic allegory the
"alien man" is a figurative projection of psychic self-alienation, so
in Baldwin's autobiography and fiction the Exiled African-American
projects inner self-exile.

Gnostic allegory provides a model of alienation through which
Baldwin's biographical estrangement can be seen as allegory. It becomes a paradigm for split subjectivity, which is transcendent, theological, and metaphysical rather than historical. Baldwin draws a
parallel duality between the double narrative of human alienation—
historically, in Marxist terms, and metaphysically, in Gnostic terms—
and the duality of divided subjectivity.[53] It is true that on a certain
level, and sometimes throughout an entire text, the divided and

complex fictional character is molded only by categories of hyphenation. However in other texts, on which I focus below, the structure of the split subject cannot be understood without recourse to metaphysical, allegorical discourse, and these texts provide a template for reading other texts as well.

The dialectical tension of opposed ideologies in Baldwin's discourse is evident already in his early short story, "Sonny's Blues." The story's double-layered structure underscores black music as a reservoir of creative energy for African-American self-fashioning, both within and as an escape from historical time. In this Baldwin handles the topos of jazz in a way that differs from its more familiar deployment. Beyond the commonplace view that jazz provided African-Americans with a language of their own as refuge from the master language, he underscores in jazz a dimension of escape from history, including the history of jazz itself. In other words, conceived through the commonplace paradigm within historical time, the African-American exists in two worlds—that of white discourse, and that of black music. The added, more transcendent dimension, depicts gnostic awakening, which liberates from *all* historical existence, and *all* variations of historical self, showing them to be mere illusions. Through the idiom of jazz, Baldwin transposes in "Sonny's Blues" the historical duality of hyphenated identity to an allegory of a totally different duality, beyond temporal existence:

> The music seemed to soothe a poison out of them; and time seemed, nearly to fall away from the sullen, belligerent, battered faces, as though they were fleeing back to their first condition, while dreaming of their last.[54]

Baldwin's narrative underscores the alienated subject's dread of history and temporality, and its craving for liberation. Yet it equally foregrounds a sense of commitment and responsibility to one's community and its heritage, within temporal existence. Each jazz musician, as Ellison explains, must "learn the best of the past, and add to it his personal vision . . . with a fluid style that reduced the chaos of living to form."[55] Thus, when Sonny becomes an accomplished jazz musician, he can offer *momentary* solace to his community of listeners, by helping them restructure their historical existence: "But the man who creates the music . . . is dealing with the roar rising from the void and imposing order on it as it hits the air. . . . And his triumph, when he triumphs, is ours" (139).

The narrative of Baldwin's musician resounds both with a Marxist call for change within history, and with a gnostic awakening call for liberation beyond time, just as Baldwin's own narratives perpetuate both levels of the duality:

> He and his boys up there were keeping it new, at the risk of ruin, destruction, madness and death, in order to find new ways to make us listen. For, while the tale of how we suffer, and how we are delighted, and how we may triumph is never new, it always must be heard. . . . it's the only light we've got in this darkness. (141)

A different treatment of sociopolitical as opposed to metaphysical alienation is evident in Baldwin's "Previous Condition," whose very title breeds gnostic possibilities.[56] In "Sonny's Blues" the "first condition" is mentioned only in passing, as the place where true subjectivity can be recovered. Here, too, "previous condition" can no more be found in the story, than gnostic salvation can be found in history. What the story does foreground is precisely the multi-labeled identity, fashioned by *autrui*, and *pour autrui*, and inspiring ambivalent responses in Peter, the narrator. Just as Baldwin is split between responsibility towards his own historically-labeled group on the one hand, and the horrors of historical labels on the other, so the narrator is split between African-American identification, which a white observer would project, and his own need to get rid of all labels and all homes. Baldwin's strategies of self-deconstruction break down the protagonist's historical selfhood, in order to reconstruct his elusive, invisible, yet ethically responsible and responsive selfhood. To a committed member of the African-American community, a "previous condition" beyond historical identity is not an open option. As an artist, however, Peter knows that there is something false even about group commitment. Entering a bar in Harlem, and accosted by an old, sullen-faced African-American woman, the narrator is at once repelled and rebuked for his repulsion by the old woman's identification: "I was standing by somebody's grandmother. 'Hello, papa. What you puttin' down?' 'Baby, you can't pick it up,' I told her. . . . 'Nigger,' she said, 'you must think you's somebody' " (98).

At the outset, Peter's narrative seems an Existential tale of anxiety and call for revolt:

> I would go to sleep frightened and wake up frightened and have another day to get through with the nightmare at my shoulder. . . . I had got to

the point where I resented praise and I resented pity. . . . I'm sick to death. (82–83, 88, 92)

Towards the end of the story, a gnostic perspective is added to Peter's narrative, underpinning the view that there is no solution to anxiety, and no hope for liberating revolt within historical existence.

The duality of Marxist commitment and Marcionite alienation is hinted at in the above mentioned Harlem bar scene which concludes the story. At home by sociological categories, yet painfully alienated by gnostic categories, the narrator's experience remains double-edged and ambiguous, just like the dualities Baldwin is committed to share with his readers:

> I longed for some opening, some sign, something to make me part of life around me. But there was nothing except my colour. A white outsider coming in would have seen a young Negro drinking in a Negro bar, perfectly in his element, in his place, as the saying goes. But the people here knew differently, as I did. I did not seem to have a place. So I kept on drinking by myself . . . (99)

Despite his commitment to an essentially Marxist ideology of temporality, which demands mastery of history, and not an escape from it, Baldwin's model of historical selfhood is closer to Jonas's model of gnostic subjectivity than either to Bloom's or the Marxist mode of selfhood. "It is certainly true," Baldwin asserts, "that all the identities coming out of history with a capital H are proven to be false, to be bankrupt. . . . In one way or another, one is very much a prisoner of his time" (*Conversations*, 192).

Baldwin's dilemma is created by two possible assumptions of subject-construction and deconstruction. The first is the Marxist-historicist assumption that individuals construct themselves, with or without obstruction by others. The second is the Marcionite-metaphysical assumption that individual identity is innate. As used by Marxist sociologists, double consciousness refers to different kinds of constructed subjectivity, such as the historical self that others make for the individual, or that the individual makes for himself; either way, these are man-made identities. The prevailing theories of African-American studies usually opt for this possibility.

When dual subjectivity is treated in gnostic terms, the categories are metaphysical or theological, not historical or political. The split self is partly created by an evil demiurge, and partly by a good God, but certainly not by itself. The task of gnostic enlightenment is to help candidates for self-knowledge (Gnosis) distinguish between lies, used by the demiurge to create their false subjectivity, and the origin of their true subjectivity, beyond historical existence.

To hold such opposite models of dual subjectivity, is, needless to say, to be inconsistent. Bloom, like most readers of Baldwin, easily discerns the historical discourse of subjectivity, and does not venture beyond that. Yet Baldwin works with both models, as he tells Ida Lewis in an interview: "Yes, I played two roles. I never wanted to be a spokesman, but I suppose it's something that had to happen. . . . And I discovered that . . . the necessary time to get myself together, was not possible in America" (*Conversations*, 84). When criticized, he can only say like Emerson's subject: "Suppose you should contradict yourself; what then?" Aware of the entanglement for both writer and reader, Baldwin still chooses to speak both in the Marxist discourse of constructed identities and in the Marcionite discourse of innate and metaphysical elusive selfhood: "On a very serious level, the trap I'm in is that I can't afford the historical point of view. And yet I know something about time present and time now" (*A Rap on Race*, 169).

6

Alice Walker's Poetics: Ethic Narratives and Their Gnostic Double

One thing I try to have in my life and in my fiction is an awareness of an openness to mystery, which to me is deeper than any politics, race or geographical location.

Alice Walker, "An Interview with Alice Walker"

I

Harold Bloom's theory, as introduced in *Anxiety of Influence* and *Poetry and Repression,* admits into his canon of prophets of selfhood only writers who, from Valentinus to Emerson, uphold their solipsistic Promethean self by resurrecting their precursors only to repress them. Alice Walker's resurrection of Zora Neale Hurston, without the resistance one expects from American writers in general, and black women writers in particular, leads Bloom perceptively to ask:

> But what has Walker subverted by imitating and so repeating a revisionist moment that she has not originated? No feminist critic will admit the legitimacy of that question, but it abides and will require an answer.[1]

Why, in other words, does Walker not conform to Bloom's model of rebellious repetition of precursors? Why does she not imitate subversively, or repress by repeating?

Since Bloom is committed to a narcissistic hence subversive model of the relation between the prophetic self and her precursor, he cannot conceive of a gnostic, yet not solipsistic aesthetics. Walker can, and *does,* and so cannot be read by Bloom's dual (American and gnostic) model of poetics of repressive repetition. Analyzing the dualities and complex poetics of her writing requires taking Bloom's question seriously, rather than rhetorically. Why, indeed, does she construct a prophetic or individual subject by resurrecting its precursor without repressing? And how do her modern reconstructions show traces of their gnostic precursors? These are the questions that this chapter will explore.[2]

Bloom suggests yet another line of exploration. In his essay on Flannery O'Connor, he makes a distinction between writer and gnostic prophet: "The essayist and letter writer denounces Manichaeism . . . , while . . . O'Connor's fictive universe [is] essentially Gnostic."[3] O'Connor is another precursor alluded to by Walker, to hint at her own poetics. Like Bloom, Walker senses that O'Connor's poetics are fraught with inscrutable dualities—a mystery beyond the manners (*Mothers' Gardens*, 8, 53). The duality of manner-persona and mystery-person in Walker crosses with the duality of gnostic spirit and historical "body" to produce a model of prophetic selfhood which can imitate on one level, and yet remain mysteriously isolated on another. Going far beyond Bloom or O'Connor in deliberately constructing a space of mystery for her prophetic self, Walker devises what might be called a gnostic strategy for staging her own split between political self (body) on one level, and transcendent, disentangled poet (spirit), on another.

In her loving journey through her mothers' gardens in search of self, Walker is committed to a less aggressive, less narcissistic response to precursors than Bloom's model of prophetic American poetics requires. As an African-American woman, and as supporter of womanist[4] ideology, she pledges allegiance to communities of selfhoods (ethnic and gendered). As American individualist, and as American poet, she needs her own alien self. "E.T.," she admits, "remains the character with whom I most identify."[5] For staging this dual commitment and the dual self that it produces and presupposes, Walker creates a highly complex poetics, for which neither Bloom, nor even more admiring readers, give her credit. Blinkered, perhaps, by his own model of American poetics (of repressive repetition), and by his stubbornly solipsistic reading of the gnostic model of repetitive rebellion, Bloom misreads Walker's own version of gnostic poetics, and her model of prophetic selfhood.

The following analysis pursues the development of Walker's nonsubversive revisionary poetics of prophetic selfhood. Her neo-gnostic strategies will be shown to generate a poetic persona aesthetically as gnostic as Bloom's, but ethically more ambiguous.

What double and conflicting needs does Walker believe such dualistic poetics serve? As shown in previous chapters, I agree with Bloom's claim that American theology and aesthetics figure a strong gnostic tradition, which often serves the needs of America's prophets of selfhood.[6] Walker should not be excluded from either tradition, though my reasons for including her are based on a reading of Gnosticism which differs from Bloom's. For Walker, as for Baldwin, Gnosticism furnishes an aesthetic solution to her rival commitments to history on the one hand, and to history-free art on the other. On the one hand she professes an "addiction to art that transcends time" (*Mothers' Gardens*, 44), and on the other hand, her work clearly reflects "strong feelings about history and the need to bring it along."[7] Walker's essays on womanist prose are shot through with this duality. On the one level, Walker fulfills her political-historical and communal duties by protesting against institutional repression of African-Americans' and women's voices. But on another level, often marked by a shift from prose to poetry, Walker confesses the wish to transcend history, and historicist-political categories of identity, in quest of a secret that "has purged my face from history and herstory, and left mystory just that, a mystery" (*Mothers' Gardens*, 392). More poetically and more esoterically, Walker hints at "mysteries / that lure me to a keener blooming / than I know / and promise a secret / I must have."[8]

Where does Walker locate her secret mystical self? Why does its exposure require release from history and historical identities? In what aesthetic space can she reveal her poetic-prophetic selfhood, without betraying the commitments of her historical self?

Walker does not provide any conceptually stated answers. A reading confined to the historical level of her work, moreover, will not decode the inherent contradictions of acceptance and rejection of political and social identities. The basic premise of my reading is that Walker writes on two levels of reference to selfhood. On the political-historical ("horizontal") level, as Bloom, other readers, and Walker herself have pointed out, she joins "these times of group-think and the right-on chorus" (*Mothers' Gardens*, 36). Her work delineates, in normative discourse—by *consciously* imitating models and precursors—the specificities of the group identities to which she feels committed as an African-American woman writer. By the same token, however, Walker mistrusts all variations of constructed selfhood, and claims they create a confined rather than liberating inwardness. They seem to her to be formed, or deformed, by false and enslaving images of the political myths inherent in the postmodernist "culture so in love with flash, with trendiness, with superficiality" (*Mothers' Gardens*, 36). Constricted and confused by the walls of her ethnic and gendered phenomenal self, Walker seeks doors which may lead to an imagined spiritual space, and an untainted, truly liberated inner self (*Same River*, 32).

Influenced by Flannery O'Connor—an admired precursor—she feels directed "away from sociology . . . and further into mystery, into poetry, and into prophecy . . . [as] our only hope . . . of acquiring a sense of essence, of timelessness, and of vision."[9] This vision, which verges on betrayal of her overt group loyalties, cannot be expressed in any of her accepted political languages, which engender the very deceiving images she defies. Walker tends, instead, "towards the unknown otherness"[10] of gnostic, esoteric aesthetics, and finds in the double poetics of their gospels a possible doorway to her imagined spiritual space. Any inklings of the vision which she wishes to share with the reader are merely hinted at through intertextual allusions, "written in a very foreign tongue," or language of the unsayable.[11] "If you are silent for a long time," Walker tells Gloria Steinem, "people just arrive in your mind. It makes you believe the world was created in silence."[12] Indeed, the Gnostics, who rejected all accepted tropes, elevated Silence (Sophia-Wisdom) to be the female co-Creator, consort of Fore-Father, and Mother of Mind.[13]

In more than one essay Walker has pointed to Flannery O'Connor as a source for her double-layered poetics—the split between historical consciousness and a mystical one, between normative narratives and an essential prophetic vision. As mentioned above, Harold Bloom, who denies Walker a complex poetic structure, foregrounds the aesthetics of dualities in O'Connor's work. He relates it, moreover, to O'Connor's use of gnostic elements, the predominant existence of which he overlooks in Walker's fiction and poetry. I find in Walker's prophetic figure, more than in O'Connor's, characteristics of the gnostic rather than the Biblical vision.[14] As Bloom shows in the vast scope of his studies, some American visionaries herald laws which transcend accepted norms in order to present and preserve their essential self, even at the cost of possible betrayal of constructed communities. Emerson's "spiritual laws" and Thoreau's "higher laws" are two conspicuous examples, to which Walker's means of "purging her face" can be added.

Like Grace Paley, Walker constructs her prophetic/poetic persona as a careful listener.[15] Unlike Paley, however, and more like O'Connor and Updike, Walker's prophetic persona is split between the listening, socially oriented subject, and the mystical, isolated one. Walker's prophetic subject thus resembles neither Levinas's exposed and easily invaded subject, nor Bloom's narcissistic reading of the gnostic one. Rather, true to an inherent contradiction in gnostic aesthetics itself, Walker's prophetic figure remains detached from all outer political communities while striving to belong to an inner spiritual community of inspired entities beyond the phenomenal world.[16] Less firm in her faith in institutionalized religion than O'Connor or Updike, perhaps as disillusioned by black church ethics and rhetoric as Baldwin, Walker is less secular than one would perhaps assume, and her skepticism reverberates more with the religious variant of Kierkegaard and O'Connor than with the Nietzschean humanist one.[17]

Bloom rightly notes that O'Connor's final visions are equivocal. So, I argued above are Baldwin's, and so I believe, are Walker's. And unlike Bloom, I suggest that ambivalence, dualities, and contradictions, so predominant in gnostic speculations, are intentional in the vision of these writers. Where Bloom finds fault, I see a deliberate strategy of prophetic rhetoric to construct and deconstruct a text. Bloom finds in O'Connor a tendency to perpetuate "the American version of cosmological emptiness that the ancient Gnostics called the *kenoma*."[18] By contrast, I see in both Walker and her precursor the attempt to find a version of the fullness beyond the abyss—the gnostic *pleroma*. For both writers it resounds with the notion of the Kingdom of God as a state of transformed consciousness. For O'Connor it is the vision of a transcendent "true country," arrived at through a violent process of awakening to true faith. For Walker it is a desire for transcendent knowledge which can counterbalance postmodernist blinding fragmentation: "[E]verything around me is split up, deliberately split up. History split up . . . and people are split up too. It makes people do ignorant things."[19]

The search for a transformed consciousness, which would redeem the essential self from the state of splitting and enslaving ignorance, is at the basis of gnostic speculations in general, and of the Valentinian school in particular. When seeking redeeming knowledge to restore and preserve her "essence," Walker may be seen as resorting to the Valentinian system, rather than to the more familiar Manichaean system of gnostic speculations. To accept the Manichaean division of colors—black as evil and white as pure—would require Walker to co-opt into dominant (biblical) white narratives, which her own prophetic vision rejects. To transvaluate blackness and whiteness—evil and purity—would still leave her vision entrapped in the same discourse. Manichaean dualism cannot furnish Walker with the space beyond categories that she so desperately tries to create and conserve. Her work centers, rather, on the duality of constructed and essentialist identities, and expresses hope for liberating knowledge—regardless of the color (or gender) any outer form exhibits.[20] Similarly, on the historical level, Walker refuses to see colorism as the sole source of evil. Like Harriet, the protagonist of "We Drink the Wine in France," Walker feels annihilated by the range of colors offered by normative myths.[21] When asked to distinguish between black and white literature, Walker expresses her resentment saying "it is not the difference between them that interests me, but, rather, the way black writers and white writers seem to be writing one immense story" (*Mothers' Gardens*, 5).

II

The Valentinian school of gnostic speculations "differed essentially from dualism," as expressed in the Manichaean split between good and evil, light and darkness, male and female. It centered, rather, on contrasting "those who are gnostics, 'children of the Father,' with those who are uninitiates, offspring of the demiurge."[22] This distinction seems more pertinent for Walker, whose work delineates the split between those who are blinded by history and its false myths of self, and those who may be instructed to rediscover their transcendent essential self beyond their historical conditioning. Another reason why the Valentinian school appeals to Walker may be that, unlike Manichaeism, it does not derogate the feminine. Indeed, its master narrative figures a female deity—Sophia—who represents Wisdom, Grace, and Silence.[23]

In the Valentinian system, Hans Jonas explains in *The Gnostic Religion*, "knowledge is the original condition of the Absolute, the primary fact, and ignorance not simply the neutral absence of it . . . but a disturbance befalling a part of the Absolute."[24] This aberration is responsible for the creation of the lower world by a demiurge, who observes the reflected image of the Absolute Father and his world, and tries to imitate it. Ignorant of the pneumatic, divine element, however, his re-creation of imitated images is merely material and psychic, hence false and deceiving. The pneumatic spark—essential self—is implanted in created individuals by the Mother/Sophia, and remains imprisoned by the shells of material and psychic existence.[25]

The Valentinians narrate the allegory of this displaced pneumatic spark who, ignorant of her true origin in the Absolute, is kept in a state of intoxicating sleep and is drunk, numb, and haunted by the nightmare of her earthly existence.[26] To be liberated from her captivity the spark must receive an awakening call from a divine alien messenger. The call reveals to the spark her estrangement in the world of deceiving matter, and her true origin in the Absolute:

> What liberates is the knowledge of who we were, what we became, where we were, whereinto we have been thrown; whereto we speed, wherefrom we are redeemed; what birth is, and what rebirth.[27]

True to the paradoxes and doubling inherent in gnostic aesthetics, the alien savior is seen as a duplication both of his redeeming Gnosis (knowledge), and of the enslaved spark it comes to liberate. It is an inner voice, a "saved savior," and "a kind of double or alter ego."[28] Thus, in "The Hymn of the Pearl," a didactic allegory found in the "Apocryphal Acts of the Apostle Thomas," the awakened subject likens her newly received Gnosis and its bearer to a mirror image of herself, the encounter with which enables a restitution of the fragmented self: "Myself entire I saw in it, and it entire I saw in myself. I saw that we were two in separateness, and yet again one in the sameness of our forms."[29]

The liberating call has a twofold purpose, affecting both the individual self and the divine fullness. As ignorance causes suffering, displacement, and captivity on both cosmic and anthropological planes, so knowledge of one's origins in the godhead enables the self-discovery of the individual spark, and her partaking in the restoration of divine fullness:

> Thus the seed remained for a while assisting [him] in order that, when the Spirit comes forth from the holy aeons, he may raise him up and heal him from the deficiency, that the whole pleroma may again become holy and faultless.[30]

Walker's familiarity with the Valentinian allegory of captivity and liberation is made evident through her choice of epigraph for the second chapter of *In Search of Our Mothers' Gardens:* "If you bring forth what is within you, what you bring forth will save you. If you do not bring forth what is within you, what you do not bring forth will destroy you." This text of Christ's teaching appears in the gnostic

"Gospel of Thomas," though Walker claims to have found this passage in Elaine Pagels's *The Gnostic Gospels* (*Mothers' Gardens*, 118). Pagels introduces Christ's words in a chapter in which she centers on the Valentinian allegory of the imprisoned pneumatic spark, and underscores its governing principle—self-ignorance as a form of self-destruction, and self-discovery as liberation.[31]

It is significant that, though Walker is acquainted with *The Nag Hammadi Library*—the major publication of gnostic tractates, which includes "The Gospel of Thomas"—she chose to quote Pagels's slightly different translation of Christ's saying.[32] In the *Nag Hammadi* version, Jesus distinguishes between an indwelling knowledge which saves, and its *absence* which annihilates. Pagels's version, by contrast, stresses the concept of "saved savior," and the responsibility of the entrapped spark in the redeeming process. It underscores the (Socratic) rediscovery of an *existing*, though dormant, *indwelling* Gnosis, and the need to *return* to one's origins through the renewed awareness of the true self.

Walker's choice points to the significance she attributes to the process of self-discovery through the call of the twin, or "alien man." It equally alludes to the emphasis on origins, predominant in both the esoteric and historical levels of her writing. Gnostic speculations (Bloom's theory notwithstanding) advocate forgetting neither one's divine genealogy nor transcendent abode, but only the history of one's earthly existence:

> Jesus said, "Whoever does not hate his father and his mother as I do cannot become a (disciple) to Me. And whoever does not love his father and his mother as I do cannot become a disciple of me. For My mother (gave me falsehood), but (My) true (Mother) gave me life.[33]

Jesus' call for constructive continuity with one's spiritual ancestors seems to concur with Walker's insistence, throughout her work, on the need to reunite with the spirit of forgotten ancestors, mothers and grandmothers, in order to transcend all divisions.[34] It should be noted, and will be further dealt with below, that Walker's keen interest in, and commitment to ancestral communities and their cultural heritage, may indicate a modern adaptation of the gnostic pleroma, and a careful qualifying of the gnostic split between historical (this world) and spiritual (transcendent world) genealogy. In translating the gnostic guiding spirit to ancestral spirits of African paganism, however, Walker does remain faithful to gnostic syncretism which, as Pagels and Jonas have shown, freely fused pagan and Christian elements in their speculations.[35]

Walker adapts the Valentinian allegory of captivity and displacement to her own narrative of historical-political captivity, and escape to mystery. Like the Gnostic alien man (or woman), Walker represents herself as an outcast whose very alienation became the starting point for illumination:

> I believe that it was . . . from my solitary, lonely, position, the position of an outcast, that I began to really see people and things. . . . I felt at the mercy of everything, including my body, which I had learned to accept as a kind of casing, over what I considered my real self.[36]

Unlike Bloom, who puts a solipsistic construction on gnostic isolation, Walker foregrounds the spiritual twin, who provides companionship inside, to balance the alienation outside. Thanks to this twin, a channel to ancestors is opened in Walker as in the Valentinian speculation. The experience is described at the outset of *The Same River Twice*, in a passage I find worth quoting at length:

> I was aware that throughout my struggles . . . I had never been truly alone. Always with me was the inner twin: my true nature, my true self. . . . This was the self that came in dreams, visions, and spiritual revelations of extraordinary power. There was developed in me a spontaneous way of knowing that seemed more like remembering than learning. There were things I just suddenly seemed to know, about life, about the world. As if my illness had pushed open an inner door that my usual consciousness was willing to ignore. I found myself in easy contact with my ancestors. (32)

In the spirit of gnostic contradictions, Walker defines her rediscovered essential self as "[b]oth more committed and more detached." Having encountered her "inner twin," Walker, like the gnostic "saved savior," sends out her tales of instruction to oblivious readers, who are still lamentably "devoted to copies." This she does in a layered allegorical discourse, in which the political level narrates the conflicts of captivated ethnic and gendered identities, and the mythological level offers a way to emancipation from exile to true selfhood.[37]

III

In the 1987 "Afterword" to her first novel, *The Third Life of Grange Copeland* (1973), Walker alludes to the book's double-layered structure. Its political interest, she claims, is an attack on "violence among all black people in the black community at the same time that all black people . . . were enduring massive psychological and physical violence from white supremacists."[38] Though her labeled communities expect of her loyalty and a deceiving silence, her political observations unfold the oppressive effects of the stereotypes of patriarchal narratives, and defiantly underscore "the writer's duty to those who fall, pitiful, poor, ill-used, under the embarrassed pall of silence" (*The Third Life*, 345).

Beyond the overt political critique of flawed and tyrannical norms, however, Walker alludes already in her first novel to a mystical layer—a gnostic tale of rebirth and awakening to the possibility of escape, though desolate and painful, beyond phenomenal existence. In his "third life," Grange Copeland awakens to the call of his inner spark, or twin. He sets himself free from poisoning external stereotypes, as well as from his enslaved psyche, deformed by images of normative discourse. Once liberated, Copeland delivers the redemptive message to his son: "I'm talking to *you*, Brownfield . . . and most of what I'm saying is *you got to hold tight a place in you where they can't come*" (*The Third Life*, 290, italics in text). The son remains impervious to the call to free his soul from the degradation and oppression imposed by "them"—those who rape and conquer the spirit with their stereotypes. But as Walker asserts at the end of the afterword, the saved savior's call does reach his granddaughter, Ruth, and shields her inner self against the onslaught of enslaving myths.

Walker ends her afterword by weaving together the plea for liberation heard in slave narratives (historical) and the gnostic allegory of enslaved sparks (mystical). As gnostic spark and as cultural Other, the captive self is initiated into an interior space whose mystery and gifts are mirrored only in the esoteric fringes of the narrative:

> I believe wholeheartedly in the necessity of keeping inviolate the one interior space that is given to all. . . . There are some people who could never be slaves; many of our enslaved ancestors were among them. That is part of the mystery and gift passed on to us that has kept us generation after generation going. This is the understanding that is encoded in the lives of the "soul survivors" of this novel, Grange Copeland and his granddaughter, Ruth. (*The Third Life*, 345–46)

No postmodern genre would allow the artist to keep the mutually exclusive narratives of constructive and essentialist identities. Gnostic aesthetics, by contrast, offers a stratified allegorical discourse, in which each scene of instruction records the errors of the phenomenal self, then doubles back to transcendent spaces, where blindness and error of false communities are exchanged for insight and true being in a transcendent fullness of isolated spirits.

Thus viewed, Walker's narrative spells neither unequivocal, shameless escape to solipsistic solitude, nor wholehearted merging with any constructed community, but an alien space aesthetically open to both the political commitments and the imagined spiritual selfhood. Within this space, her instructing persona—resembling that of the Valentinian rather than of Bloom's prophet—teaches that the advent of liberation involves a process of discarding those "negative images that are permitted to proliferate," and that serve the Other in oppressing the self. Though the shedding of false shells causes "pain," "grief," and a sense of loss, it should be seen as liberating escape and not suicide (*The Same River*, 33). This is explicitly expressed in Walker's aptly-entitled poem "On Stripping Bark From Myself." The poem features a chain of gnostic dualities:

> I could not live
> silent in my own lies
> hearing their "how *nice* she is!"
> whose adoration of the retouched image
> I so despise . . .
> I find my own
> small person
> a standing self
> against the world . . .
> My struggle was always against
> an inner darkness: I carry within myself
> the only known keys
> to my death—to unlock life, or close it shut
> forever . . .
> I am happy to fight
> all outside murderers
> as I see I must.[39]

As the subversive Gnostics rewrote the New Testament allegories to "fight outside murderers" threatening the pneumatic self, so Walker's art re-presents accepted ethnic and gendered myths in order to criticize their stereotypes and alert implied readers to their confining discourse. This subversive tendency is accomplished through intertextual allusions, transpositions, contradictions, and paradoxes which inwardly rock the seemingly solid historical level of her writing.

Most studies of Walker's work relate exclusively to this historical-political level in which her commitment to various constructed communities seems predominant. This may explain Bloom's reduction of her writing to ideology, and his misreading of the trans-political layer implicit in Walker's response to Zora Neale Hurston. Bloom's complaint against Walker's non-subversive imitation of Hurston misses the point of her gnostically opened text.

Readers have rightly noted Walker's conscious indebtedness to Hurston as a precursor in whose work she found "a sense of black people as complete, complex, *undiminished* human beings" (*Mothers' Gardens*, 85, italics in text).[40] This newly defined personal and collective identity, created in what Bloom calls Hurston's moment of revision, has served Walker in her own quest for self-expression. Her search for Hurston's grave—posing as her niece—may be seen as an attempt to resurrect her precursor's spirit, and enact what Bloom calls genealogical metalepsis. "Properly accomplished," he claims, "this stance figuratively produces the illusion of having fathered one's own fathers."[41] Yet unlike the agon of Bloom's poets, Walker's poetic persona suffers precisely for lack of spiritual parents, and seeks to preserve rather than narcissistically repress any heritage she may discover. Unlike the gnostic-teaching prophet who discards historical precursors, unlike Emerson who denounces the *retrospective* vision of his age, and unlike Bloom's scene of instruction which demands the annihilation of precursors,[42] Walker's revolutionary call instructs the black artist-prophet to imitate and store ancestral heritage:

> The work of the black artist is to create and to preserve what was created before him. . . . *We must cherish our old men.* We must revere their wisdom, appreciate their insight. . . . For that is also the role of the black revolutionary artist. He must be a walking filing cabinet of poems and songs and stories, of people, of places, of deeds and misdeeds. (*Mothers' Gardens*, pp. 135–36, italics in text)

This conviction has underscored her own commitment to "give voice to centuries not only of silence, bitterness and hate but also of neighborly kindness and sustaining love" (*Mothers' Gardens*, 21). Her voice resonates both with the "sense of community . . . the solidarity and sharing a modest existence can sometimes bring," and the community's struggle against the threats of racism and sexism (*Mothers' Gardens*, 17). In *The Third Life of Grange Copeland*, she claims, "it is the women and how they are treated that colors everything," and her second novel, *Meridian*, recaptures the spirit of feminist and civil rights activists. Indeed readers have noted Walker's group solidarity. Thus, *Ms.* magazine defined *Meridian* as "a classic novel of feminism and the Civil Rights Movement." And McDowell, in her essay on *Meridian*, notes that Walker expresses a feminist challenge of society's role definition, and attempts to break down gender boundaries.[43] These "badges of group membership" mark her affiliation with the "vital range of micropolitical movements"—gendered, ethnic, ecological, and class oriented. As such they may denote a certain compliance (her idea of "correctness"), not merely with myths produced by her sociopolitical discourse, but also with some constitutive features of postmodern culture, which reject "the monadic subject" in favor of "a collective 'objective spirit.' "[44]

In an attempt to encode the specificities of African-American women's experience—as distinct from that of white women—Walker has even coined a special badge—Womanist—borrowed "from the Black folk expression of mothers to female children. . . . Womanist to feminist as purple to lavender" (*Mothers' Gardens*, xi–xii). This expression has been integrated into different African-American discourses, such as "Womanist Theology" in black church experience. It is interesting to note that Walker's careful scrutiny of all existing labeled communities is echoed even here. For, as Lincoln and Maniya explain, womanist theology

> agrees with the critique of white racism and the need for black unity expressed in black liberation theology, and it agrees with the criticism of sexism and the need for the unity of women in feminist theology. However womanist theology *moves beyond both,* by providing its own critique of racism in feminist theology, and of sexism in black theology.[45]

Deploring the fact that white literary and political rhetoric has ridiculed and so stolen African-American folklore, Walker underscores it in her work, "because folklore is at the heart of self-expression and therefore at the heart of self-acceptance."[46] This she does in "Black folk English," imitating Hurston who "took the trouble to capture the beauty of rural black expression." As inherited language of a community of belonging, it preserves, for future generations, the spirit of ancestors who "have carried us *safely* to where we are today," and who provide clues for origins.[47]

Walker's work can and has been read as molded by the politically and historically demarcated groups to which she is related. But her aesthetic relations to group identities is far more complex than has been noted. She engages in an attentive dialogue with postmodern narrative strategies of containment, which herald the confines of historical space. Her recourse to stereotypes of constructed communities, moreover, resounds with elements of postmodern image-culture, introduced, as Jameson argues, through "media and specialized or expert language . . . [which] seek tirelessly to classify and categorize, to transform the individual into the labeled group."[48]

Walker shares not only Jameson's underscoring of postmodernism as "media culture," but also his critique of that culture. Both Walker and Jameson see in the culture industry a means to produce subjects, whose nature is determined by the image held by the consumer of that culture. Jameson is interested mainly in the consumer of cinema and photography, while Walker's stories center more on television and magazines. Unlike Jameson, perhaps, she believes that just as the media can create a deformed and enslaving self-image, it can be used to refashion that self-image. Thus, for example, she tells how the television her mother bought in 1960, introduced to the viewers both fair-skinned black women trying to "pass," and the charismatic image of Martin Luther King, "who gave us back our heritage" (*Mothers' Gardens*, 143–44). The audience Jameson addresses is literate, not to say intellectual, while Walker caters also to an audience that reads only magazines. The media is therefore seen as a very significant tool for molding a self-consciousness different from that formed (or deformed) by white, patriarchal mainstream culture.

Jameson's view of the "visual deceptiveness of the photograph" and spurious reification represented in journals, films, and television[49] is reiterated in Walker's writing, and evidenced, for example, in her dual evaluation of the cinematic medium: "I believe movies are the most powerful medium for change on earth. They are also a powerful medium for institutionalizing complacency, oppression and reaction" (*The Same River*, 282). The powerful effect of movies is in counteracting the numbing effect of the popular media.[50]

Like Jameson, Walker sees in the physical spaces of nature and the human body loopholes through which writer and reader can transcend the constrictions of society, politics, and history. She would seem, in other words, to agree with Jameson's view that the postmodernist insistence on "place and landscape, including the human body . . . may take away in the capacity to think time and History." As a poet and as a storyteller, however, Walker goes much further than Jameson in her effort to actually create aesthetic figures of this liberating space. One metaphor she may find suitable for this space is a door "if not to pry open, at least to peer through" the prisonhouse of historical space, and the trap of constructed identities.[51]

IV

Jameson's categories are confined mainly to the politics of what he calls utopian spaces. Metaphysical or theological categories for such utopias do not figure in his models. By contrast, Walker's aesthetic space is frankly metaphysical, often theological, not necessarily Christian. Aesthetically, it is related to the heritage of the gnostic religion, albeit she does not speak openly of the duality of two gods, nor of the division of human beings to three classes. Least of all does she read the natural and physical world as though they were the kingdom of the demiurge—the evil god. Aesthetically her debt to the gnostic tradition involves adaptation of its allegorical inversions of authoritative mystic discourse. She may have been attracted to the Gnostics by their pre-modern recognition of the enslaving power of false images, and their radical rebellion against the historical subject such false images create.

Walker distrusts the sovereignty of constructed identities and subverts the languages by which they are molded. As for herself, she resists confinement within the boundaries of any political-historical discourse. Her rebellion goes beyond a protest against social and historical injustice. Rather, her campaign of consciousness-raising requires pursuit of a true self, transcending any empirical identity, let alone the titles and labels by which it is recognized:

I have not labeled myself yet. I would like to call myself revolutionary. . . . It seems necessary for me to forget all the titles, all the labels, and all the hours of talk, and concentrate on the mountain of work I have before me. . . . *there must be an awareness of what is Bull and what is Truth.* (*Mothers' Gardens*, 133, italics in text)

My assumption that the gnostic tradition is crucial to an interpretation of Walker's aesthetics and ideology is based on her determination to seek the source of slavery beyond any historical or social ambience as the core of the soul's misinterpreted and misconstructed empirical identity. Walker uses the term "revolutionary" in a sense that cannot be exhausted by its ethnic and gendered definitions. Unlike feminists who, for all the differences between them, reject at least the very idea of essential human nature or human truth, Walker clearly envisages a space where real, metaphysical, transcendent truth can be experienced. I do not mean to deny by this her complete agreement with feminism that official identities are dangerous "badges of affirmation," which must be laid bare as "Bull." Having exposed the "Bull," however, her multilayered aesthetics imagines a space—possibly of silence—for a truth her art serves to reveal.

Her revolutionary activism, Walker claims, has been for some time centered in her writing and not in any organized political movement. Part of that activity involves careful scrutiny of images and stereotypes relating predominantly to racism and sexism, and produced by the media—journals, television, and the movies:

> One of the things that I've been doing more in San Francisco is writing about things like pornography and sadomasochism, and it is through writing about those things that I join with women who are more active.[52]

She refers here specifically to the stories "Porn," "A Letter of the Times," and "Coming Apart," written at that time and collected in *You Can't Keep a Good Woman Down* (1981).

My conviction is that Walker's assault on pornography is double-edged, working both on a social and political level directly, and on a cognitive level indirectly. An example of her political commitment is furnished by her response to the mixed reception of the movie adaptation of *The Color Purple*. Rape and the resistance it provokes encapsulates for Walker the devastating power of the culture industry at its worst. Here is what she says about the pornography industry and her cinematic response to it:

> The pervasiveness of the degradation and brutality women are subjected to in this society screams out at you from every direction. Rape, women being battered by *their* men, a multi-billion-dollar pornography industry trading in violence against women. . . . And all of this is a sharper prob-

lem for Black women because this all interpenetrates with the oppression they face as Black people. . . . It is the portrayal of women's
resistance to this that gives *The Color Purple* its power. And it is exactly
that that those attacking the movie object to. (*Same River*, 192)

As for the cognitive level, Walker's exposition of rape and pornography in her revolutionary writing is paradigmatic of the inherent
split in her poetics, between literal and figurative layers, which the
alert reader is expected to reveal. Read on the political-historical
level, her castigation of pornography as degrading and enslaving
marks her allegiance to her labeled community. Read allegorically,
however, these acts of brutal obscenity are shown to have their beginnings in a much earlier tradition, and their effects to be much
deeper, and more enslaving than any literal-political act of sexism.
Readers who miss Walker's prompting to move from the literal to
the figurative register resemble the political activists whom she accuses of misreading the "real chains of subjugation." Such activists
(and readers) repeatedly "place in power a new group of exploit-
ers" and "euphemize" rape, instead of stripping away the lies which
mask its atrocity.[53] Allegorically illiterate readers miss her gnostic assault on existing psychic and spiritual rape and pornography, caused
by alien falsehoods which enslave, degrade, and destroy the soul.
  Walker's figurative tales resemble the gnostic allegories which tell
of evil Archons—progeny of the deceiving demiurge—who, detect-
ing in their domain of evil the reflection of Eve, declare: "Now come
let us seize her and let us cast our seed on her, so that when she is
polluted she will not be able to ascend to her light."[54] These Archons duplicate through forced intercourse "copies of the bodies,"
to further disperse the pneumatic sparks, enslaved by the powers of
darkness.[55]
  Alice Hall Petry's reading of Walker's deployment of sexual abuse
as merely dull, "interminable monologues on pornography, abor-
tion, sadomasochism and rape," seems to center on the literal level
of her stories, without venturing deeper into her allegorical narratives.[56] The same can be said for Petry's classifying Walker merely as
a labeled, political artist, who addresses readers of "black- and femi-
nist-oriented magazines."[57] The berating views of both *The Color Purple* (novel and movie), and *You Can't Keep a Good Woman Down*, which
Walker notes in *The Same River Twice* (38–39, 192), exemplify this
misreading of Walker's highly complex poetics. Some readers not
merely ignore the allegorical intertext, but object to it. A salient case

in point is Petry's hostile objection to the passage from Hesse, which Walker chose to cite as epigraph for *You Can't Keep a Good Woman Down*: "It is harder to kill something / that is spiritually alive / than it is to bring the dead / back to life." Petry's reading of the epigraph marks it as irrelevant to the stories, since none of the heroines qualify as "spiritually alive" by "most informed standards." All are, rather, "self-absorbed" and "dull." A related charge is that the characters who "speak almost ad nauseam on the subjects of pornography and sadomasochism, . . . are simply spokespersons for particular attitudes regarding contemporary sexual mores."[58]

A more allegorically oriented reading of the tales would show that they elaborate, on another level, the action which might seem dull on the literal level. Allegorically interpreted, these stories stage what Bloom calls a scene of instruction, whose purpose is not only to transmit information but to enable transformation of the learner. One might say that Walker's so called "simple spokespersons" are figuratively creative disciples who turn scenes of instruction to scenes of construction. Like the unnamed "jazz-poet" in Walker's story "The Lover,"[59] they are "excellent listener[s]," whose attention is split between outer and inner existence. They hear, politely, the "pompous bullshit" produced by the colonizing fantasies of their communities, and are casually aware of "[w]hat others minded at the Colony." Their attention, however, is mostly directed inwardly, to an inner voice of Truth, which calls for "self-preservation" (*You Can't Keep*, 32).

At the outset of "The Lover," the protagonist seems intoxicated by the Colony's climate of fantasies and false images—drinking wine, the narrator explains, is "a fine old Colony tradition" (*You Can't Keep*, 35).[60] She dreams of a lover who will make a dishonest woman out of her, so that she can "be truly a woman of her time"— one more duplicate of the stereotypes engendered by her culture. At the end of the story, she exchanges this fantasy with the less "illicit" one "of her husband making love to her." Though still enclosed in a state of self-oblivious dream, the protagonist seems to begin the process of casting off popular stereotypes. Since in the past she did not include her own husband in her fantasies, the present dream may indicate a wish for retreat from trendy constructs imposed by others. On the metaphoric level, here as elsewhere, Walker's narrative is open-ended and less than optimistic. At the end of the tale the individual entity is still nameless, and not yet awakened from the entrapping fantasies of "daring adventures."[61]

The one tentative hope for liberation is the allusion to "faraway countries," as a doorway to a transcendent space beyond the lies and colonizing images of her mundane existence (*You Can't Keep*, 37–39).

The claim made by Alice Hall Petry that "its title notwithstanding, 'The Lover' has nothing to do with love"[62] may be true, but hardly because Walker is incapable of distinguishing between love and lust. Rather, she assaults the popular fantasy of eros molded by the media culture and colonized by the stereotypes "of her time," which turns love to mere lust. Walker has no other way to express her critique than by imitating the "informed standards" of popular discourse, and subversively repeating the "contemporary sexual mores" accepted by her audiences.[63] She specifically warns both her fictional artists, and the revolutionary black artists her tales aim to instruct, "not to be tricked, seduced, or goaded into verifying by imitation or even rebuttal, other people's fantasies" (*Mothers' Gardens*, 312).

"The Lover" can be seen as an apt example of the ironic critique which Walker's allegories launch at the "flash, trendiness, and superficiality" of her culture, and at her target audience. The epigraph of *You Can't Keep a Good Woman Down*, moreover, is highly relevant to this story, as to others in the collection, since it calls artists and readers to take a step beyond the empirical surface of the text and the self.

From the point of view of my thesis, it is imperative to lay bare Walker's gnostic strategies, for these hold the clue to the link between her poetics and the prophetic tradition Bloom exemplifies as the prophets of selfhood. Bloom's question, presented at the outset of this chapter, is, in what way does Walker's poetics merit the title of rebellion? He does not even ask in what way she produces a prophetic self through this poetic rebellion. Like the readers mentioned above, Bloom is blinded by his reduction of Walker to a political ideological level of discourse and intention. The gnostic prophetic self is to be sought beyond this level, in implied allegorical meanings.

The restrictiveness of a political reading can be illustrated by Walker's "A Letter of the Times, Or Should Sado-Masochism Be Saved."[64] Here Walker stages the split between the political and figurative layers of the narrative and of prophetic selfhood. On the literal level her first person narrator—a university instructor—tries to teach her students

to be unable . . . to think of enslaved women as exotic, picturesque, removed from themselves, deserving of enslavement . . . to be able to repu-
diate all the racist stereotypes about black women who were enslaved:
that they were content. (*You Can't Keep*, 120)

The narrator draws a parallel between the narrative of enslaved contemporary women—deformed by the colonizing fantasies of their
society—and slave narratives of black women, "captured, enslaved,
sexually abused" by white colonialists. "[T]elevision," she warns, "is
a lot more subtle than slaveships," yet it is just as much an abusive
vehicle of enslavement:

Whoever saw that television program [on sado-masochism] can now look
at me standing on the corner waiting for a bus and not see *me* at all, but
see instead a slave, a creature who *would* wear a chain and lock around
my neck for a white person—in 1980—and accept it. *Enjoy* it. (*You Can't
Keep*, 122–23, italics in text)

The only way to escape from "abused consciousness," she claims, is
offered by the "twin self who saved [slaves]. . . . and that twin self is
in all of us, waiting only to be summoned" (*You Can't Keep*, 119).
    The gnostic allusion in this passage treats the "Letter" of which
the title speaks as the redeeming note for/by the gnostic instructor,
in direct analogy with gnostic texts. As shown above, the gnostic narrative "The Hymn of the Pearl," figures as its protagonist a subject
alienated from his or her transcendent kingdom, and sunk in intoxicating slumber. The subject is rescued by Gnosis, in the form of a
messenger / letter / "robe of glory," sent to him or her by the
Father. Jonas explicates this story:

The ascent . . . is guided and spurred on by the letter. . . . The letter is
the embodiment of the call. . . . The caller in gnostic symbolism is the
messenger, and the called, the sleeping soul. Here, however, the called
sleeper is himself the messenger, the letter therefore a duplication of his
role, as he on his part duplicates that of the divine treasure he came to
retrieve from the world . . . his mirror image with which he is reunited
at the completion of his mission . . . a kind of double or alter ego preserved in the upper world. . . . Thus the encounter with this divided-off
aspect of himself . . . and the reunion with it signify the real moment of
his salvation.[65]

In her "Letter of the Times" Walker seems to use the twin as the
door opening on to an intertextual space, in which the captive spark

in the "scene of instruction," in the instructor and the students, and in the writer and the reader finds reassuring support in a companion spirit. She avoids open elaborations perhaps because, as she puts it in a rhetorical question, "who dares talk seriously of 'religious' matters these days?" (*You Can't Keep*, 120). Cautious intertextual allusion serves as a veiled access to the rebellious metaphysics, out of fashion among her implied readers.

Furthermore, Walker draws by intertextual allusion another parallel with Gnosticism that goes beyond historical slave narratives. The scene of instruction establishes a line of descent between the political-historical captivity narrative and the spiritual gnostic allegory of the captive spark. Women who "could see nothing wrong with what we'd seen on TV," and who proclaim that "slavery, real slavery is over," are as blindfolded and entrapped as the community of uninitiates scorned by the Gnostics.

Jonas tells us that, as persecuted heretics, the Gnostics produced no written texts of their own, but rather conveyed their rebellion by ironically perverting and inverting the narratives of the official institution. Similarly, Walker leaves the gnostic world and the prophetic self virtually unsaid, except as spaces opened by her assault on official images and narratives. Thus she seems to repeat without subverting. But that is because first of all, repetition itself is subversion, and secondly, given her audience, gnostic metaphysics would be best left unsaid.

Walker's subversive repetition is illustrated in her story "Coming Apart."[66] Here she openly cites media language in which excerpts of feminist journal articles are inserted. At the same time, she refashions the narrative into a hybrid fable which undercuts or puts in question the cited text. Her overt aim is to instruct implied readers not "to swim with the tide" but to fight entrapping "self images," presented in movies and popular journals (*You Can't Keep*, 43).

Alice Hall Petry denounces "Coming Apart," as "unsuccessful" —a "magazine editorial which masquerades as a short story."[67] The gnostic prophetic paradigm I offer places Walker's choice of journalistic discourse as a literal layer designed to mask a metaphoric second layer, which blinkered readers have neglected to discern. Walker's complex poetics presents a political fable about sexist "conquest" through pornography, and at the same time alludes figuratively to the conquest of the essential self by all existing mundane fables. The equivocal ending of the story serves to remind the attentive reader that conquerors are not easily defeated, and that

essential identity cannot be as easily constructed and deconstructed
as postmodernist theories argue. The couple in "Coming Apart,"
like the twins in the gnostic "Hymn of the Pearl," are captured and
liberated together. Once the wife's consciousness rises to the poison
of media images and of the fantasies they evoke (she "is unable to
fake response"), her husband is partially liberated by the three feminist texts she instructs him to read.[68]

One of these texts makes an intertextual allusion to Frantz Fanon,
which Walker leaves unexplicated. It is for the reader to consult
Black Skin, White Masks, where Fanon calls for "the liberation of the
man of color from himself."[69] Though Fanon claims that "what is
often called the black soul is a white man's artifact,"[70] he insists that
images of blackness are just as dangerous as white mythical constructs and that ultimately, for the black self entrapped by false images, the tom-tom hardly "chatters out the cosmic message." He
warns against the danger of all "obscenity of dances and words,"
and calls for freedom from all false gods.[71] Fanon resorts to the Manichaean metaphor of black/white dualism to warn against the dangers of all cultural binarisms and advocate liberation through
release from their poisoning clutches. Walker's gnostic allegories go
beyond Fanon's deconstruction of cultural Manichaeism. Her pref-
erence for Valentinian rather than Manichaean discourse balances
subversive image-breaking with an affirmative element of Valentinian myth, namely the pleroma, or fullness. This includes the Valentinian call for renewal of contact with the spirits of dead ancestors:
"Light the light within you. . . . Raise your dead who have died, for
they lived and have died for you. Give them life."[72]

V

Unlike Bloom's patriarchal model of discontinuity, Walker's neo-
gnostic model—maternal and adhesive—interlocks the liberation of
the spark-self with the rebirth of ancestral spirits, weaving a figurative narrative of continuity. Thus, for Fanny in *The Temple of My Familiar,* ancestral spirits "open doors inside me. To rooms inside myself
. . . and my heart starts to expand. . . . It becomes a light, and the
light enters me, by osmosis, and a part of me which was not clear
before is clarified."[73] That part of the self, the reader learns from
what Lissie tells Fanny's estranged husband, Suwelo, is intimately occupied by familiar and ancestral spirits. Suwelo is advised to open

the door to the memory of parents, because "if our parents are not present in us . . . our very flesh is blind and numb. . . . And more important, the doors into the ancient past, the ancient self, the pre-ancient current of life itself, remains closed."[74]

Any reading which perpetuates a single-layered political ideology in Walker's poetics and neglects to record her allusions to gnostic transcendent space will fail to understand her indebtedness, on both levels of selfhood, to "all my teachers, ancestors, and spirits," who inhabit her pleroma.[75] However, unlike the familiar spirit (or double, twin, alter ego) in gnostic myth, Walker's familiars are situated in this world, in African and African-American cultural space. African culture serves Walker as a figurative substitute for the transcendent pleroma of ancient Gnosticism. The significance of African space, myth and ritual in Walker's neo-gnostic allegories gains by reference to the gnostic tradition in general, and its American prophetic version in particular.

According to Barbara Christian, Walker's recording of Africa aims at deconstructing the romantic image of "motherland" generated by contemporary militant black activists. Christian rightly observes that Walker deflates the idealistic myth of Africa in order to show its deceiving hence destructive effect on the black political struggle for liberation.[76] However, readers like Christian do not yet venture beyond the political level of interpretation. Figuratively, Walker's Africa is not celebrated as origin or "home" of some historical religion, since so far as consciousness-raising is concerned, all the historical religions that flourish in Africa—Christian, Islamic, or pagan—seem to her equally blinding and enslaving. Her neo-gnostic discourse enables Walker to allude to Africa and its community of pagan spirits as her liberating space beyond all entrapping images. There, Walker constructs for herself, her readers, and her fictional characters an inner temple which turns "herstory" into "mystery," and reunites her prophetic self with its transcendent twin.[77]

Why Africa? Walker's Africa is a co-term for the pagan primitive rival of white Christian civilization. However, Paganism as an official institutional system is no more viable a faith for Walker than it was for the Gnostics, who abused Homer as freely as they did Moses.[78] It is more difficult in our own multicultural critical environment to notice that Walker abuses African paganism just as freely as she does Christian sacramentalism. Walker herself creates this difficulty since she is sincerely committed to resurrecting her African ancestors. She cannot, for example, treat African jazz as freely as the Gnostic

treated pagan Jove and Juno. On the contrary, among other tributes
to Zora Neale Hurston—her resurrected precursor—Walker almost
plagiarizes Hurston's use of jazz as a figure of liberating release from
white cultural captivity.

In the Hurston reader she edited, Walker included "How It Feels
to be Colored Me." In this text Hurston celebrates jazz as what
might be called her cultural redeemer. Her description of jazz resonates with elements anticipating Walker's use of African space in her
story "The Diary of an African Nun."[79] Hurston writes:

> The orchestra grows rambunctious, rears on its hind legs and attacks the
> tonal veil with primitive fury, rending it, clawing it until it breaks
> through to the jungle beyond. I follow those heathen. . . . I dance wildly
> inside myself. . . . I am in the jungle, and living in the jungle way. My
> face is painted red and yellow and my body is painted blue. My pulse is
> throbbing like a drum.[80]

Once the music ends, Hurston admits, "I creep back slowly to the
veneer we call civilization,"[81] which perpetuates the conquest by stereotypes, like Fanon's White Mask, and Walker's cultural artifacts.

In "The Diary of an African Nun," the African jungle that jazz
elicits for Hurston furnishes the mystical space for the self-discovery
of a cosmic true self, beyond all constricting rituals and masks—
white or black. Within this space, moreover, Walker can collapse the
differences between pagan myths and gnostic allegories, and translate the gnostic pleroma into the mythic idiom inhabited by ancestral pagan communities. Thus viewed, her stratified narrative and
intertextual allusions accord this aesthetic space a theological, redemptive function, which neither a constricted historicist reading
nor Bloom's solipsistic one can detect. In her attempt to redeem the
essential self from its splintered state, and to reconstruct her version
of gnostic fullness, Walker's prophetic character resurrects and preserves, rather than represses, the spirit of precursors and pagan ancestors in a mythic African space.

On the literal level of the story, the African jungle is evoked both
by its geographical setting—"the foot of the lovely Uganda moun-
tains"—and its jazz-like narrative structure. A major theme is introduced in the first and last parts of the story, and is improvised in the
four middle parts. Even a narrow literal reading can detect that the
major theme spells a pronounced split—a duality of whiteness and
blackness, cold (reason) and heat (passion), barrenness and fertil-

ity, art and nature, Christian and Pagan rituals. The narrating persona, an African nun "shrouded in whiteness," is equally presented as split along these lines: "I am a wife of Christ, a wife of the Catholic church. . . . I was born in this township, a village 'civilized' by American missionaries" (*In Love and Trouble*, 114). The split, so overt and emphasized on the literal level, should alert the attentive reader to Walker's ironic exposition and critique of popular Manichaean dualism. Her almost cliched presentation alerts us to a warning that all aspects of the dualities presented are illusory, false, and hence deceiving and entrapping, and that the reader should look beyond them to a space or temple which can offer an inkling of restored fullness.

In a language of mutual African and American mythologizing, the African nun presents herself as an artifact—a projection of narcissistic myths held by opposing Others. Thus, Promethean Americans are perturbed by her seeming self-abnegation; Germans consider her "a work of primitive art . . . the incarnation of civilization, anti-heathenism," and the French see her as an object to be interpreted through painting (*In Love and Trouble*, 113).[82] None of the Western guests at the mission school see the nun beyond their own projection of cultural myths. Molded by their diverse stereotypes, the young nun is kept in the prison-house of the mission, its barren existence, and its prayers perpetuating, in dead language, her enslaved state: "Pater noster . . . fiat voluntas tua, sicut in caelo et in terra" (*In Love and Trouble*, 115). By the same token, the African villagers impose on her their own perception of an admired "civilized" work of art, and are as reverent of her as of her white instructors. Thus they too, uphold the imprisoning myth.[83]

The young African nun juxtaposes the myths of the civilized West with the pagan rituals of her ancestors, and is aware of the pronounced binarism created. What function is filled by this "contradiction that divides the world"? (*In Love and Trouble*, 118) On the political-cultural level of the narrative the contradiction is illusory; the effect of ritual on its victim is less contradictory than cultural binarisms might lead readers to expect. After participating in a Christian ritual and the pagan dance she learns that people are just as imitative in either frame:

To assure life for my people in this world I must be among the lying ones and teach them how to die. I will turn their dances into prayers to an empty sky. . . . In this way the wife of a loveless, barren, hopeless Western marriage broadcast the joys of an enlightened religion to an imitative people. (*In Love and Trouble,* 118)

Read on the historical-political level only, the story aims as Walker herself has noted, to criticize "Christianity as an imperialist tool used against Africa."[84] Yet the counterpointed pagan rituals that Walker unfolds in the story are far from liberating, and the beating drums are no more messengers of a cosmic selfhood for Walker's African nun than they are for Fanon's Negro. Walker's depiction of the pagan ritual does not leave out its threat of intoxication and violent conquest of passion. Her representation of opposing myths serves to remind the implied reader that all cultural artifacts are enslaving, that none produce a space of redemption.

The imitative effects of cultural splits can be undone only by awakening to the spiritual, metaphysical split that they conceal. This is never as openly asserted by Walker as it was by the Gnostics. She does not, in so many words or images, divide the self into hylic, psychic, and pneumatic aspects.[85] Nor does she insistently divide her poetic persona into political-historical and prophetic-mystical. Instead, since no known discourse can serve Walker in her attempt to give inklings of her imaginary space, she resorts to intertextual allusions to lead the reader away from history and into the mystery of liberated selfhood. In "The Diary of an African Nun" her clue is the "sacred dance" metaphor.

On the literal level the dance serves to distinguish between the opposing rituals, and so underscore the split world of colonized historical Africa (*In Love and Trouble,* 115). Obviously, the violently physical and orgiastic nature of the dance in the jungle appears diametrically opposed to the ascetic and barren spiritual sacrament in the mission school. Figuratively, however, Walker goes beyond the physical implications of dance to the spiritual meaning that dancing acquires, for example, in "The Round Dance of the Cross," a heretic text which is part of the gnostic tractate, *Acts of John.* Walker's gnostic intertextual poetics invokes a different figure of Christ, who is not the alien, imposing, "pale lover who never knew the dance and could not do it" (*In Love and Trouble,* 115). Instead, he is a prophet who instructs, precisely through the dance in which his disciples take part.[86]

During the dance the gnostic disciple is awakened to the saved savior, his redeeming message and the twin self, all reflected in the dancing Christ:

To the universe
Belongs the dancer
Whoever does not dance
Does not know what happens. . . .
I am a mirror to you
Who know me. Amen. . . .
Now if you follow
My dance
See yourself
In me who am speaking.[87]

The redeeming Christ, Pagels notes, further makes the distinction between mundane and extramundane existence—between history and mystery.[88]

The gnostic subversive reading of Christ's prophetic image, as the dancing double or twin, opens up a mystical space within which the pneumatic spark can find her twin and be liberated. Walker's foregrounding of the dance in the historical narrative of "The Diary of an African Nun" enables her to allude through her gnostic poetics to such mystical space in which her prophetic selfhood can join a pleroma of dancing ancestral spirits. Only by linking, beyond the text, the Christ delineated in part 3 of the story to the dance foregrounded in part 4 can the reader even ask, let alone answer the question: How can one and the same narrative persona, without falling apart psychically and ethically, participate in two such seemingly opposed symbolic actions? Only by consulting the gnostic intertext does one discover a strangely hybrid figure of Christ who asks questions instead of giving answers, who dances instead of sermonizing, and who yet dismisses the physicality of the dance as a mere illusion. The prophetic self Walker projects through a spiritually dancing narrator can thus indirectly suggest a way of searching for the self in which body and soul become figures of endless questioning:

Do I care? Must I still ask myself whether it was my husband, who came down bodiless from the sky . . . ? Must I still long to be within the black circle . . . ? Must I still tremble at the thought of passions . . . ? How long must I sit by my window before I lure you down . . . ? . . . . How to teach a barren world to dance? (*In Love and Trouble*, 115–18)[89]

In her diary, which conforms to no institutional confession, the silent, isolated speaker of "The Diary of an African Nun" offers a series of questions. They discard, as enslaving, the images constructed by all accepted discourses—black and white, civilized and primitive, Christian and pagan—and offer no alternative badges of affirmation.

The nun's questions are not rhetorical. They should be read as providing the only strategy for constructing a transcendent space of possible liberation. Unlike Bloom's gnostic prophet of selfhood who sustains a narcissistic, self-enclosed self by repressing precursors, and more like Fanon's prayer: "O my body, make of me always a man who questions!"[90], Walker's prophetic figure seeks a community of isolated selfhoods not by singing herself, but rather by constantly asking about her present existence, her origins and precursors, and her inner twin. Walker's prophetic self, striving to understand "who we are," and "who we have been"—beyond historical selfhood[91]—resembles the gnostic saved savior/twin self, whose message centers on asking "who we are, where we've been, or why, where we are going."[92]

Can Walker's questioning prophetic self find inklings of a transcendent space for liberated selfhood? In a poem entitled "Reassurance," Walker asserts that any tentative assurances of such space are paradoxically transmuted only by questions:

> I must love the questions
> themselves
> as Rilke said
> like locked rooms
> full of treasure
> to which my blind
> and groping key
> does not yet fit
> and await the answers
> as unsealed
> letters
> mailed with dubious intent
> and written in a very foreign
> tongue.[93]

Notes

Chapter 1. Introduction

1. For hybridity see Homi Bhabha, e.g., "Of Mimicry and Man: The Ambivalences of Colonial Discourse"; "Sly Civility"; and "Signs Taken For Wonders" in *The Location of Culture* (New York: Routledge, 1994), pp. 85–122. Bhabha demonstrates that the uncanny and imaginary play a central role in the politics of postcolonial resistance to and subversion of identities, imposed by the oppressing stranger. In the encounter between colonized and colonizer a certain hybridity (double consciousness or vision) is created. Hybridity serves Bhabha to describe the "part object that articulates native and colonial knowledge, and which can, it is now claimed, enable active forms of resistance" (114). Underscoring the "continual slippage between civil inscription and colonial address" (99), Bhabha intimates that oppressors are no less hybridized than the oppressed.

2. Ralph Ellison, *Invisible Man* (New York: Vintage Books, 1989).

3. See Michel Foucault, "Technologies of the Self," *Technologies of the Self: A Seminar with Michel Foucault*, eds. L. Martin, H. Gutman & P. Hutton (Amherst: University of Massachusetts Press, 1988), pp. 16–49.

4. For a discussion of postmodernist subjectivity, see Fredric Jameson, "Imaginary and Symbolic in Lacan," *The Ideologies of Theory: Essays, 1971–1986*, vol. 1 (Minneapolis: University of Minnesota Press, 1988). I do not pretend to define postmodern subjectivity. My book traces a *pre*-modern prophetic subjectivity, diversely constructed by different American traditions. My concern is with pre-modern origins of the vanishing American self in postmodern American writing.

5. Paul Ricoeur, *Oneself as Another*, trans. Kathleen Blamey (Chicago: University of Chicago Press, 1992), pp. 166–67. On narrative identity, see Ricoeur, *Oneself As Another*, pp. 113–202.

6. Ricoeur, *Oneself*, pp. 23–25. On prophetism as genre see Meir Sternberg's monumental study, *The Poetics of Biblical Narrative: Ideological Literature and the Drama of Reading* (Bloomington: Indiana University Press, 1987), pp. 78–112, 505–15.

7. Ricoeur, *Oneself*, p. 167.

8. "New Americanist" is a term coined by Frederick Crews in his essay, "Whose American Renaissance?" *The New York Review of Books* (October 27, 1988): 68–81. Crews's essay is closely examined below.

9. *Fiction and Historical Consciousness: The American Romance Tradition* (New Haven: Yale University Press, 1989); *Engendering Romance: Women Writers and the Hawthorne Tradition, 1850–1990* (New Haven: Yale University Press, 1994); *Nineteenth-Century American Romance: Genre and the Construction of Democratic Culture* (New York: Twayne Publishers, 1996).

10. On Cavell see section IV in this chapter.

11. Stanley Cavell, *Senses Of Walden* (New York: Viking Press, 1972), pp. 61–67. Quoted in Miller-Budick, *Nineteenth-Century American Romance*, p. 169.

12. The New Americanist position is presented in Crews's "Whose American Renaissance?" examined below. Crews discusses works by Walter Benn Michaels, Donald E. Pease, Russel J. Reising, Sacvan Bercovitch, Jane Tompkins, David Reynolds, and Philip Fisher.

13. Crews, p. 70. Davidson and Moon argue that "what constitutes a canon at a particular moment reflects current assumptions about what or who represents the nation . . . issues of race and gender challenge nationalist paradigms and realign the borders of both the nation and the field of American literary history." Cathy Davidson and Michael Moon, eds., *Subjects and Citizens: Nation, Race, and Gender from 'Oroonoko' to Anita Hill* (Durham: Duke University Press, 1995), p. 1. See also Hannan Hever, "The Struggle over the Canon of Early-Twentieth-Century Hebrew Literature: The Case of Galicia" *Interpreting Judaism in a Postmodern Age*, ed. Steven Kepnes (New York: New York University Press, 1996), pp. 243–77.

14. Crews, p. 75. Donald Pease, Crews argues, is a typical New Americanist precisely because of "his eagerness for moral certainties about the relation between the books and the politics that he admires. . . . Pease feels compelled to invent new politically upbeat intentions for nineteenth-century works so as to purge them from their distasteful irresoluteness and irony" (p. 77).

15. Crews, p. 79

16. Ibid., p. 74.

17. Donald E. Pease, "National Identities, Postmodern Artifacts, and Postnational Narratives" *Boundary 2* 19, no. 1 (spring 1992): 1–13.

18. Ibid., p. 9.

19. Walter Benn Michaels, *Our America: Nativism, Modernism and Pluralism* (Durham: Duke University Press, 1995), p. 69.

20. Ibid., p. 24. Michaels goes on to quote a Klan leader claiming that the Jew "is a stranger to the emotion of patriotism as the Anglo-Saxon feels it" (p. 47).

21. "From the standpoint of the 'native'," Michaels argues, pluralism "must involve the repudiation of any attempt to blur differences, which is to say, the repudiation of any effort of Americanization" (Ibid., p. 69).

22. Ibid., p. 79.

23. Ibid., p. 139.

24. Ibid., p. 180, note 240. In "Introduction: Who Needs 'Identity'?" Stuart Hall asks: "What, then, is the need for further debate about 'identity'? Who needs it?" S. Hall and P. Du Gay, eds., *Questions of Cultural Identity* (London: Sage Publications, 1996), p. 1. Likewise, Derek Parfit states in *Personal Identity*: "Certain important questions do presuppose a question about personal identity. But they can be freed of this presupposition. And when they are, the question about identity has no importance." *Personal Identity*, ed. J. Perry (Berkeley and Los Angeles: University of California Press, 1975), p. 200

25. R. W. Emerson, "Spiritual Laws," *The Works of R. W. Emerson* (New York: Tudor Publishing Company, 1968), p. 86.

26. William Faulkner, *Light In August* (Harmondsworth: Penguin Books, 1960), p. 296.

27. See Stanley Cavell, *Conditions Handsome and Unhandsome: The Constitution of Emersonian Perfectionism* (Chicago: University of Chicago Press, 1990), p. 59. Subsequent quotations from this work are cited parenthetically in the text as (*Conditions*).

28. Ricoeur, *Oneself*, p. 214.

29. James Baldwin, "Previous Condition," *Going to Meet the Man* (Harmondsworth: Penguin Books, 1991), pp. 79–100; Alice Walker, *The Temple of My Familiar* (New York: Pocket Books, 1989). According to Cavell, Kant's ethical model of the subject as a citizen of two worlds underpins Emerson's and Thoreau's discourse of self alienation. (*The Senses of Walden*, pp. 92–93).

30. Julia Kristeva, *Strangers to Ourselves*, trans. Leon Roudiez (New York: Columbia University Press, 1991). In *This New Yet Unapproachable America* (Albuquerque: Living Batch Press, 1989), Cavell quotes a passage from Nietzsche's *The Genealogy of Morals*: "We are unknown to ourselves, we men of knowledge—and with good reason. We have never sought ourselves—how could it happen that we should ever *find* ourselves?" (p. 24).

31. Emmanuel Levinas, *Otherwise than Being*, trans. Alphonso Lingis (The Hague: Martinus Nijhoff, 1981), and Paul Ricoeur, *Oneself as Another*.

32. *The Puritan Origins of the American Self* (New Haven: Yale University Press, 1975), p. 19. Bercovitch explains the derivation of auto-machia from medieval psychomachia. Subsequent quotations from this work are cited parenthetically in the text in the abbreviated form (*Puritan Origins*).

33. Sacvan Bercovitch, *The American Jeremiad* (Madison: University of Wisconsin Press, 1978), p. 15.

34. "As a true American," Bercovitch argues, "Emerson never wearied of repeating the familiar story—how the continent was 'kept in reserve from the intellectual races until they should grow to it,' how Boston in particular, Winthrop's city on a hill, was 'appointed in the destiny of nations to lead . . . civilization,' and how the present generation was 'continuing (the) holy errand into the wilderness.' " These tropes, however, served Emerson to unfold a "personal and national divinity, whose substance *is* the Emersonian-American self" (*Puritan Origins*, pp. 166–67). Italics in text).

35. Sacvan Bercovitch, "Emerson The Prophet: Romanticism, Puritanism, and Auto-American-Biography," in *Emerson: Prophecy, Metamorphosis and Influence*, ed. David Levin (New York: Columbia University Press, 1975), p. 22.

36. Stanley Cavell, *The Senses of Walden*, 19. Subsequent quotations from this work are cited parenthetically in the text in the abbreviated form (*The Senses*).

37. The difference between the two types of Puritan response to the dual structure of prophetic discourse can be illustrated by the use made by Cotton Mather and Jonathan Edwards, respectively, of the city as trope for the community that the individual either identifies with or withdraws from. In Edwards's personal narrative, the city is a scene for staging separation and withdrawal: "I very frequently used to retire into a solitary place . . . at some distance from the city. . . . My heart seemed to sink within me, leaving the family and city . . ." ("Personal Narrative," 213). In *Magnalia Christi Americana*, Mather presents the city on a hill as a scene for collective identification. Bercovitch argues that Mather presents John Winthrop— "Nehemiah Americanus"—as a leader in the *public* role of the Old Testament prophet: "Mather's hybrid American Nehemiah . . . is not . . . a man whose divine call sets him apart from others . . . . The obvious connection between the terms of Mather's title lies in the hero's public role" (*Puritan Origins*, pp. 1–2).

38. Bercovitch's central argument is that, as ideological trope, the errand into the wilderness "was a mode of consensus designed to fill the needs of a certain social order." *The Rites of Assent*, (New York: Routledge, 1993), p. 32.

39. *The Senses*, p. 29. Cavell goes on to say that "knowing that, Jesus fulfilled them, but the kingdom of heaven is not entered into; knowing that, the Founding Fathers brought both testaments to this soil, and there is no America; knowing that Jonathan Edwards helped bring forth a Great Awakening, and we are not awake" (29).

40. In *This New Yet Unapproachable America*, p. 39, Cavell quotes Kierkegaard's description of self-alienation as a journey to foreign lands: "Most men live in relation to their own self as if they were constantly out, never at home. . . . Spiritually and religiously understood, perdition consists in journeying into a foreign land, in being 'out'."

41. See Cavell *Conditions*, pp. 9–12, 30; *This New Yet Unapproachable America*, p. 116; *The Senses*, pp. 100–103.

42. In *The Claim of Reason: Wittgenstein, Skepticism, Morality and Tragedy* (Oxford: Clarendon Press, 1979) p. 87, Cavell argues that respect and responsibility for the stranger are built into the search for the unapproachable self in American philosophy and fiction from its invention by Emerson and Thoreau, down to its adaptations in American film genres: "There is a natural form of conceptual disappointment which underlies a philosophical surmise about other minds (and thereby shows it not to be 'merely' philosophical). The idea of the other as stranger; the possibility that he may be 'different from me'."

43. See also *The Senses*, p. 51; *This New Yet Unapproachable America*, pp. 39–42.

44. Thus for example, in *This New Yet Unapproachable America* Cavell reads Emerson's "Experience" as "the effort to imagine—to fancy—giving birth" (103). In *The Senses*, pp. 45–50, Cavell highlights Thoreau's journey of loss and rebirth.

45. *This New Yet Unapproachable America*, p. 116. Cavell highlights the centrality of "the affinity of . . . [Wittgenstein's] narrations of exile from oneself with what from the nineteenth-century we learn to call alienation" (pp. 37–39).

46. In *The Varieties of Religious Experience* (New York: Collier Books, 1961), discussing Tolstoi's conversion, William James describes his gloom as feeling withdrawn from an "uncanny" and "unhomelike" world, leading through gnawing and carking questioning to a "satisfying religious solution" (pp. 130–32).

47. *In Quest of the Ordinary: Lines of Skepticism and Romanticism* (Chicago: University of Chicago Press, 1988), pp. 184, 187. Cavell further notes that "Thoreau's claim for the uncanny for philosophy is thus the idea of the reader's willingness to subject himself or herself to taking the eyes of the writer, which is in effect yielding his or her own." On the uncanny in Emerson and Thoreau see also Cavell's *Conditions Handsome and Unhandsome*, pp. 7–8.

48. Cavell, *Conditions Handsome and Unhandsome*, pp. 8–9. For an entirely different use of the trope "city of words" see Tony Tanner, *The City of Words: American Fiction, 1950–1970*, (New York: Harper and Row, 1971). Bercovitch underscores the fact that the American Puritan entity, and its central trope, "city on a hill" were created "ex verbo, by the word", through a particular narrative: "The Puritans' vision of New England was quintessentially literary, a product of the myth-making imagination." Unlike Cavell and the tradition he follows from Plato to Kant, Bercovitch does not detect in this city-creating narrative the shattering of the historical dual self by an agent beyond history. See Bercovitch, "The Modernity of American Puritan Rhetoric," *American Letters and the Historical Consciousness*, ed. J. G. Kennedy & D. M. Fogel (Baton Rouge: Louisiana State University Press, 1987), pp. 42–66.

49. Discussing Cavell's concept of aversion/conversion, Emily Miller-Budick argues that in Cavell's reading, the elusive self can relate to other selves "through a mutual recognition of strangeness, of establishing such a relationship, and of reestablishing it again and again" (*Nineteenth-Century American Romance*, pp. 169–70). In "Bercovitch, Cavell, and the Romance Theory of American Fiction," *PMLA* 107, no. 1 (January 1992): 84, Miller-Budick elaborates on Cavell's "aversive possibilities of consent."

50. Jean-Paul Sartre, *What Is Literature?* trans. Bernard Frechtman (London: Mathuen and Co., 1949), p. 201. Subsequent quotations from this work are cited parenthetically in the text in the abbreviated form (*Literature*).

51. Sartre, *Literature*, p. 191. See section III in this chapter.

52. *What Is Literature?*, pp. 216, 203–4. See also p. 237: "As we have no means of actions against these strangers, it is as beggars that we shall present ourselves before them, that we shall beg them to lend us the appearance of life by using us as they like."

53. Harold Bloom, *The American Religion* (New York: Simon & Schuster, 1992).

54. Harold Bloom, *Poetry and Repression: Revisionism From Blake to Stevens* (New Haven: Yale University Press, 1976), pp. 262–63. Subsequent quotations from this work are cited parenthetically in the text in the abbreviated form (*Poetry and Repression*).

55. In discussing James Baldwin's prophetic voice, Bloom distinguishes between two rival models of Old Testament prophetic figures. The first is Jeremiah-like—individual, isolated and private. The second is like Amos or Micah or Isaiah—a public, socially connected figure. Baldwin, Bloom goes on to say, "is of the authentic lineage of Jeremiah, most inward of prophets." Introduction to *James Baldwin* (New York: Chelsea House Publishers, 1987), p. 1.

56. Hans Jonas, *The Gnostic Religion* (Boston: Beacon Press, 2d ed., 1963), chapter 3. On Valentinian Gnosticism see the chapter on Alice Walker below.

57. Harold Bloom, "Emerson: The American Religion," *Modern Critical Views on R. W. Emerson,* ed. Harold Bloom (New York: Chelsea House Publishers, 1985), p. 97.

58. In *Rhetoric, Power and Community* (Louisville, Kentucky: Westminster John Knox Press, 1993), pp. 94–98, David Jasper deploys the "central theological metaphor for God, that is the breaking in of otherness". He argues that the "vertical model becomes the perfect instrument for introducing the theological metaphors of the inbreaking of otherness."

59. Both Updike and O'Connor acknowledge Barth's influence on their narratives of horizontal breakdown and vertical judgment. Updike attributes his view of God as "the totally inscrutable Other" to his reading Barth (James Plath, ed., *Conversations With John Updike* [Jackson: University Press of Mississippi, 1994], p. 251), and in his memoirs he asserts that he learned "from Kierkegaard and Barth to say the worst about our earthly condition, which was hopeless without a scandalous supernatural redemption" (*Self Consciousness* [New York: Fawcett Crest, 1989], p. 156). Though a devout Catholic, O'Connor finds that "Barth's description of the wonder, concern and commitment of the evangelical theologian could equally be a description of the wonder, concern and commitment of the ideal Catholic life." Flannery O'Connor, *The Presence Of Grace* (Athens: University of Georgia Press, 1983), p. 165.

60. Karl Barth, *The Epistle to the Romans*, trans. Edwyn Hoskyns (Oxford: Oxford University Press, 1968), p. 149. Subsequent quotations from this work are cited parenthetically in the text in the abbreviated form (*Romans*).

61. Anzia Yezierska, *Bread Givers* (New York, 1975), p. 125, quoted in Michaels, *Our America*, p. 69.

62. Paley says: "I do write with an accent. I did have three languages spoken around me when I was a kid: English and Russian and Yiddish. Those were my languages," in Neil David Isaacs, *Grace Paley: A Study of the Short Fiction* (Boston: Twayne, 1990), p. 116. See also Bonnie Lyons, "Grace Paley's Jewish Miniatures," *Studies In American Jewish Literature* 8, no. 1 (spring 1989): pp. 26–33.

63. *The Collected Stories* (New York: Farrar, Straus Giroux, 1994), pp. 146–60. Subsequent quotations from this work are cited parenthetically in the text in the abbreviated form (*Collected Stories*).

64. Emmanuel Levinas, *Beyond the Verse*, trans. Gary D. Mole (London: The Athlone Press, 1982); *In the Time of the Nations*, trans. Michael B. Smith (London: The Athlone Press, 1994); *Outside the Subject*, trans. Michael B. Smith (Stanford: Stanford University Press, 1993).

65. See for example Levinas's essay "Politics After," in *Beyond the Verse*, pp. 188–95.

66. *Beyond the Verse*, 50. Subsequent quotations from this work are cited parenthetically in the text in the abbreviated form (*Beyond*).

67. In "The Philosophy of Franz Rosenzweig" Levinas writes: "In that shattering of totality-within which pure inwardness does not succeed in getting out of the Myth and crossing the absolute interval that separates it from the Other . . . we can find the basis for the priority of language over 'pure thought.' And this is so . . . because the ultimate bond of the psyche is not the one securing the unity of the subject, but the binding separation, so to speak, of society, the dia- of the dialogue, of dia-chrony, of . . . the binding separation known by the well-worn name of love" (*In the Time of the Nations*, 160). In chapter 4 below I relate to the distinction between Bakhtin's dialogism and Levinas' diachrony.

68. Levinas, *In the Time of the Nations*, p. 2. Subsequent quotations from this work are cited parenthetically in the text in the abbreviated form (*In the Time*).

69. Emmanuel Levinas, *Totality and Infinity*, trans. Alphonso Lingis (Pittsburgh: Duquesne University Press, 1969), p. 39.

70. In *Otherwise Than Being*, Levinas says: "The ego stripped of the trauma of persecution of its scornful and imperialistic subjectivity, is reduced to the 'here I am,' in a transparency without opaqueness. . . . As a given sign to the other . . . the 'here I am' signifies me in the name of God, at the service of men that look at me" (pp. 146, 149). See also pp. 79, 121.

71. For Emerson's use of giantism see "Self Reliance," *The Works of R. W. Emerson*; Bloom, *Poetry and Repression* p. 251. See also chapter 2 to follow.

72. In *Difficult Freedom*, trans. Sean Hand (Baltimore: The Johns Hopkins University Press, 1990), pp. 30–38.

73. Emmanuel Levinas, *Existence and Existents*, trans. Alphonso Lingis (Dordrecht/Boston/London: Kluwer Academic Publishers, 1988), pp. 85–93. Emphasis in text.

74. Levinas, *Existence and Existents*, p. 93.

75. Levinas, *Difficult Freedom*, p. 33. For feminist critique of Levinas see chapter 4, section V to follow.

76. "Colored" is the term Zagrowsky uses in Paley's story (*Collected Stories*, pp. 353, 359).

77. See for example Victoria Aarons, "A Perfect Marginality: Public and Private Telling in the Stories of Grace Paley," *Studies in Short Fiction* 27, no. 1 (winter 1990): 35–43; Jacqueline Taylor, *Grace Paley: Illuminating the Dark Lives* (Austin: University of Texas Press, 1990); Emily Miller-Budick, *Engendering Romance*.

78. Paley, *Collected Stories*, pp. 352–53. See Miller-Budick, *Engendering Romance*, pp. 239–40.

79. See Miller-Budick, *Engendering Romance*, pp. 219–20.

80. " 'Thou shalt not abhor an Edomite, for he is thy brother; thou shalt not abhor an Egyptian, because thou wast a stranger in his land' (Deut. 23:8). Fraternity (but what does it mean? Is it not, according to the Bible, a synonym of humanity?) and hospitality: are these not stronger than the horror a man may feel for the other who denies him in his alterity?" (*In the Time*, 97). Cf. above Walter Benn Michaels on xenophobia in America.

81. See Levinas's essay, "The Rights of Man and the Rights of the Other," *Outside the Subject*, pp. 116–25.

82. For Levinas's discussion of the prophetic response "Here I am!" see *Otherwise Than Being*, pp. 146–49, 185. For a powerful analysis of the aesthetics and ideology governing dialogic confrontation between Samuel and Saul see Meir Sternberg, *The Poetics of Biblical Narrative*.

83. See Ricoeur's analysis of the question "who?" in *Oneself As Another*, pp. 57–61; 166–68.

84. Levinas, *Outside the Subject*, pp. 117–18.

CHAPTER 2. JOHN UPDIKE'S POSTMODERN APOCALYPSE AT MIDPOINT

1. James A. Schiff, "Updike Ignored: The Contemporary Independent Critic," *American Literature* 67, no. 3 (September 1995): 531–52.

2. Harold Bloom, introduction to *John Updike*, ed. Harold Bloom (New York: Chelsea House Publishers, 1986), p. 7; Harold Bloom, introduction to *Modern Critical Views on R. W. Emerson*, ed. Harold Bloom (New York: Chelsea House Publishers, 1985), p. 10.

3. See, for example, John Updike, *Picked Up Pieces* (New York: Fawcett Crest, 1975), pp. 47, 54. Subsequent quotations from this work are cited parenthetically in the text.

4. Barth's influence on Updike has been studied by many readers. Yet, to the best of my knowledge, none of the readers have presented Updike's ambivalent treatment of Barth that my analysis exposes. See for example Joseph B. Wagner, "John Updike and Karl Barth: An Insistent 'Yes.' " *Cithara* 18 no. 1 (1978): 61–69; George Hunt, *John Updike and the Three Great Secret Things: Sex, Religion and Art* (Grand Rapids: William B. Eerdmans Publishing Company, 1980).

5. See chapter 1, section III.

6. Karl Barth, *The Word of God and the Word of Man*, trans. Douglas Horton (New York: Harper and Brothers, 1957), pp. 203, 170. Subsequent quotations from this work are cited parenthetically in the text in the abbreviated form (*The Word of God*).

7. Two conspicuous examples are Reverend Dobson in "Pigeon Feathers," *Pigeon Feathers and Other Stories* (New York: Fawcett Crest, 1963), pp. 84–105, and Jack Eccles the Episcopalian minister in *Rabbit, Run* (New York: Fawcett, 1961). On Updike's comments on American ministry see John Updike, *Odd Jobs* (London: Andre Deutsch, 1992), p. 147. Subsequent quotations from this work are cited parenthetically in the text.

8. Updike was well acquainted with the writing of both Rimbaud and Nietzsche. On Rimbaud see, for example, John Updike, *Hugging the Shore* (Harmondsworth: Penguin Books, 1985), p. 556. Subsequent quotations from this work are cited parenthetically in the text in the abbreviated form (*Hugging*). On Rimbaud and Nietzsche see *Hugging*, p. 542; *Odd Jobs*, pp. 162–63; 439.

9. In John Updike, *Assorted Prose* (New York: Fawcett Crest, 1966), p. 212. Subsequent quotations from this work are cited parenthetically in the text. Quoted from Karl Barth, *The Word of God*, p. 204.

10. Karl Barth, *A Barth Reader*, ed. Yoachim Erler & Reiner Marquard (Grand Rapids: William B. Eerdmans Publishing House, 1986), pp. 101–3.

11. Updike, *Assorted Prose*, p. 220. See also Plath, ed., *Conversations With John Updike*, p. 75. Subsequent quotations from this work are cited parenthetically in the text in the abbreviated form (*Conversations*). Updike's critique of liberal theology may relate him to the ancestral line Barth draws from his own theology back "through Kierkegaard to Luther and Calvin, and so to Paul and Jeremiah." The antithetical, humanistic tradition Barth delineates, runs back from Schleiermacher "through Martensen to Erasmus," and the (false) "prophets of Judea" (Barth, *The Word of God*, pp. 195–96). As American affiliates to this lineage, I believe, Updike would add not only Niebuhr, but also Emerson and Whitman, as prophets of the American sublime best introduced in Harold Bloom, *Poetry and Repression*.

12. In one of his earlier essays on Barth's theology, Updike defines it as confessional in *Assorted Prose*, p. 216. The review opens with a quote from Barth's *The Word of God and the Word of Man*, which underscores the unbridgeable gap between God and man.

13. Barth, *The Word of God*, pp. 210, 168, 204.

14. See also chapter 1, section V.

15. Bloom, *Poetry and Repression*, pp. 254, 244.

16. R. W. Emerson, "Self-Reliance," *Selections from R. W. Emerson*, ed. Stephen Whicher (Boston: Houghton Mifflin, 1960), p. 164.

17. Bloom, *Poetry and Repression*, p. 251.

18. Barth conflates the figure of the prophet with the state of humanity experiencing crisis. In *The Epistle to the Romans*, he more explicitly associates the trope of crisis as a metaphysical frontier experience of self-annihilation, with the death and resurrection of Christ. The prophets, Barth contends, debunk human titanic aspirations; they "see what men in fact are; . . . they see them arrogantly and illegitimately daring the impossible and raising themselves to equality with God." In order to awaken self-inflated individuals to their gnomic being on the one hand, and to the possibility of redemption on the other, the prophet "leaps into the void" at the moment of "prophetic crisis," which is the line of death that the sinful individual cannot cross unaided from without (pp. 183, 243–44).

19. R. W. Emerson, "The Divinity School Address", *Selections*, p. 106.

20. Barth, quoted in Plath, ed., *Conversations*, p. 14.

21. Updike, "Cruise", *The Afterlife and Other Stories* (New York: Fawcett Crest, 1994), pp. 290–304. Subsequent quotations from this work are cited parenthetically in the text.

22. Gore Vidal, "Rabbit's Own Burrow: The Comfortable Patriotism of John Updike and His Fiction," *TLS* (April 26, 1996): 3–7. For critical views see also Robert Gingher, "Has John Updike Anything to Say?" *MFS* 37, no. 1 (spring 1991): 97–105. Gingher claims that Updike's characters prefer "self-aggrandizement" and "self-indulgence" to dauntless self-questioning (p. 103).

23. Updike, *Self-Consciousness: Memoirs*, p. 240. Subsequent quotations from this work are cited parenthetically in the text.

24. Updike, "Still Life," *Pigeon Feathers*, pp. 27–40.

25. Schiff, "Updike Ignored," p. 537.

26. Updike, *Self Consciousness*, p. 231. In an early story, "Packed Dirt, Church Going, A Dying Cat, a Traded Car," Updike denounces American giantism, which bred "docile Titans—guileless, competent, mildly earnest . . . [with] the instinctive optimism of the young animal" (*Pigeon Feathers*, p. 179). In "Joyce's Poldy/Updike's Rabbit," *Cimarron Review* (January 1995): 92–101, Sanford Pinsker provides an example of a misreading of Updike's refashioning of Emersonian subjectivity: "And isn't this our fascination with the protagonist of *Rabbit, Run* precisely what Emerson had in mind when he talked about the transcendental self—shining, radiant, altogether imperial—locked inside the most inconspicuous heart?" (p. 94)

27. John Updike, "Pigeon Feathers," *Pigeon Feathers*, pp. 84–105. Subsequent quotations from this work are cited parenthetically in the text.

28. In the closing story of *Pigeon Feathers*, the reader meets David, now a grown man, in yet another wasted point of crisis. Like his earlier self, the protagonist of "Packed Dirt, Church Going, a Dying Cat, a Traded Car" experiences a moment of horror. Updike retains, however, the sustained duality between the Barthian No and the American self-affirming voice, and David remains at midpoint, advocating rituals and not annihilating confessions: "We in America need ceremonies, is I suppose, sailor, the point of what I have written" (p. 189).

29. Bloom, introduction, *Modern Critical Views on Emerson*, pp. 1–11.

30. Updike, "George and Vivian," *The Afterlife and Other Stories*, pp. 160–96. Subsequent quotations from this work are cited parenthetically in the text.

31. Michel Foucault, *The Foucault Reader*, ed. Paul Rabinow (New York: Pantheon Books, 1984), pp. 41–42.

32. Emerson, "Illusions", *Selections*, p. 294.

33. Plath, ed., *Conversations With John Updike*, p. 103. See Emerson's essays, "Illusions" and "Experience." In "Illusions," Emerson talks about "the beneficent illusions of sentiment and of the intellect," and cheerfully declares that "it is all phantasm" and that "life is an ecstasy." Unlike Sacvan Bercovitch, who does not emphasize the contradiction in Emerson between his Puritan precursors and his Romantic contemporaries, Updike radicalizes their mutual exclusiveness. Juxtaposing Emerson to Hawthorne, he applauds the latter for his loyalty not to transcendentalist "boastful optimism," but rather to "the Puritan sense of guilt and intrinsic limitation which Emerson so exultantly wished to banish" (*Odd Jobs*, p. 151).

34. Updike's conservative views, his non-marginal voice, and his refusal to comply with politically correct discourse, has put him at odds with academic circles,

whom he refers to as "Eastern establishment; Cambridge professors." He has, likewise, criticized the anti-Vietnam protests of "a favored enlightened few hiding behind college deferments . . . snootily pouring pig blood into draft files, writing deeply offended Notes and Comments, and otherwise pretending that our great nation hadn't had bloody hands from the start" (*Self-Consciousness*, pp. 125, 141). Updike does not attempt, however, to gloss over the plight of minorities in American society. In a letter to his half-black grandsons, he voices his genuine concern about the problems of minority groups in America. His tone is realistic and pragmatic, without resorting to radical rhetoric (*Self-Consciousness*, pp. 171–222). See also *Conversations*, pp. 224–25.

35. John Updike, *In the Beauty of the Lilies* (New York: Fawcett Crest, 1996), p. 457.

36. Barth, *The Epistle to the Romans*, p. 203. John Updike, *Telephone Poles* (New York: Alfred A. Knopf, 1979), p. 72. As will be shown, Updike examines the Barthian trope of crisis in a story entitled "Short Easter" (*Afterlife and Other Stories*, pp. 95–106).

37. Barth, *Barth Reader*, 32–34.

38. Emerson, "Circles", *Selections*, p. 68.

39. Vidal, "Rabbit's Own Burrow," p. 4.

40. See for example Tanner, *City of Words*, p. 47.

41. *Conversations*, p. 11. In *John Updike and the Three Great Secret Things*, George Hunt discusses Updike's delight in ambiguities and indeterminacies. While he attributes to Updike a dialectical discourse, he finds its expression merely in the non-reductionist explication of reality (pp. 15–21).

42. In *The Word of God*, pp. 203–5, Barth postulates that self-criticism is not enough since it is too human. He demands a total negation which only God can bring about.

43. Updike, *Conversations*, pp. 37, 103; *Self-Consciousness*, p. 158.

44. In *Readings in the Canon of Scripture: Written For Our Learning* (New York: St. Martin's Press, 1995), David Jasper studies readings of scriptural and postmodern apocalypse: "The tradition of apocalyptic writing, coming after prophetic literature, precisely recognizes that it must act as a warning against its own fulfillment— that judgment is both in the present, when the chaos which we may not be fully aware of, actually is the chaos that we fear. . . . Judgment Day is now, and yet perhaps it can be avoided even so. . . . The postmodern voice perhaps is a lament over an age which narcissistically merely sees its own face reflected in all things and in the frenzy of consumerism which rushes to its own destruction without difference and without originality" (pp. 113, 129).

45. Updike, "Short Easter," *The Afterlife and Other Stories*, pp. 95–106. Subsequent quotations from this work are cited parenthetically in the text.

46. See David Jasper, "Living in the Reel World: The Bible in Film," *Readings in the Canon of Scripture*, pp. 83–95.

47. In *Self-Consciousness* Updike accuses the media of presenting apocalyptic catastrophes as harmless and unmenacing: "We cannot imagine a Second Coming that would not be cut down to size by the televised evening news, or a Last Judgment not subject to pages of holier-than-Thou second-guessing in the *New York Review of Books*" (p. 227).

48. *In the Beauty of the Lilies*, epigraph. Quoted from Julia Ward Howe's poem "The Battle Hymn of the Republic."

49. Brooke Allen, "Losing Faith," *The New Criterion* 14 no. 5 (January 1996): 57–60. Quote on p. 59.

50. In *The Epistle to the Romans*, Barth castigates the wavering of the unbeliever as a stutter: "In the presence of His 'Yes' and His 'Amen,' our stammering 'As If,' our muttered 'Yes' and 'No' cannot stand" (p. 229).

51. Vidal, "Rabbit's Own Burrow," pp. 3–4.

52. Ibid., pp. 5, 3.

53. *Foucault Reader*, pp. 362–63. Foucault claims that the stoic autobiographical texts served as exhibitionist displays of self, free from self-questioning: "They do not constitute an 'account of oneself'; their objective is not to bring the *arcana conscientiae* to light, the confession of which . . . has a purifying value." For the Christian self, by contrast, autobiography is an exercise in self-examination, part of the "necessity of renouncing the self and deciphering its truth" (pp. 365–66).

54. *The New York Times Magazine* (May 12, 1996). Quote from p. 27. In one of the essays in this issue—"Confessing For Voyeurs: The Age of The Literary Memoir is Now," (pp. 25–27)—James Atlas traces both confession and autobiography to Emersonian literary tradition, and defines the contemporary notion of confession in a formulation which for Augustine, Kierkegaard, and Barth would be a contradiction in terms: "What Christopher Lasch famously labeled 'the culture of narcissism' has been replaced by the culture of confession" (26). For Atlas, as for other contemporary American readers and writers, the term confession, interchangeable with autobiography, becomes free from self-questioning; both denote a study in exhibitionism. I read Updike's *Self-Consciousness* as a self-questioning confession rather than as the exhibitionist account of a "journey from there to here."

55. See my discussion of Updike's story "Cruise" earlier in the chapter.

56. *Self-Consciousness*, p. 243. In his more recent collection of essays, *Odd Jobs*, Updike reaffirms his faith in God's Yes: "I still have them, these visitations of joy and gratitude, and still associate them with the Good News. 'Know too,' Matthew's Gospel ends, 'that I am with you every day to the end of time' " (p. 239).

CHAPTER 3. VISION WITHOUT PROPHETS

1. Flannery O'Connor, *Mystery and Manners*, ed. Sally and Robert Fitzgerald (New York: Farrar, Straus and Giroux, 1989), p. 32. Subsequent quotations from this work are cited parenthetically in the text in the abbreviated form (*Mystery*).

2. Miller-Budick, *Engendering Romance*, p. 162. To mention only a few of the critical studies which center on O'Connor's religious consciousness: Linda Munk, "Understanding Understatement: Biblical Typology and 'The Displaced Person'," *Literature & Theology* 2, no. 2 (September 1988): 237–53; Kathleen Feeley, *Flannery O'Connor: Voice of the Peacock* (New York: Fordham University Press, 1982); Most recently *Literature and Belief* 17 (1997) devoted an entire issue to *Flannery O'Connor and the Christian Mystery*, ed. John J. Murphy.

3. Richard Giannone, "Flannery O'Connor Tells Her Desert Story," *Religion & Literature* 27, no. 2 (summer 1995): 47–67. Quote on p. 50.

4. Paul Nisly, "The Prison of the Self: Isolation in F. O'Connor's Fiction," *Studies in Short Fiction* 12, no. 2 (1974): 49–54. Quote on p. 50.

5. Claire Katz-Kahane, "Flannery O'Connor's Rage of Vision," *American Literature* 46, no. 1 (March 1974): 54–67. Quote on pp. 56–57.

6. From their respective viewpoints, both Miller-Budick and Katz-Kahane refer to O'Connor as a woman writing within a patriarchal theological tradition. Miller-Budick, who situates the Catholic writer in the American romance tradition, highlights O'Connor's attempt to free herself from the constraints of both theological and generic patriarchal traditions (*Engendering Romance*, p. 163). In Katz-Kahane's psychological reading, O'Connor's degrading portrayal of female characters who seek autonomy projects "fantasies of castration" and "repugnance towards femaleness" (p. 64).

7. Flannery O'Connor, *The Habit of Being*, ed. Sally Fitzgerald (New York: Farrar, Straus and Giroux, 1988), p. 372. Subsequent quotations from this work are cited parenthetically in the text in the abbreviated form (*Habit*).

8. Updike, *Hugging The Shore*, p. 291; Updike, *Odd Jobs*, p. 455; Plath, ed., *Conversations With Updike*, p. 95. The phrase "pinpoint of light" appears three times in the last chapter of O'Connor's *Wise Blood* in *Three by Flannery O'Connor* (New York: Signet Classic, 1983) discussed below. It is noteworthy that when Updike expresses his view that contemporary "reality so diminished proves the existence of a great Diminisher," his immediate association is to O'Connor's writings, and her emphasis on divine judgment (*Odd Jobs*, p. 455).

9. Reference is made here to the adversaries in the "Apocalypse of Enoch," whose namesake is demolished in O'Connor's *Wise Blood*.

10. Herman Melville, *Moby Dick* (New York: Macmillan, 1962), chapters 28, 41, 82, 83.

11. Flannery O'Connor, *Wise Blood*, pp. 3–120, reference to p. 71; *The Violent Bear it Away* in *Three by Flannery O'Connor*, pp. 121–267, reference to p. 252. Subsequent quotations from these works are cited parenthetically in the text.

12. For the Emersonian giant that destroys itself see above, chapter 2, section I.

13. O'Connor, *The Presence of Grace*, pp. 74–75.

14. In her introduction to *Three By Flannery O'Connor* Sally Fitzgerald highlights Eliot's influence on O'Connor's work in general and on *Wise Blood* in particular. Fitzgerald suggests, however, that "the work that seemed to move [O'Connor] powerfully was *The Waste Land* (ix–x).

15. Jean Baudrillard, *Simulacra and Simulation*, trans. Sheila Faria Glaser (Ann Arbor: University of Michigan Press, 1994).

16. See chapter 2, section V above for Updike's treatment of American film industry and its role in the aftermath of Auschwitz and Hiroshima.

17. In 1918 Jung wrote: "As the Christian view of the world loses its authority, the more menacingly will the "blond beast" be heard prowling about its underground prison, ready at any moment to burst out with devastating consequences." Quoted in Susan Acheson, "Esoteric Eschatology of H. D.'s Trilogy," *Literature & Theology*, 12, no. 2 (June 1998): 187–204, quote on p. 203 n. 23. Jung's nightmare predicts that the gospel of no-God heralds the age of the "blond beast." Likewise, in O'Connor's *Wise Blood*, prophesies of no-God (84) are framed by scenes of jungle beasts and film monsters, entertaining pleasure-seeking audiences. Only such a pain-fleeing culture could produce entertaining murderous monsters such as King Kong or the dinosaurs of *Jurassic Park*. Jung's nightmare is peopled with dying gods and released beasts. Cleansed of nightmare, O'Connor's scene replaces vanished

gods with blank skies and blank eyes while comfortably placing the king of the beasts in containing cages or celluloid simulacra. In *Mystery and Manners* O'Connor says: "St. Cyril of Jerusalem wrote: 'The dragon sits by the side of the road, watching those who pass. Beware lest he devour you. We go to the Father of Souls, but it is necessary to pass by the dragon.' No matter what form the dragon may take, it is of this mysterious passage past him, or into his jaws, that stories of any depth will always be concerned to tell" (p. 35).

18. James, *Varieties of Religious Experience*, pp. 80, 90.

19. On vision-resisting, reluctant, and hostile readers see *Habit*, p. 361; *Mystery*, pp. 48, 112, 161–63, 185.

20. Miller-Budick, *Engendering Romance*, pp. 169–74.

21. See Levinas, *Proper Names*, trans. Michael B. Smith (Stanford: Stanford University Press, 1996), pp. 66–75; Soren Kierkegaard, *Fear and Trembling*, trans. Walter Loweie (Princeton: Princeton University Press, 1941).

22. "To bear responsibility rather than to be borne away by violence is the urgent message of O'Connor's text." Miller-Budick, *Engendering Romance*, p. 177.

23. On apocalyptic scenes as violent invitations to parabolic insight, see Barth, *The Epistle to the Romans*, pp. 333, 500. Subsequent quotations from this work are cited parenthetically in the text in the abbreviated form (*Romans*).

24. Quentin Anderson, *The Imperial Self: An Essay in American Literary and Cultural History* (New York: Alfred A. Knopf, 1971). For Bloom's giant see chapters 1 and 2 above.

25. Harold Bloom, introduction to *Flannery O'Connor* (New York: Chelsea House Publishers, 1986), p. 4.

26. Bloom, introduction, to *Flannery O'Connor*, p. 3. O'Connor herself frequently stresses in her nonfiction that her strategies of violence are not violence for its own sake but rather theological strategies for awakening hardened sinners with perversely closed eyes and minds. See, for example, *Mystery*, pp. 34, 112–13.

27. See, for example, Jefferson Humphries, "Proust, O'Connor and the Aesthetic of Violence," in *The Otherness Within: Gnostic Readings in Proust, O'Connor and Villon* (Baton Rouge: Louisiana State University Press, 1983), pp. 95–111; Katz-Kahane, "Flannery O'Connor's Rage of Vision"; Andre Bleikasten, "Heresy of Flannery O'Connor," *Critical Essays on Flannery O'Connor*, eds. Melvin Friedman and Beverly Clark (Boston: G. K. Hall, 1985), pp. 138–58. Bloom admits that his own reading "dissents from the sensitive reading of Jefferson Humphries" (Introduction to *Flannery O'Connor*, p. 5). See note 57 below for the significance of the title and epigraph for O'Connor.

28. Bloom, *The American Religion* p. 24.

29. See Jonas, *The Gnostic Religion*, pp. 68–73.

30. Bloom, introduction, *Flannery O'Connor*, p. 8.

31. Ibid., p. 6. O'Connor was critical of her critics. In a letter to John Hawkes, O'Connor wryly comments on academic reviews of *The Violent Bear It Away*: "I've been busy keeping my blood pressure down while reading various reviews of my book. . . . most reviewers seem to have read the book in fifteen minutes and written the review in ten . . ." (*Habit*, p. 389).

32. Perhaps Bloom is more lenient with O'Connor because he finds that, unlike Updike's narratives and against O'Connor's better judgment, her art is touched by Emersonian Sublime.

33. In *Blake's Apocalypse: A Study in Poetic Argument* (Ithaca: Cornell University Press, 1963), Bloom offers a brilliant analysis of Blake's visionary works, and uses apocalypse as a guiding metaphor. Bloom, however, uses the metaphor in the sense of vision, and certainly not as destruction of self. In my reading of O'Connor, I relate only to the specifically Christian connotation of apocalypse, namely to self-under-Judgment. It is in this light that I read O'Connor's *The Violent Bear It Away* at the end of the present chapter. For Updike's and Barth's concepts of the apocalypse see chapter 2 above.

34. Feeley, *Flannery O'Connor: Voice of the Peacock*, p. 45. For hostile readers see above, note 19.

35. O'Connor's letters testify to her deep interest in radical protestant theology in general and particularly in that of Karl Barth. In a letter to John Hawkes she admits to accepting "the same fundamental doctrines of sin and redemption and judgment that [radical Protestants] do" (*Habit*, p. 350). To her friend "A" she writes: "I am surprised you don't know anything about the crisis theologians. . . . They are the greatest of the Protestant theologians writing today. . . . We have very few thinkers to equal Barth . . . perhaps none (*Habit*, 306).

36. Barth, *The Word of God and the Word of Man*, p.204; Plath, ed., *Conversations With John Updike*, p. 14.

37. *Habit*, p. 302. In this letter, addressed to a correspondent curious to learn her concept of Original Sin, she writes: " 'How we have fallen' means the Fall of Adam, the fall from innocence, from sanctifying grace."

38. *Mystery*, p. 227. For further reference to Updike, see chapter 2, section III above.

39. Jonathan Culler, "On the Negativity of Modern Poetry: Friedrich, Baudelaire and the Critical Tradition," *Languages of the Unsayable: The Play of Negativity in Literature and Literary Theory*, ed. S. Budick and W. Iser (Stanford: Stanford University Press, 1987), p. 191.

40. David Jasper, "Living in the Reel World: The Bible in Film," pp. 83–95, and "Apocalypse Then and Now," in *Readings in the Canon of Scripture*, pp. 106–21. See also Baudrillard, *Simulacra and Simulation*, p. 126.

41. Jasper, "Apocalypse," pp. 112–13.

42. I borrow the term "added dimension" from O'Connor, who asserts that belief in Christian dogma "will add a dimension to the writer's observation" (*Mystery*, p. 150).

43. O'Connor, *The Presence of Grace*, p. 168.

44. Miller-Budick, *Engendering Romance*, pp. 163–64.

45. In *Mystery and Manners*, p. 72, O'Connor talks about three kinds of meaning of sacred texts introduced by Medieval commentators on Scripture: "One they called allegorical, in which one fact pointed to another; one they called tropological, or moral, which had to do with what should be done; and one they called anagogical, which had to do with the Divine life and our participation in it."

46. For the term "twice-born" see William James, *Varieties*, p. 80.

47. See *Mystery*, p. 30, for O'Connor's assertion that there can be no moral judgment without religious faith.

48. Emerson, "Self-Reliance," *Selections From Ralph Waldo Emerson*, p. 150.

49. In *The Violent Bear It Away*, for example, Rayber tries to avoid hearing the "prophet child": "He was groping fiercely about him . . . not able to find the switch

that would cut off the voice. Then his hand touched the button and he snapped it. A silent dark relief enclosed him like shelter after a tormenting wind" (p. 204). See note 63 below.

50. In *Mystery* O'Connor says: "I have found . . . that my subject in fiction is the action of grace in territory largely held by the devil." The novel's "center of destruction," she continues, "will be the devil" (pp. 118, 197).

51. Emerson, "Spiritual Laws," *The Works of R. W. Emerson,* p. 86.

52. O'Connor sees the prophet as "a realist of distances," and prophetic moments of vision as radically realistic, while satanic imagination derealizes distances: "True prophecy in the novelist's case is a matter of seeing near things with their extensions of meanings and thus seeing far things close up. . . . Prophecy, which is dependent on the *imaginative* and not the moral faculty, need not be a matter of predicting the future. *The prophet is a realist of distances* and it is this kind of realism that goes into great novels." M. Friedman and L. Lawson, eds., *The Added Dimension: The Art and Mind of Flannery O'Connor,* (New York: Fordham University Press, 1966), p. 252; O'Connor, *Mystery,* p. 179.

53. O'Connor, "The Displaced Person," *The Complete Stories of Flannery O'Connor* (London and Boston: Faber & Faber, 1990), pp. 194–235. Reference on p. 209. Subsequent quotations of this work are cited parenthetically in the text in the abbreviated form ("Displaced"); *The Violent Bear it Away,* p. 128.

54. Jacques Derrida, "At This Very Moment in This Work Here I Am," *Re Reading Levinas,* ed. Robert Bernasconi and Simon Chritchley (Bloomington: Indiana University Press, 1991), pp. 11–48. References on pp. 25–27.

55. In Mark Twain's "The Mysterious Stranger" the narrator describes his "enchanting" encounters with an angel called Satan whose earthly name is Traum (dream). While Satan makes the narrator "drunk with the joy of being with him," he ruthlessly attacks "the weakness and triviality of [the human] race." The appalled narrator's way to avoid the angst caused by Satan's revelations is to make him unreal—a dream from which one awakens to "other dreams and better." Thus the story ends with Satan's assuring the narrator: "I am but a dream—your dream, creature of your imagination. In a moment you will . . . banish me from your visions and I shall dissolve into the nothingness out of which you made me . . ." (*The Mysterious Stranger and Other Stories* [New York: Signet Classic, 1962], pp. 161–253). Quotes on pp. 169, 171, 252. See O'Connor, *Mystery,* p. 161, for Emerson's "vaporization of religion in America."

56. Emerson, "Spiritual Laws"; In "Experience" Emerson claims that "every evil and every good thing is a shadow which we cast." *Selections,* pp. 254–74, quote on p. 269.

57. O'Connor, *Mystery,* p. 51. In *Habit,* p. 382, O'Connor emphasizes the sig- nificance of her chosen title, claiming that "the title is the best thing about the book."

58. O'Connor notes that the "pervert who gives Tarwater a lift" at the end of *The Violent Bear It Away* is a diabolic figure (*Habit,* p. 375).

59. See Miller-Budick, *Engendering Romance,* pp. 169–72.

60. See Barth, *Romans,* pp. 196–97.

61. Commenting on Emerson's "vaporization of religion in America," O'Connor stresses his decision not to "celebrate the Lord's Supper unless the bread and wine were removed" (*Mystery,* p. 161).

62. In *Romans* Karl Barth shows the correlation between crucifixion, baptism, and the burial of the old self. See pp. 197–98. In *Wise Blood* Enoch buries his clothes before putting on a gorilla outfit. Yet O'Connor makes clear that "burying his old clothes was not a symbol to him of burying his former self" (p. 101).

63. Rayber is hard of hearing, having been shot by old Tarwater when he attempted to retrieve his nephew. At crucial instances O'Connor shows him to switch on or off his hearing aid. See pp. 175, 205, 242.

64. See, for example, *Habit*, 331, 343; *Mystery*, 165.

65. O'Connor explicitly notes that the "Tempter, the Devil . . . becomes actualized" in that driver (*Habit*, 375).

66. Romantic writers prided themselves on being prophetic figures. (Both Sacvan Bercovitch and Harold Bloom introduce Emerson and Whitman as American prophets. See chapter 1 above). Though O'Connor complains that the Romantics are too subjective (see *Habit*, 456) she does not reject a subjective attitude as such.

67. Barth reads baptism as the core of the "psychology of grace." (*Romans*, p. 197). He uses the frontier metaphor when he discusses baptism and crucifixion: "The barrier marks the frontier of a new country, and what dissolves the whole wisdom of the world also establishes it. . . . Faith is the incomparable and irrevocable step over the frontier separating the old from the new man and the old from the new world (*Romans*, 38, 201).

68. O'Connor does not relate to the assault on Tarwater as rape but as "violation." See, for example, *Habit*, 368.

CHAPTER 4. FOOTSTEPS AND ECHOES

1. For silence and postmodern discourse after Auschwitz see David Carroll, *Paraesthetics: Foucault, Lyotard, Derrida* (New York: Methuen, 1987), pp. 107–13, 126ff, 169–72, 183, 199 n. 23, 205 n. 11. See especially chapter 7, "Auschwitz and the Signs 'of History'," pp. 169–73.

2. Grace Paley, "Dreamer in a Dead Language," *The Collected Stories*, pp. 265–83. Subsequent quotations from Paley's stories are cited parenthetically in the text, and refer to this edition.

3. See Levinas on honoring the right of the other to exist in *In the Time of the Nations*, pp. 171, 178.

4. See chapter 1 above; Levinas, *Existence and Existents*, p. 93.

5. See Levinas, *In The Time of the Nations*, p. 97. See my discussion in chapter 1 above.

6. The aesthetics of dialogism can, of course, be read through Bakhtin's prism. However, diachrony as Levinas defines it and Paley practices it, introduces a distinctly Jewish element into the larger category of dialogism. Critics such as Jacqueline Taylor have recognized the relevance of Bakhtin's dialogism to Paley's techniques, but what remains to be observed and analyzed is Levinas's diachronic model. See Taylor, *Grace Paley: Illuminating the Dark Lives*, p. 21. The term "non-allergy" is borrowed from Emmanuel Levinas. See for example *Beyond the Verse*, p. 190; *Totality and Infinity*, p. 51.

7. See Emerson, "The Poet," *Selections From R. W. Emerson*, pp. 260–61.

8. See for example Taylor, *Grace Paley: Illuminating the Dark Lives*. Kathleen

Hulley, "Grace Paley's Resistant Form," *Delta* 14 (1982): 3–18; Lyons, "Grace Paley's Jewish Miniatures," pp. 26–33; Miller-Budick, *Engendering Romance,* pp. 219–45.

9. Paley, *The Collected Stories,* pp. 232–37.

10. For Levinas's use of "allergy" see note 6 above; Harold Bloom, *The Anxiety of Influence: A Theory of Poetry* (London: Oxford University Press, 1973).

11. Bloom, *Anxiety,* pp. 85, 122–23.

12. Walt Whitman, "As I Ebbed with the Ocean of Life" in *The Complete Poetry and Selected Prose* ed. James Miller (Boston: Houghton Mifflin Co., 1959), p. 186. It is strange that in his study of Whitman's sublime Bloom does not cite these lines. Zephyra Porat, in *Prometheus Among the Cannibals: Adventures of the Rebel in Literature* (in Hebrew), discusses Whitman's Promethean self in a chapter entitled, precisely, "What Is Yours Is Mine, My Father." (Tel Aviv: Am Oved Publishers, 1976), pp. 46–59.

13. Foucault, *The Foucault Reader,* p. 362.

14. Emmanuel Levinas, *Basic Philosophical Writings,* ed. Adrian Peperzak, Simon Critchley, and Robert Bernasconi (Bloomington: Indiana University Press, 1996), pp. 115–17.

15. Miller-Budick, *Engendering Romance,* p. 231.

16. Ibid., pp. 223, 227.

17. Ibid., p. 230.

18. For a comprehensive discussion of the issue, see Hana Wirth-Nesher, ed., *What is Jewish Literature* (Philadelphia and Jerusalem: The Jewish Publication Society, 1994).

19. Harold Bloom, "The Sorrows of American-Jewish Poetry," *Commentary* 53, no. 3 (March 1972): 69–74; Cynthia Ozick, "Judaism & Harold Bloom," *Commentary* 67, no. 1 (January 1979): 43–51.

20. Bloom, "The Sorrows," p. 71; Ozick, "Judaism," pp. 49–50.

21. It is interesting to note that Levinas argues that in order to find the self, the Jewish prophetic subject must be found in advance by an Other, not necessarily a father: "All my inwardness is invested in a form of a despite-me-for-another. Against my will for-another, that is signification par excellence and the sense of oneself . . . of the self . . . that accusative that derives from no nominative; it is the very fact of finding oneself while losing oneself." *Basic Philosophical Writings,* p. 118.

22. In "Poetry and Resurrection: Notes on Agnon," Levinas defines Jewish fictional writing both as a mourning community that has vanished and, precisely as such, providing the light of continuity in the very act of writing and listening. *Proper Names,* pp. 7–16.

23. Bloom, "The Sorrows," pp. 70–71.

24. Ibid., p. 71.

25. Cynthia Ozick, "A Translator's Monologue," *Metaphor & Memory: Essays by Cynthia Ozick* (New York: Alfred A. Knopf, 1989), pp. 199–208; "S. Y. Agnon and the First Religion," *Metaphor & Memory,* pp. 209–22.

26. Ozick, "A Translator's Monologue," pp. 201–2.

27. Ozick, "S. Y. Agnon and the First Religion," pp. 213–22.

28. Ozick, "Judaism & Harold Bloom," pp. 45–46.

29. Harold Bloom, introduction to *Cynthia Ozick,* ed. H. Bloom (New York: Chelsea House Publishers, 1985), p. 1.

30. Ibid., p. 5.

31. Ibid., p. 2.

32. Ibid., p. 5.

33. Ozick, "Judaism," pp. 47–48.

34. Ozick, "Usurpation (Other People's Stories)," quoted in Bloom, introduction, *Cynthia Ozick*, p. 4.

35. Ibid., p. 5.

36. In "Memory and Metaphor" Ozick links prophetism, Jewish prophetism, and historic memory. See, for example, "Memory and Metaphor," *Metaphor & Memory*, pp. 281–83.

37. Bloom, introduction, *Cynthia Ozick*, p. 6.

38. Since my reading of Paley is inspired by Levinas it is worth noting here that Levinas distinguishes between "sacredness" and "holiness," and centers on the ethical rather than on the sacred. In *Of God Who Comes to Mind*, trans. Bettina Bergo (Stanford: Stanford University Press, 1998), p. 51, Levinas underscores "the reversion of the waiting for God into the proximity of another, into my responsibility as a hostage; a reversion of this fear, as foreign to fright before the Sacred as it is to the anguish before Nothingness, into fear for the neighbor." (See also p. 196 n. 12). I find that like Levinas, Paley calls for transcendence to an ethical rather than to a sacred space.

39. Ozick, "Judaism," pp. 48–49.

40. Ibid., pp. 49–50. Italics in text.

41. Cynthia Ozick, "Envy; or Yiddish in America," p. 48.

42. Ozick, "Envy," pp. 60–61. Quoted in Bloom, introduction, *Cynthia Ozick*, p. 6.

43. For Emerson's aversion to history see "Self Reliance," *Selections*, pp. 152, 155; "History," *Essays and Lectures* (New York: The Library of America, 1983), pp. 239, 251. Nietzsche's aversion to history is elaborated at great length in "The Use and Abuse of History," *Untimely Meditation*, trans. R. S. Hollingdale (Cambridge: Cambridge University Press, 1983), pp. 57–125.

44. Ozick, "Envy," p. 61.

45. Bloom, introduction, *Cynthia Ozick*, p. 6. Italics in text.

46. I borrow the metaphor from Ozick. See "Ruth," *Metaphor & Memory*, pp. 240–64. Reference to pp. 263–64.

47. In this respect Paley's Jewish characters feature a dimension to which Ozick would object, considering her criticism of Updike's only Jewish character Bech. In "Bech, Passing," *John Updike*, ed. H. Bloom, pp. 127–38, Ozick accuses Updike of denying Bech the religious transcendental dimension which he grants all his other religious characters. Unlike Christian characters who are all "touched by the transcendental," Updike's Jew is all "sociology," ethnicity and local American anthropology. Paley's Jews are not manifestly touched by the transcendental. But, I believe, neither are they all ethnicity, sociology, and anthropology (Reference to pp. 133–37).

48. Joan Lidoff, "Clearing her Throat: An Interview With Grace Paley," *Shenandoah* 32, no. 3 (1981): 3–26.

49. Paley, *The Collected Stories*, p. x. "I do write with an accent," Paley admits in her interview with Lidoff, "I did have three languages spoken around me when I was a kid. . . . That's what's in my ear" (Lidoff, "Clearing Her Throat," p. 4).

50. Rosemary O'Sullivan, "Listening and Telling in Counterpoint: A Conversation With Grace Paley," *Plotting Change: Contemporary Women's Fiction* (London: Edward Arnold, 1990), p. 106.

51. In *Difficult Freedom*, Levinas argues that the Jewish ethical approach to history and heritage is anachronistic and diachronic: "Judaism is a non-coincidence with its time, within coincidence: in the radical sense of the term it is an *anachronism*. The simultaneous presence of a youth that is attentive to reality and impatient to change it, and an old age that . . . is returning to the origin of things" (p. 212, italics in text). On Levinas and "anachronism" see also Susan Handelman, *Fragments of Redemption: Jewish Thought & Literary Theory in Benjamin, Scholem, & Levinas* (Bloomington: Indiana University Press, 1991), pp. 277, 316.

52. I use here Ricoeur's term expounded in *Time and Narrative*, trans K. McLaughlin & D. Pellauer (Chicago: University of Chicago Press, 1984–1988), vol. 2, pp. 3–34.

53. O'Sullivan, "Listening and Telling," p. 104.

54. Kathleen Hulley, "Interview with Grace Paley," *Delta* 14 (1982): 19–40. Quote on p. 38.

55. Jameson, "The Vanishing Mediator; Or, Max Weber as Storyteller," *The Ideologies of Theory*, vol. 2, pp. 3–34.

56. Jameson, "The Vanishing," p. 20.

57. Here again I borrow terms from Ricoeur's *Time and Narrative*.

58. In an interview with Ruth Perry, Paley says that throughout the *Collected Stories* the character of the father is based on her own father, while the daughter/narrator and the plots are imaginary. Ruth Perry, "Grace Paley," *Women Writers Talking*, ed. J. Todd (New York: Holmes and Meir Publishers, 1983), pp. 35–56. Quote on p. 42. For a critical discussion of the story see, for example, Ronald Schleifer, "Chaste Compactness," *Contemporary American Women Writers: Narrative Strategies*, ed. C. Rainwater and W. Scheik (Lexington: University Press of Kentucky, 1985), pp. 31–47; J. Meier, "The Subversion of the Father in the Tales of Grace Paley," *Delta* 14 (May 1982): 115–27; Nicholas Humy, "A Different Responsibility: Form and Technique in Grace Paley's 'A Conversation with my Father'," *Delta* 14 (May 1982): 87–95; Miller-Budick, *Engendering Romance*, pp. 220–24.

59. Ricoeur, *Time and Narrative*, vol. 3, p. 141.

60. Wolfgang Iser, *The Fictive and the Imaginary: Charting Literary Anthropology* (Baltimore: The Johns Hopkins University Press, 1993), pp. 50–51.

61. O'Sullivan, "Listening and Telling," p. 104.

62. Hulley, "Interview," pp. 33–34.

63. Ricoeur, *Time and Narrative*, vol. 2, p. 97.

64. Ibid., vol. 1, p. 68.

65. Ibid., vol. 1, p. 199.

66. Hana Wirth-Nesher, "Afterword: Between Mother Tongue and Native Language in *Call It Sleep*," in Henry Roth, *Call It Sleep* (New York: Farrar, Straus and Giroux, 1991), p. 460.

67. Hulley, "Interview," p. 25.

68. Grace Paley, introduction to "A Conversation With My Father," in *Fathers, Reflections By Daughters*, ed. U. Owen (New York: Pantheon Books, 1985), p. 233.

69. Perry, "Grace Paley," p. 42.

70. Noelle Batt and Marcienne Rocard, "An Interview with Grace Paley," *Caliban* 25 (1988): p. 122.

71. Ibid.

72. R. W. Emerson, "Nature," *Selections*, p. 21. In "Self Reliance," for example, Emerson says: "In history our imagination plays us false. . . . Why all this deference to Alfred and Scanderbeg and Gustavus?" *Selections*, pp. 147–68, quote on p. 155; See also "History," pp. 239, 244, 256, in *Essays & Lectures*, pp. 237–56. See reference in note 43.

73. Bloom, *Anxiety*, p. 21.

74. Ibid., p. 26.

75. Perry, "Grace Paley," p. 55.

76. Paley, "Zagrowsky Tells," *Collected Stories*, pp. 348–64.

77. Ricoeur, *Time and Narrative*, vol. 1, p. 198.

78. The inclusion of African Americans in this debate is not accidental. In an earlier story, "Faith In The Afternoon," one of the characters declares: "The war made Jews Americans, and Negroes Jews" (158). See reference to Walter Benn Michael's analysis of ethnic alienation in America in chapter 1.

79. Paley's heteroglossic narrative voice obviously invites analysis with reference to Bakhtinian categories. See M. M. Bakhtin, *The Dialogic Imagination*, trans. Caryl Emerson and Michael Holquist (Austin: University of Texas Press, 1981). My interest, however, focusing as it does on the prophetic *tradition*, requires analyzing a diachronic mode of dialogue, for which Levinas is more relevant than Bakhtin. On the difference between the philosophy of dialogue, which Levinas claims is very old, and his own philosophy of diachrony, see Levinas's conversations with Buber in *Proper Names*, pp. 17–39; *Outside the Subject*, pp. 4–19.

80. Grace Paley, "Of Poetry and Women and the World," *TriQuarterly* 65 (winter 1986): 247–53. Quote on p. 252.

81. O'Sullivan, "Listening and Telling," p. 102. As the writer exposes herself to other voices, art opens up to politics and social intercourse: "[a]ll of art is political; if a writer says this is not political . . . [t]hat's a statement of an alienation problem." Evading the accessibility of aesthetics to politics is implicitly an outgrowth of the narcissistic aversion to intersubjective relations, inherent in the American social scene.

82. Grace Paley, "Symposium," *Shenandoah* 2 (winter 1976): 29. For my discussion of Cavell's model of American prophetic subject see chapter 1 above, section IV.

83. Perry, "Grace Paley," pp. 53–55.

84. See note 47 above.

85. Levinas, *Beyond the Verse*, p. 112.

86. Ibid., pp. 129–31.

87. Levinas, *In the Time of the Nations*, p. 176.

88. Ibid., p. 171.

89. See Fredric Jameson for the inevitable hostility to the stranger, generated by politics of group identity, in *The Political Unconscious: Narrative as a Socially Symbolic Act* (Ithaca: Cornell University Press, 1981), p. 290.

90. Levinas, *In the Time Of the Nations*, p. 181; *Otherwise Than Being*, p. 121. It is worth noting here that Ricoeur resorts to linearity, albeit somewhat differently, in discussing Levinas's idea of open subjectivity: "In this intimate conversation, the self appears to be called upon and in this sense to be affected in a unique way. . . . [T]his affection by another voice presents a remarkable dissymmetry, one that can

be called vertical, between the agency that calls and the self called upon. It is the vertical nature of the call, equal to its interiority, that creates the enigma of the phenomenon of conscience." Ricoeur, *Oneself As Another*, p. 342.

91. Levinas, *Otherwise Than Being*, p. 119. In *Oneself as Another* Ricoeur points to the correlation in Levinas's theory between responsibility and response to a call of the other. According to Levinas, Ricoeur claims, "the other constitutes me as responsible, that is capable of responding. In this way, the word of the other comes to be placed at the origin of my acts," p. 336.

92. Levinas, *Otherwise Than Being*, p. 15.

93. Ibid., pp. 4, 185. Paley equally sees "vanity (as) the destroyer of truth," and negates self-love as fighting "too much against the important factor of attention to what's outside" (Hulley, "Interview," p. 27). In *Oneself as Another* Ricoeur quotes Bernanos in what could serve here as an interplay on Paley's name: "Grace means forgetting oneself. But if all pride were dead in us, the grace of graces would be to love oneself humbly" (p. 24 n. 31).

94. Levinas, *Proper Names*, p. 6.

95. Ibid., p. 6.

96. Ibid., p. 94.

97. See note 92 above.

98. Levinas, *Beyond the Verse*, p. x; *Otherwise Than Being*, pp. 5, 114, 146–49, 185 (italics in original).

99. Levinas, *Beyond the Verse*, p. xiii.

100. I borrow here terms introduced by Bakhtin. For dialogism and diachrony see notes 6 and 79 above.

101. In emphasizing the priority of diachrony in relation to dialogue in Paley's fiction my interpretation of the conversational relationship she introduces diverges from that of Miller-Budick. While, like Miller-Budick, I stress the close link Paley draws between conversation and moral responsibility, I add that, as in Levinas, for Paley conversation does not induce responsibility unless it is well-anchored in a diachronic heritage (Miller-Budick, *Engendering Romance*, pp. 243–44).

102. In *Proper Names*, pp. 67–77, Levinas exposes two related flaws in Kierkegaard's image of religious selfhood. One is the egomaniac violence of his obsession with self, the other is the verbal violence he deploys in sermonizing about it. Disputing Kierkegaard's divorce of faith from ethics, Levinas rejects his interpretation of Abraham's sacrifice of Isaac. Abraham, he remarks, was forbidden to kill his son. For Jews, sacrifice consists in binding: "Instead of destroying the I, the putting in question binds it to the Other" (p. 73).

103. See Miller-Budick, *Engendering Romance*, pp 239–40; "Zagrowsky Tells," p. 354.

104. Levinas, *Proper Names*, p. 6.

105. Exotopy is the term Tzvetan Todorov uses to define Bakhtin's notion of the writer's external position to his character; the returning "within oneself at one's place, outside of the one suffering." Tzvetan Todorov, *Mikhail Bakhtin: The Dialogical Principle*, trans. Wlad Godzich (Minneapolis: University of Minnesota Press, 1984), p. 99.

106. For Emerson's aversion of the past see notes 43 and 72 above.

107. Jameson, *The Political Unconscious*, pp. 69–70.

108. Paley, "Dreamer in a Dead Language," p. 275.

109. Ozick denounces contemporary Jewish readers and writers as illiterate generation. See Elaine Kauvar, "An Interview with Cynthia Ozick," *Contemporary Literature* 34, no. 3 (1993): 359–94. Quote on pp. 375–77.

110. Paley, *Collected Stories,* pp. 195–98.

111. In Hulley, "Interview," p. 38. On the loss of children and on maternal responsibility see Paley's stories "Friends," "Ruthy and Edie," and "The Expensive Moment."

112. In his essay "Judaism and Christianity," *In the Time of the Nations,* pp. 161–66, Levinas recalls having seen in church, at a funeral of a friend's child during the *Shoah,* a painting of Hannah "leading her son Samuel to the Temple." In the story of Hannah's sacrifice Levinas reads "authentic relation, the concreteness of soul, the very personification of the relation. . . . What closeness!" He compares the closeness permeating Hannah's dialogue with God, to the charity which he personally found in the Church during the *Shoah,* when the nuns of St. Vincent de Paul rescued his wife and daughter from death in Nazi concentration camps. (Reference on p. 163).

113. See Sternberg, *The Poetics of Biblical Narrative,* pp. 156–57.

114. Levinas, *Otherwise Than Being,* p. 77. For a discussion of maternity in Levinas's prophetic ethics see Handelman, *Fragments of Redemption,* pp. 206, 255–56. To reinforce my position, which does not deal with feminist theories but recognizes the controversy between feminism and Judaism on the ground of excessive patriarchy, suffice it to quote Simone de Beauvoir's harsh critique of Levinas, mentioned by Handelman. De Beauvoir, says Handelman, "attacked Levinas' association of alterity with femininity . . . as 'an assertion of masculine privilege,' but she neglects or misunderstands his central critique of the narcissistic logic of identity. . . . Levinas seems to have anticipated by many years the recent poststructuralist feminist embrace of alterity as the undoing of the 'privilege of phallogocentrism' " (p. 206).

115. Levinas, *Otherwise than Being,* pp. 75–78. On Levinas's concept of the feminine "caress of consolation" see chapter 1 above, section VIII.

116. Levinas, *Otherwise Than Being,* p. 78.

117. For different interpretations of the name Immanuel see J. Hastings, *Dictionary of the Bible,* vol. 2, (Edinburgh: T. & T. Clark, 1899), p. 454. In the context of Isaiah's prophecy Immanuel is a sign of a dual message. On the one hand it carries the prophet's warning to autonomous, dominant subjects: "And the mean man shall be brought down, and the mighty man shall be humbled" (Isaiah 5:15). On the other hand, it signifies the fulfillment of the promise that the name incorporates ("God is with us"). As such it is a combination of a sign in time and for eternity. *Biblical Encyclopedia* (Jerusalem: Bialik Institute, 1971), p. 294 (in Hebrew). The promised child of the Old Testament is often seen as the type of the child Jesus. The Hebrew *almah* is understood as virgin (Matthew 1:23). This reading, however, is pertinent to my discussion only insofar as Paley parodies the paradigm by letting the mentally disturbed (Jewish) Cissy sing in the street "Look, a virgin will conceive a son" (p. 356). To the best of my knowledge, none of the studies dealing with this story examines the implications of the name Emanuel.

118. Levinas, *Otherwise Than Being,* p. 164.

119. Some years before, Zagrowsky's hostility was cause for a demonstration by young liberal women including his present interlocutor: "They're out there with signs. ZAGROWSKY IS A RACIST. YEARS AFTER ROSA PARKS, ZAGROWSKY REFUSES TO SERVE BLACKS" (352).

120. Levinas, *In the Time of the Nations*, pp. 97–106. See also note 5 above; and chapter 1 above.

121. The same prophetic, ethical decree to love the stranger is explicitly expressed by Faith herself in "Midrash on Happiness." Paley, "Midrash on Happiness," *Triquarterly* 65 (winter 1986): 151–53: "By work to do she included the important work of raising children righteously up. By righteously she meant that along with being useful . . . they must do no harm. By harm she meant not only personal injury to the friend . . . but also the stranger; she meant particularly the stranger in all her or his difference, who, because we were strangers in Egypt, deserves special goodness for life or at least until the end of strangeness" (p. 152). In "Metaphor and Memory" Ozick emphasizes the ethical significance of the biblical "precept of loving the stranger, and treating the stranger as an equal both in emotion and under the law" (279).

122. Lidoff, "Clearing Her Throat," p. 7.

123. I refer to Levinas's essay "Judaism and the Feminine," in *Difficult Freedom*, pp. 30–38.

124. See Levinas, "Poetry and Resurrection," *Proper Names*, pp. 7–16.

125. Levinas, *In the Time of the Nations*, p. 168.

126. Levinas, *Existence and Existents*, pp. 88, 93.

127. Levinas, *Difficult Freedom*, p. 33. See chapter 1, section VIII above.

128. Levinas, *Proper Names*, pp. 91–93.

129. In "Faith in the Afternoon" Faith is described as "seasick with ocean sounds" and as "all ears . . . , born in Coney Island" (145).

130. "Havdalah," *The Metsudah Siddur*, trans. Rabbi Avrohom Davis (New York: Metsudah Publications, 1983). See also Isaiah 48:19, Genesis 32:12

131. Whitman, "Out of the Cradle Endlessly Rocking," p. 184, and "As I Ebb'd With the Ocean of Life," pp. 184–86, in *Complete Poetry*. Quote on p. 185.

132. Whitman, "As I Ebb'd With the Ocean of Life," *Complete Poetry*, p. 186. See note 12 above.

133. Paley, *Collected Stories*, pp. 378–86.

134. Cynthia Ozick, "America Towards Yavne," *What is Jewish Literature?*, ed. Hana Wirth-Nesher, pp. 20–35; "Metaphor and Memory," *Metaphor & Memory*, pp. 265–83. Reference to p. 278. Like Ozick's, Paley's liturgical stance is not exactly religious but neither is it merely rhetorical or aesthetic. Liturgical in Ozick's sense is a way of giving the self to the Other and a responsibility of self to Other that requires making one's private voice a vessel of collective voice. Paley does not go so far as to call her listening a liturgical act, even though she frames her acts of listening with allusions to prayers learned in childhood. Ozick, who refers to Paley in her roll call of Jewish American writers, introduces a distinction between Jewish liturgical and American lyrical voice, which Bloom rejects but Paley seems to accept. According to Ozick the American voice is lyrical, aesthetic, pagan, in the sense of being private and solitary. The Jewish liturgical voice, Ozick argues, is never private, always collective; never practicing art for art's sake, always ethical although not necessarily religious. Most crucial for Ozick and Paley is the diametrically opposed relation to history of pagan oracles and Jewish prophecy. Jewish liturgical or prophetic discourse is nothing if not historical. Pagan poetry is detached from history, and its Emersonian heir openly expresses strong aversion to history. The voice of lyric speakers is the voice of rupture. The voice of liturgical speakers is the voice of continuity, generosity, fecundity, and forgiveness.

135. Levinas, *Totality and Infinity*, pp. 239–40.

136. Handelman, *Fragments of Redemption*, pp. 204–5.

137. O'Sullivan, "Listening and Telling," p. 103. See also Taylor, *Grace Paley*, p. 127, where Paley says: "You hear, but listening is another matter."

138. Miller-Budick, *Engendering Romance*, p. 219.

139. Ibid., p. 243.

140. Paley entitled her first collection of stories, published in 1959, *The Little Disturbances of Man*.

141. See for example Paley, "Faith in the Afternoon," *The Collected Stories*, pp. 146–60.

142. "Havdalah," *The Metsudah Siddur*. See reference to Havdalah and note 130 above.

143. In Levinasian prophetic ethics, grace is inherently related to diachronic devotion. The responsibility for the other, Levinas writes, "does not have a 'synchronic' structure. In its devotion—in its devoutness—it is gratuitous or full of grace; it is not concerned with reciprocity. It is younger than the order of the world. . . . It brings to mind the dia-chrony of time, i.e., the ultimate secret of its very order." *In the Time of the Nations*, p. 183.

144. Ozick, "Ruth," *Metaphor & Memory*, p. 264.

145. See Bloom, "The Sorrows"; "Jewish Culture and Jewish Tradition," *Poetics of Influence*, ed. John Hollander (New Haven: Henry R. Schwab, 1988), pp. 347–68.

146. See note 68 above.

147. See Jonas, *The Gnostic Religion*, pp. 48–91.

148. Charles Reznikoff, quoted in Bloom, "The Sorrows," p. 71.

149. In Paley's "Faith in the Afternoon" the daughter remains indifferent to the pain and suffering of her mother, Mrs. Hegel-Shtein, and the old people they talk about. The mother by contrast says "I'm sorry for the old people" (pp. 154–55). Miller-Budick reads the missing pain in Faith's response on the personal level, and even the mother's compassion is seen as "pointing the story directly back to herself" (*Engendering Romance*, p. 227). This reading does not relate to the pain of collective loss (absent in Faith's response and present in her mother's) which is at the core of Jewish prophetic ethics.

150. Quoted in Bloom, "The Sorrows," p. 73.

151. Ibid., p. 73.

152. Paley, "The Expensive Moment," *The Collected Stories*, pp. 365–77. Reference to p. 371.

153. Paley, "Midrash on Happiness," p. 153.

154. In her interview with Elaine Kauvar, Ozick argues with much more pathos than Bloom, that there cannot be a Jewish writer as writer, without dealing with the "years given to mourning, two thousand years of grieving over the razed and violated Temple," p. 367.

155. Paley, "The Expensive Moment."

156. Paley, "Faith in the Afternoon," *The Collected Stories*, p. 148.

CHAPTER 5. JAMES BALDWIN'S SCHIZOPHRENIC ALIENATION

1. Harold Bloom, introduction to *James Baldwin*, ed. Harold Bloom (New York: Chelsea House Publishers, 1987), pp. 1–9. References to pp. 1–3, 8.

2. Bloom, introduction, *James Baldwin,* p. 1.

3. Ibid., p. 3.

4. See chapter 1, section VI.

5. Bloom regards Baldwin's castigation of Church and God in *The Fire Next Time* as the "superb instance . . . of prophetic authority." (p. 4).

6. See chapter 4, section II for the argument between Bloom and Ozick on this issue.

7. Henry Louis Gates, *Loose Canons: Notes on the Culture Wars* (New York: Oxford University Press, 1992). In a recent essay, K. Anthony Appiah examines the problem of split subjectivity from his position as "a gay black man." Appiah's interest lies predominantly in the distinctions between "collective and personal dimensions of individual identity." Although he questions the validity of "large categories—gender, ethnicity, nationality, 'race,' sexuality" for the construction of authentic individual identities, Appiah's alternative set of categories remain within the sphere of social sciences. "Identity, Authenticity, Survival," *Multiculturalism,* ed. Amy Gutmann (Princeton: Princeton University Press, 1994), pp. 149–63.

8. Gates, *Loose Canons,* p. xii. In "The Challenge to American Literary History," Heide Zeigler examines the attempt made in cultural studies to redefine American literature in multicultural terms. She claims that the editors of two recent literary histories—*Columbia Literary History* and *Cambridge Literary History*—"feel the need to attest to the lack of unifying perspective." *Multiculturalism and the Canon of American Culture,* ed. Hans Bak (Amsterdam: Vu University Press, 1993), pp. 57–64.

9. Erving Goffman, *Stigma: Notes on the Management of Spoiled Identity* (Harmondsworth: Penguin Books, 1968); Nathan Rotenstreich, *Basic Problems of Marx's Philosophy* (Indianapolis: The Bobbs Merrill Company Inc., 1965), pp. 144–61; and Kristeva, *Strangers to Ourselves.* For Marxist approaches to African American problems see also Cornel West, *Prophetic Thought in Postmodern Times* (Monroe, Maine: Common Courage Press, 1993); *Race Matters* (New York: Vintage Books, 1994).

10. Rotenstreich, *Basic Problems,* pp. 158–60.

11. Tracing the changing contents of the concept, Rotenstreich notes that "St. Augustine conceived of alienation as a state of ecstatic contemplation in which the human soul or spirit is elevated." Rotenstreich likewise introduces a dialectical paradox in the relation between alienation, knowledge, and individual identity: "The ideal of the identity brought about through the act of knowing, then, goes hand in hand with the idea of alienation. The state of identity is the positive correlative of the state of alienation" (*Basic Problems,* pp. 147–48).

12. Even before the Civil War, Frederick Douglass links his awakening to the experience of homelessness and estrangement in which he grew. He does not present it as a penalty, but rather as a privilege, enabling him to reject the mentality of the slave which allowed the master narrative of punishment. Likewise, Sundquist reads Nat Turner's revolt as a prophetic awakening to a state of subjugation and alienation. Turner harnessed the sense of estrangement to the ideology of revolt. Eric Sundquist, *To Wake The Nations* (Cambridge: Harvard University Press, 1993), pp. 56–83.

13. Throughout this chapter I use the term Marxist as a label, or telegraphic shorthand, for a philosophy of history which sees in alienation an effect of human causes. It asserts that human freedom can and must overcome alienation within temporal existence, and turn history from man's exile to his kingdom. My study

of Baldwin presents two dichotomous concepts of history. The first is the gnostic metaphysical one, which claims that history cannot be changed, and that it is the creation of an evil demiurge. The second is the Marxist one, which claims that history is man-made and therefore man-remediable. "Marxist" does not denote, in this context, an affiliation to any political party or ideology. I am well aware, moreover, of the critique Baldwin launched, in his essay "Many Thousands Gone," at Richard Wright (who was a card-holding Communist) for using Communist ideology in *Native Son*. See, for example, F. Standley & L. Pratt, eds., *Conversations With James Baldwin* (Jackson: University Press of Mississippi, 1989), p. 203. Subsequent quotations from this work are cited parenthetically in the text in the abbreviated form (*Conversations*).

14. Richard Goldstein, " 'Go the Way Your Blood Beats': An Interview With James Baldwin," *James Baldwin: The Legacy*, ed. Quincy Troupe (New York: Simon & Schuster, 1989), pp. 173–85. Quote on p. 175.

15. Margaret Mead and James Baldwin, *A Rap on Race* (Philadelphia: J. B. Lippincott Company, 1971), p. 134. Subsequent quotations from this work are cited parenthetically in the text.

16. Goldstein, "Go the Way," p. 178.

17. Quincy Troupe, "The Last Interview," *James Baldwin: The Legacy*, pp. 186–212. Quote on p. 210.

18. A former slave, Lucretia Alexander, quoted in Albert Robateau's "Exodus and the American Israel," *African-American Christianity*, ed. Paul Johnson (Berkeley and Los Angeles: University of California Press, 1994), p. 8. Robateau deploys the particular strategies used by African-American Christians to appropriate the story of Exodus (9–15). Eric Sundquist observes that while "numerous slaves . . . found the Bible an instrument of comfort or salvation rather than oppression," others protested that "the Bible and Jesus / Made slave of the nigger." *To Wake the Nations*, p. 57.

19. Werner Sollors, *Neither Black Nor White, Yet Both: Thematic Explorations of Interracial Literature* (New York: Oxford University Press, 1997).

20. James Baldwin, *The Price of the Ticket: Collected Nonfiction, 1948–1985* (New York: St. Martin's Press, 1985), p. 347. Subsequent quotations from this work are cited parenthetically in the text as (*The Price of the Ticket*).

21. Sartre, *What Is Literature?*, p. 59.

22. For the prophetic narrative of obedience see John Barton, *Oracles of God* (New York: Oxford University Press, 1986), p. 13.

23. *The Rap On Race*, p. 174. Elsewhere Baldwin explains that he may be read as a prophetic writer only insofar as his work projects his position as witness: "I don't try to be prophetic, as I don't sit down to write literature. It is simply this: a writer has to take all the risks of putting down what he sees" (*Conversations*, p. 254).

24. Bloom, *Poetry and Repression* and *The American Religion*. In the latter Bloom suggests that African-American religion can serve as a paradigm of the Gnostic-American creed as a whole (chapter 15). Yet in his studies of individual African-American writers, such as Baldwin and Walker, he does not mention a gnostic influence.

25. *The American Religion*, p. 49. In *Omens of the Millennium; The Gnosis of Angels, Dreams, and Resurrection* (New York: Riverhead Books, 1996), Bloom examines the issue of the gnostic double, or twin. See chapter 1, section VI above for a discussion of Bloom's gnostic model of prophetic subjectivity.

26. Bloom openly acknowledges his heavy debt to Freud, in *The Anxiety of Influence* and *Poetry and Repression*. My own focus, however, is theological rather than psychoanalytical, and so, I believe, is Baldwin's.

27. See chapter 3, section III and chapter 6, section I for further discussion of Bloom's narrow interpretation of the gnostic religion.

28. Jonas, *The Gnostic Religion*, pp. 320–40. In the introduction to her *The Gnostic Gospels* (New York: Random House, 1979), Elaine Pagels refers to Jonas's major contribution to the study of Gnosticism, and underscores the parallel he draws between Gnosticism and Existentialism (pp. xxx–xxxi).

29. Jonas, *The Gnostic Religion*, p. 329.

30. Ibid., p. 330.

31. Albert Camus, *The Rebel* (Harmondsworth: Penguin Books, 1962); *The Myth of Sisyphus*, in W. Kaufmann, ed., *Existentialism From Dostoevsky to Sartre*, (Cleveland and New York: Meridian Books, 1969).

32. Camus, *The Rebel*, p. 29.

33. Ibid., p. 29.

34. See for example *Conversations*, pp. 203, 224–25.

35. In an interview with Allen Geller, Ellison talks about the centrality of American literary heritage to contemporary African-American writers such as himself, and criticizes Baldwin's recourse to French rather than classical American writers. Maryemma Graham and Amritjit Singh, eds., *Conversations With Ralph Ellison* (Jackson: University Press of Mississippi, 1995), pp. 83–84. For gnostic elements in Melville's work see Lawrence Thompson, *Melville's Quarrel With God* (Princeton: Princeton University Press, 1952); Zephyra Porat, "Towards the Promethean Ledge: Varieties of Skeptic Experience in Melville's *Clarel*," *Literature & Theology*, 8, no. 1 (March 1994): 30–46.

36. James M. Robinson, ed., *The Nag Hammadi Library*, (San Francisco: Harper & Row, 1977), pp. 110, 115.

37. Jonas, *The Gnostic Religion*, p. 67.

38. Ibid., p. 95.

39. Pagels, *The Gnostic Gospels*, p. 25.

40. See for example his treatment of God's covenant with Noah, above.

41. *Conversations*, pp. 162–63. Ellison likewise emphasizes, though in a less militant formulation, the creative process of inverting one's only available language by resorting to black religion and music: "In my own case, having inherited the language of Shakespeare and Melville, Mark Twain and Lincoln and no other, I try to do my part in keeping the American language alive and rich by using in my work the music and the idiom of American Negro speech, and by insisting that the words of that language correspond with the reality of American life as seen by my own people." *Shadow And Act* (New York: Vintage Books, 1972), p. 267.

42. Toni Morrison, "Life In His Language," *James Baldwin: The Legacy*, ed. Quincy Troupe (New York: Simon & Schuster, 1989), p. 76.

43. Henri Charles Puech, "Gnosis and Time," *Christian Backgrounds of English and American Literature*, ed. Zephyra Porat. Department of English, Tel Aviv University, Tel Aviv, photocopy, p. 253.

44. Rudolf Bultmann, *Primitive Christianity in Its Contemporary Setting* (New York: Meridian Books, 1957).

45. Bloom, *The American Religion*, p. 242. In numerous interviews Baldwin is re-

ferred to as spokesman for the African-American community. See for example *Conversations*, pp. 71, 84, 139, 142, 174, 240. On betraying one's community of affiliation see chapter 1, sections III, V above.

46. Marcion, Jonas tells us, was the most Christian of Gnostics. His gospel is "of the alien and good God, the Father of Jesus Christ, who redeems from heavy bonds to eternal life wretched mankind, who are yet entire strangers to him. . . . He . . . freely adopts strangers to take them from their native land of oppression and misery into a new Father's house." Jonas emphasizes the fact that Marcion's gospel does not present Christ's sacrifice as a means for "the remission of sins or the cleansing of mankind from guilt" (*The Gnostic Religion*, pp. 138–39).

47. Du Bois's "sociological definition of black identity" centers on race "as a phenomenon of color with biological roots." Double consciousness, he claims, generates "this sense of always looking at one's self through the eyes of another." Sundquist, *To Wake the Nations*, pp. 459–62; Meyer Weinberg, ed., *W. E. B Du Bois: A Reader* (New York: Harper Torchbooks, 1970).

48. James Baldwin, *Just Above My Head* (New York: Dell Publishing, 1990), p. 480. Subsequent quotations from this work are cited parenthetically in the text.

49. Jonas, *The Gnostic Religion*, p. 45.

50. See Sartre, "Self-Deception," in Kaufman, ed., *Existentialism From Dostoevsky to Sartre*, pp. 241–70. Quote on p. 243.

51. *The Price of the Ticket*, p. 852; *Conversations*, pp. 253, 71; Bloom, introduction, *James Baldwin*, p. 1.

52. For Alice Walker's similar reaction see chapter 6, section IV below.

53. For the structure of gnostic subjectivity see Jonas' study of gnostic psychology in *The Gnostic Religion*, pp. 281–88.

54. James Baldwin, "Sonny's Blues," in *Going To Meet The Man*, pp. 103–42. Quote on p. 131. Subsequent quotations from this work are cited parenthetically in the text.

55. Ellison, *Shadow And Act*, p. 189.

56. "Previous Condition," in Baldwin, *Going To Meet The Man*, pp. 79–100. Subsequent quotations from this work are cited parenthetically in the text. The Gnostics see man's origin as twofold—extra-mundane and mundane. The true self (spirit) originates in a first condition, beyond historical time, and the present, false self (soul and body), is created by the evil demiurge. Jonas, *The Gnostic Religion*, p. 44.

CHAPTER 6. ALICE WALKER'S POETICS

1. Introduction to *Alice Walker*, ed. Harold Bloom (New York: Chelsea House Publishers, 1988), p. 4. In an interview with Robert Moynihan, Bloom makes the following generalization: "Most feminist poetry, of course, is like most black poetry. It isn't poetry. It isn't even verse. It isn't prose. . . . These groups . . . are all ideologues." *A Recent Imagining* (Archon Books, 1986), p. 30.

2. As will be shown below, Walker is familiar with the gnostic tradition. She quotes from Elaine Pagels's *The Gnostic Gospels*, mentions *The Nag Hammadi Library*, and elaborates on Rebbeca Jackson's gnostic beliefs. Alice Walker, *In Search of Our Mothers' Gardens: Womanist Prose* (New York: Harcourt Brace & Company, 1984), pp.

78, 118. Subsequent quotations from this work are cited parenthetically in the text in the abbreviated form (*Mothers' Gardens*).

3. Bloom, introduction, *Flannery O'Connor*, p. 4. See also chapter 3, section III above.

4. As shown below Walker defines "womanist" in more than one way. The most relevant definition here might be: "A black feminist or feminist of color." *Mothers' Gardens*, p. xi.

5. Alice Walker, *The Same River Twice: Honoring the Difficult* (New York: Scribner, 1996), p. 283. Subsequent quotations from this work are cited parenthetically in the text in the abbreviated form (*Same River*).

6. For Bloom's study of American Gnosticism see his *The American Religion* (New York: Simon and Schuster, 1992) and *Harold Bloom: Poetics of Influence*, ed. J. Hollander (New Haven: Henry R. Schwab, 1988). See also chapters 1 and 5.

7. Claudia Tate, "An Interview With Alice Walker," *Black Women Writers at Work*, ed. Claudia Tate (New York: Continuum, 1983), p. 185.

8. Alice Walker, *Revolutionary Petunias & Other Poems* (New York: Harcourt Brace & Company, 1973), p. 52.

9. *Mothers' Gardens*, p. 8. On O'Connor's influence on Walker, see also her essay "Beyond the Peacock," *Mothers' Gardens*, pp. 42–59; O'Brien, "An Interview with Alice Walker," in *Alice Walker: Critical Perspectives Past and Present,* ed. H. L. Gates and K. A. Appiah, (New York, Amistad, 1993), pp. 326–46. Quote on p. 337; Robert Butler, "Visions of Southern Life and Religion in O'Connor's *Wise Blood* and Walker's *The Third Life of Grange Copeland*," *CLA Journal* 36, no. 4 (1993): 349–70. Bloom's misreading of Walker is apparent in his introductory remark that she is not idiosyncratic, "since the celebration of community necessarily decries individuated subjectivity, while exalting collective roaring . . . as the more moral mode." (Introduction, to *Alice Walker*, p. 3).

10. Walker, *Revolutionary Petunias*, p. 63.

11. Ibid., p. 34. I refer here to S. Budick and W. Iser, eds., *Languages of the Unsayable: The Play of Negativity in Literature and Literary Theory* (Stanford: Stanford University Press, 1987).

12. Gloria Steinem, "Do You Know This Woman? She Knows You," *Ms.* (June 1982): 36–37, 89–93. Quote on p. 90.

13. On Sophia as Silence, see Robinson, ed., *The Nag Hammadi Library*, pp. 103, 162; Jonas, *The Gnostic Religion* pp. 176–99. On the gnostic mistrust of language, see, for example, *Nag Hammadi*, pp. 32–33: "Names given to worldly things are very deceptive for they lead our thoughts from what is correct to what is incorrect . . . people do not conceive what is correct [unless] they have come to know what is correct."

14. Writing of O'Connor, Bloom makes a distinction between the biblical and the gnostic persona. Yet Walker demonstrates that they are not mutually exclusive, though somewhat conflictual. I do not swerve from the prophetic by calling Walker a gnostic visionary, because the Gnostics see themselves as prophets, although without a community of listeners. For a discussion of the gnostic prophet see for example, *Nag Hammadi*, p. 124. See chapter 1 above for a discussion of Bloom's gnostic prophet, and chapter 5 for elements of the gnostic prophetic rhetoric in Baldwin.

15. See O'Brien, "Interview," p. 346.

16. O'Brien, "Interview," p. 331. On the contradictory and paradoxical nature of gnostic rhetoric see, for example: "For I am knowledge and ignorance / I am shame and boldness / I am shameless; I am ashamed / I am strength and I am

fear" (*Nag Hammadi*, pp. 272–73). On the unity of isolated sparks in the pleroma the "Tripartite Tractate" says: "And he brings them forth in order that it might be discovered that they exist according to their individual properties in a unified way" (*Nag Hammadi*, p. 64).

17. See O'Brien, "Interview," p. 341.

18. Bloom, introduction to *Flannery O'Connor*, p. 5.

19. O'Connor's concept of transformed consciousness is reflected in the epigraph (Matt., 11:12) chosen for *The Violent Bear it Away*; see also chapter 3 above. For Walker's view, see *Mothers' Gardens*, p. 48. It seems significant that Walker describes to her mother the idea of split on their way to visit O'Connor's house in Georgia. On the gnostic idea of the Kingdom of God as transformed consciousness, see Pagels, *The Gnostic Gospels*, pp. 128–29; "The Gospel of Thomas" in *Nag Hammadi*, p. 118.

20. *Nag Hammadi*, p. 89; Jonas, *The Gnostic Religion*, pp. 174ff, 206ff. Frantz Fanon, to whom Walker relates in her story "Coming Apart," resorts to the Manichaean dualism of color to probe the problem of the perpetual conflict between whites and blacks. *Black Skin, White Masks* (London: Paladin, 1970), p. 44. The relation of Fanon's study to Walker's work is dealt with below.

21. Alice Walker, *You Can't Keep a Good Woman Down* (New York: Harcourt Brace & Co., 1981), p. 122. Subsequent quotations from this work are cited parenthetically in the text in the abbreviated form (*You Can't Keep*).

22. Pagels, *The Gnostic Gospels*, pp. 31, 40.

23. On several occasions Walker mentions Mother-Wisdom-Sophia, who is the female part of the first emanation. See her notes on the choice of the name Sofia in *The Color Purple*, "after the goddess of wisdom" (*The Same River*, p. 41). Also her journal entry for April 17, 1984, which opens *Living By The Word: Essays* (New York: Harcourt Brace & Company, 1989), and in which she describes a dream about a two-headed wise woman (Higher and Lower Sophia?) who tells her to "live by the Word"—possibly the gnostic Logos.

24. Jonas, *The Gnostic Religion*, p. 175.

25. *Nag Hammadi*, pp. 104–11; Jonas, *The Gnostic Religion*, pp. 44–46.

26. The "Gospel of Truth," a Valentinian tractate, provides a description of the displaced pneumatic sparks: "Thus they were ignorant of the Father. . . . Since it was terror and disturbance and instability and doubt and division, there were many illusions at work by means of these . . . they were sunk in sleep and found themselves in disturbing dreams" (*Nag Hammadi*, p. 43).

27. "Exc. Theod," 78.2, quoted in Jonas, *The Gnostic Religion*, p. 45. In "The Gospel Of Truth" a similar formula of salvation through knowledge is presented (*Nag Hammadi*, pp. 40, 46).

28. Jonas, *The Gnostic Religion*, p. 122.

29. "The Hymn of the Pearl," in Jonas, *The Gnostic Religion*, p. 115. In his commentary to this allegorical text Jonas cites a Mandaean source, which has a similar formula: "I go to meet my image and my image comes to meet me; it caresses and embraces me as if I were returning from captivity" (p. 122).

30. *Nag Hammadi*, pp. 1, 12. Frantz Fanon criticizes the black person's wish for "plenitude" or fullness, when sought through the image of self formed by the Other. For Fanon it is a narcissistic sense of unity, which can perhaps be seen just as false as the gnostic mundane self and as Walker's constructed identity. Fanon, *Black Skin, White Masks*, p. 212.

31. Pagels, *The Gnostic Gospels*, pp. 119–41.

32. Walker specifically mentions *The Nag Hammadi Library* when writing about Rebecca Jackson, who held Gnostic views "a hundred years before the Nag Hammadi 'Gnostic Gospels, The Secret Teaching of Christ' was found" (*Mothers' Gardens*, p. 78).

33. *Nag Hammadi*, pp. 128–29.

34. Walker, *Living By The Word*, p. 46.

35. See Pagels, *The Gnostic Gospels*, p. xxx; Jonas, *The Gnostic Religion*, pp. 3–19.

36. O'Brien, "Interview," p. 327.

37. Walker, *The Same River*, p. 33. The Gnostic Christ instructs his disciples concerning self-discovery: "He who will drink from My mouth will become like Me. I myself shall become he, and the things that are hidden will be revealed to him" (*Nag Hammadi*, p. 129). This quotation appears in Pagels's study where Walker found her epigraph. It seems plausible that Walker read Pagels's discussion of the Socratic slant of the gnostic Christ.

38. Alice Walker, *The Third Life of Grange Copeland* (New York: Pocket Books, revised edition, 1988). Subsequent quotations from this work are cited parenthetically in the text in the abbreviated form (*The Third Life*).

39. Alice Walker, *Good Night, Willie Lee, I'll See You in the Morning* (New York: Harcourt Brace & Company, 1984), pp. 23–24. In her interview with O'Brien, Walker claims that she writes poetry as a way "of celebrating with the world that I have not committed suicide the evening before" (330). On the issue of instructors, it should be noted that Walker often populates her stories with teachers ("Source," "A Letter"), and recounts her own experience in remedial teaching.

40. See for example Dianne F. Sadoff, "Black Matrilineage: The Case of Alice Walker and Zora Neale Hurston," *Signs* 2, no. 1 (1985): 4–26; Trudier Harris, "Folklore in the Fiction of Alice Walker: A Perpetuation of Historical and Literary Traditions," *Black American Literature Forum* 11, no. 1 (1977): 3–8; Deborah E. McDowell, " 'The Changing Same': Generational Connections and Black Women Novelists," *New Literary History* 18, no. 2 (winter 1987): 281–302; Thadious M. Davis, "Alice Walker's Celebration of Self in Southern Generations," *The Southern Quarterly* 21, no. 4 (summer 1983): 39–53; Alma Freeman, "Zora Neale Hurston and Alice Walker: A Spiritual Kinship," *SAGE* 2 (spring 1985): 37–40.

41. Bloom, *Poetry and Repression*, p. 20.

42. For the gnostic rejection of historical ties see Jonas, *The Gnostic Religion*, p. 51. For Emerson see "Self-Reliance," *Selections*, pp. 147–68. For Bloom's scene of instruction see *Poetry and Repression*, p. 27.

43. O'Brien, "Interview," p. 331. Deborah E. McDowell, "The Self In Bloom: Alice Walker's *Meridian*," *CLA* 24, no. 3 (1980): 262–75. For more studies of Walker's political commitments see Keith Byerman, "Desire and Alice Walker: The Quest for a Womanist Narrative," *Callaloo* 12 (spring 1989): 332–42; Harris, "Folklore in the Fiction,"; McDowell, " 'The Changing Same,' "; Bettye Parker-Smith, "Alice Walker's Women: In Search of Some Peace of Mind," in *Black Women Writers, 1950–1980*, ed. Mari Evans (Garden City, N.Y.: Anchor Doubleday, 1984), pp. 478–95.

44. I borrow these terms from Fredric Jameson, *Postmodernism, or the Cultural Logic of Late Capitalism* (Durham: Duke University Press, 1991), pp. 17, 25, 152, 160.

45. Eric Lincoln and Lawrence Maniya, *The Black Church in the African American*

Experience (Durham: Duke University Press, 1990), p. 303, italics mine. In stories, poems, and essays, Walker gives voice to womanists who "have over the last twenty years, really forged a community of readers, writers, and activists" and who consciously avoid "using the white male literary establishment or the white male political establishment." Sharon Wilson, "A Conversation With Alice Walker," *Alice Walker: Critical Perspectives Past and Present*, ed. H. L. Gates and K. A. Appiah (New York: Amistad, 1993), p. 321.

46. Walker, *Living By The Word*, p. 32.

47. Wilson, "A Conversation With Alice Walker," p. 321; *The Same River*, p. 147, italics in text; *Revolutionary Petunias*, p. 1.

48. Jameson, *Postmodernism*, pp. 6, 322.

49. Ibid., p. 125.

50. On the deceiving aspect of movies see Jasper, "Living in the Reel World: The Bible in Film," in *Readings in the Canon of Scripture*, pp. 84–85.

51. Jameson, *Postmodernism*, pp. 160–61. See Jameson's discussion of Walter Benn Michaels' view of the individual's relations with consumer culture, and of Susan Sontag's book on photography, in which "her conclusion about contemporary image culture is the classical liberal recommendation of a kind of 'diet cure' for images" (203–7). On this issue see also Roland Barthes, *Camera Lucida: Reflections on Photography*, trans. Richard Howard (New York: Hill and Wang, 1981). See Walker's use of the metaphor of a door opening to transcendent space in *The Temple of My Familiar* (section V below). The metaphor of a door possibly leading to redeeming Gnosis, reminds me of a painting by Magritte entitled *Le Savoir* (1961), in which a door opens to celestial space. The door, and a chess figure that stands by it, are covered with music notes, rather than words, which, I believe, Walker would wholeheartedly endorse.

52. In Krista Brewer, "Writing to Survive: An Interview With Alice Walker," *Southern Exposure* 9, no. 2 (summer 1981): 12–15. Quote on p. 15.

53. Walker, *The Same River Twice*, p. 192; *Living By the Word*, pp. 57–58.

54. Robinson, ed., *Nag Hammadi*, p. 173.

55. Ibid., p. 112.

56. Alice Hall Petry, "Walker: The Achievement of the Short Fiction," *Alice Walker: Critical Perspectives Past and Present*, ed. H. L. Gates and K. A. Appiah, (New York: Amistad, 1993), pp. 193–210. Quote on p. 195.

57. Ibid., 193.

58. Ibid., pp. 195–97.

59. Walker, *You Can't Keep a Good Woman Down*, pp. 31–39. Subsequent quotations from this work are cited parenthetically in the text.

60. Walker's choice of "New England Colony" for this story is not accidental. New England was, after all, the first site where the Puritan saints attempted to merge the historical and transcendent meanings of scriptural prophecies. See Bercovitch, *The American Jeremiad;* see also chapter 1 above.

61. On the subject of name as true identity, see *The Same River Twice*, where Walker describes a scene edited out from *The Color Purple*, in which Celie "begins to hum 'Sister.' Shug hears her, 'remembers her name,' and leaves Albert high and dry" (p. 145). The Gnostics put great emphasis on the name, notably that of the Father, as the sign of identity. "The Gospel Of Truth" says that "the name is invisible because it alone is the mystery" (*Nag Hammadi*, p. 47).

62. Petry, "Walker," p. 197.

63. In "Coming Apart," *(You Can't Keep,* pp. 41–53), the husband "does not know how to make love without the fantasies fed to him by movies and magazines" (p. 53). By contrast, Walker says, "I know that my religion is love." The centrality of true love comes simultaneously with leaving behind attachment to images (de)formed by others (*The Same River Twice*, p. 33). For the tainted image of eros in gnostic speculations, see "The Origin of the World," *Nag Hammadi*, pp. 168–69.

64. Walker, *You Can't Keep*, pp. 118–23. Subsequent quotations from this work are cited parenthetically in the text.

65. Jonas, *The Gnostic Religion*, pp. 120–22.

66. Walker, *You Can't Keep*, pp. 41–53.

67. Petry, "Walker," p. 205.

68. If at the outset the husband prefers fantasies generated by journal images to his own wife, by the end of the story "it is sixty percent *her* body that he moves against in the sun" (*You Can't Keep*, p. 53, italics in text).

69. Fanon, *Black Skin, White Masks*, p. 10.

70. Ibid., p. 16.

71. Ibid., pp. 124, 126, 198, 228.

72. *Nag Hammadi*, p. 356.

73. Alice Walker, *The Temple of My Familiar* (New York: Pocket Books, 1989), pp. 185–86.

74. Walker, *The Temple of My Familiar*, pp. 354–55.

75. Walker, *Living by the Word*, p. xxi.

76. Barbara Christian, "Alice Walker: The Black Woman Artist as Wayward," *Black Women Writers, (1950–1980): A Critical Evaluation*, ed. Mari Evans (New York: Anchor Press, 1984), pp. 457–77. Reference to pp. 458–59.

77. Walker, *The Temple of My Familiar*, pp. 116, 144–45.

78. Jonas, *The Gnostic Religion*, pp. 27, 92.

79. Alice Walker, "The Diary of an African Nun," *In Love and Trouble: Stories of Black Women* (New York: Harcourt Brace & Company, 1973), pp. 113–18. Subsequent quotations from this work are cited parenthetically in the text.

80. Zora Neale Hurston, "How It Feels to Be Colored Me," in *I Love Myself When I Am Laughing . . . And Then Again When I Am Looking Mean and Impressive*, ed. Alice Walker (New York: The Feminist Press, 1979), pp. 152–55. Quote on p. 154.

81. Hurston, "How It Feels," p. 154.

82. See in this context, Edward Said, *Orientalism* (London: Penguin Books, 1985), p. 7, for a discussion of writing the Orient as an image of the white, male, colonizing West: "Under the general heading of knowledge of the Orient, and within the umbrella of Western hegemony over the Orient . . . there emerged a complex Orient suitable for study in the academy, for display in the museum, . . . for theoretical illustrations in anthropological, biological, linguistic, racial, and historical theses about mankind and the universe." Walker often criticizes the tendency of white, colonizing culture to make of the other an artifact fit for the museum.

83. For the attitude of the Negro to white cultural artifacts see Fanon, *Black Skin, White Masks*, pp. 17, 26.

84. O'Brien, "Interview," p. 341.

85. Robinson, ed., *Nag Hammadi*, p. 89.

86. Elaine Pagels, "To the Universe Belongs the Dancer," *Parabola* 4, no. 2 (1979): 7–9.

87. *Acts of John*, 95.25–96.40. Quoted in Pagels, "To the Universe Belongs the Dancer." See also Pagels, *The Gnostic Gospels,* pp. 73–74. Pagels claims that the *Acts of John* presents the dancing Christ as "a spiritual being who adapts himself to human perception." The gnostic text specifies that Christ's dance takes place in Gethsemane the night before the arrest.

88. Pagels, "To the Universe," p. 9. In "The Apocalypse of Peter," Christ is revealed to the disciple and makes the distinction between historical and transcendent savior, between a laughing, living Jesus and the crucified one: "He whom you saw on the tree, glad and laughing, this is the living Jesus. But this one into whose hands and feet they drive the nails is his fleshy part" (*Nag Hammadi*, p. 344).

89. Similarly, the gnostic Christ encourages questions, and poses as one seeking for answers, rather than providing them (*Nag Hammadi*, pp. 128, 231, 236).

90. Fanon, *Black Skin, White Masks*, p. 232.

91. Walker, *Living By The Word*, p. 63.

92. Pagels, *The Gnostic Gospels*, p. xix.

93. Walker, "Reassurance," *Revolutionary Petunias*, pp. 33–34.

Bibliography

Aarons, Victoria. "Talking Lives: Storytelling and Renewal in Grace Paley's Short Fiction." *Studies in American Jewish Literature* 9.1 (spring 1990): 20–35.

———. "A Perfect Marginality: Public and Private Telling in the Stories of Grace Paley." *Studies in Short Fiction* 27.1 (winter 1990): 35–43.

Acheson, Susan. "The Esoteric Eschatology of H. D.'s Trilogy." *Literature & Theology* 12.2 (June 1998): 187–204.

Allen, Brooke."Losing Faith." *The New Criterion* 14.5 (January 1996): 57–60.

Anderson, Quentin. *The Imperial Self: An Essay in American Literary and Cultural History*. New York: Alfred A. Knopf, 1971.

Appiah, Anthony. "Identity, Authenticity, Survival." *Multiculturalism*. Edited by Amy Gutmann. Princeton: Princeton University Press, 1994.

Arcana, Judith. *Grace Paley's Life Stories*. Urbana: University of Illinois Press, 1993.

Atlas, James. "Confessing For Voyeurs: The Age of The Literary Memoir is Now." *New York Times Magazine* (May 12, 1996): 25–27.

Bakhtin, M. M. *The Dialogic Imagination*. Translated by Caryl Emerson and Michael Holquist. Austin: University of Texas Press, 1981.

———. *Problems of Dostoevsky's Poetics*. Translated by R. W. Rotsel. Ann Arbor: Ardis, 1973.

Baldwin, James. *Going to Meet the Man*. Harmondsworth: Penguin Books, 1991.

———. *Just Above My Head*. New York: Dell Publishing, 1990.

———. *Notes of A Native Son*. Boston: Beacon Press, 1955.

———. *The Price of the Ticket: Collected Nonfiction, 1948–1985*. New York: St. Martin's Press, 1985.

Barth, Karl. *A Barth Reader*. Edited by Yoachim Erler and Reiner Marquard. Grand Rapids: William B. Eerdmans Publishing House, 1986.

———. *The Epistle to the Romans*. Translated by Edwyn Hoskyns. Oxford: Oxford University Press, 1968.

———. *The Word of God and the Word of Man*. Translated by Douglas Horton. New York: Harper and Brothers, 1957.

Barthes, Roland. *Camera Lucida: Reflections on Photography*. Translated by Richard Howard. New York: Hill and Wang, 1981.

Barton, John. *Oracles of God*. New York: Oxford University Press, 1986.

Batt, Noelle, and Marcienne Rocard. "An Interview With Grace Paley." *Caliban* 25 (1988): 119–37.

203

Baudrillard, Jean. *Simulacra and Simulation.* Translated by Sheila Faria Glaser. Ann Arbor: University of Michigan Press, 1994.

Bercovitch, Sacvan. *The American Jeremiad.* Madison: University of Wisconsin Press, 1978.

———. "Emerson The Prophet: Romanticism, Puritanism, and Auto-American-Biography." *Emerson: Prophecy, Metamorphosis and Influence.* Edited by David Levin. New York: Columbia University Press, 1975.

———. "The Modernity of American Puritan Rhetoric." *American Letters and the Historical Consciousness.* Edited by J. G. Kennedy and D. M. Fogel. Baton Rouge: Louisiana State University Press, 1987.

———. *The Puritan Origins of the American Self.* New Haven: Yale University Press, 1975.

———. *The Rites of Assent.* New York: Routledge, 1993.

Bhabha, Homi. *The Location of Culture.* New York: Routledge, 1994.

Bleikasten, Andre. "The Heresy of Flannery O'Connor." *Critical Essays on Flannery O'Connor.* Edited by Melvin Friedman and Beverly Clark. Boston: G. K. Hall, 1985.

Bloom, Harold. *The American Religion.* New York: Simon & Schuster, 1992.

———. *The Anxiety of Influence: A Theory of Poetry.* London: Oxford University Press, 1973.

———. *Blake's Apocalypse: A Study In Poetic Argument.* Ithaca: Cornell University Press, 1963.

———. "Emerson: The American Religion." *Modern Critical Views on R. W. Emerson.* Edited by H. Bloom. New York: Chelsea House, 1985.

———. Introduction to *Alice Walker.* Edited by H. Bloom. New York: Chelsea House Publishers, 1988.

———. Introduction to *Cynthia Ozick.* Edited by H. Bloom. New York: Chelsea House Publishers, 1985.

———. Introduction to *Flannery O'Connor.* Edited by H. Bloom. New York: Chelsea House Publishers, 1986.

———. Introduction to *Modern Critical Views on R. W. Emerson.* Edited by H. Bloom. New York: Chelsea House Publishers, 1985.

———. Introduction to *James Baldwin.* Edited by H. Bloom. New York: Chelsea House Publishers, 1987.

———. Introduction to *John Updike.* Edited by H. Bloom. New York: Chelsea House Publishers, 1986.

———. *Omens of the Millennium: The Gnosis of Angels, Dreams, and Resurrection.* New York: Riverhead Books, 1996.

———. *Poetics of Influence.* Edited by John Hollander. New Haven: Henry R. Schwab, 1988.

———. *Poetry and Repression: Revisionism From Blake to Stevens.* New Haven: Yale University Press, 1976.

———. "The Sorrows of American-Jewish Poetry." *Commentary* 53.3 (March 1972): 69–74.

Brewer, Krista. "Writing to Survive." *Southern Exposure* 9.2 (summer 1981): 12–15.

Budick, Sanford, and Wolfgang Iser, eds. *Languages of the Unsayable: The Play of Negativity in Literature and Literary Theory.* Stanford: Stanford University Press, 1987.

Bultmann, Rudolph. *Primitive Christianity in Its Contemporary Setting.* New York: Meridian Books, 1957.

Butler, Robert. "Visions of Southern Life and Religion in O'Connor's *Wise Blood* and Walker's *The Third Life of Grange Copeland.*" *CLA Journal* 36.4 (1993): 349–70.

Byerman, Keith. "Desire and Alice Walker: The Quest For a Womanist Narrative." *Callalloo* 12 (spring 1989): 332–42.

Camus, Albert. *The Rebel.* Translated by Anthony Bower. Harmondsworth: Penguin Books, 1962.

Carroll, David. *Paraesthetics: Foucault, Lyotard, Derrida.* New York: Methuen, 1987.

Cavell, Stanley. *Conditions Handsome and Unhandsome: The Constitution of Emersonian Perfectionism.* Chicago: University of Chicago Press, 1990.

———. *In Quest of the Ordinary: Lines of Skepticism and Romanticism.* Chicago: University of Chicago Press, 1988.

———. *The Senses Of Walden.* New York: Viking Press, 1972.

———. *This New Yet Unapproachable America: Lectures After Emerson After Wittgenstein.* Albuquerque: Living Batch Press, 1989.

Charters, Ann. "Grace Paley: A Conversation With Ann Charters." *The Story and Its Writer.* Edited by Ann Charters. New York: St. Martin Press, 1987.

Christian, Barbara. "Alice Walker: The Black Woman Artist as Wayward." *Black Women Writers, (1950–1980): A Critical Evaluation.* Edited by Mari Evans. New York: Anchor Press, 1984.

Crews, Frederick. "Whose American Renaissance?" *The New York Review of Books* (October 27, 1988): 68–81.

Culler, Jonathan. "On the Negativity of Modern Poetry: Friedrich, Baudelaire and the Critical Tradition." *Languages of the Unsayable: The Play of Negativity in Literature and Literary Theory.* Edited by S. Budick and W. Iser. Stanford: Stanford University Press, 1987.

Davidson, Cathy, and Michael Moon, eds. *Subjects and Citizens: Nation, Race, and Gender From 'Oroonoko' to Anita Hill.* Durham: Duke University Press, 1995.

Davis, Thadious. "Alice Walker's Celebration of Self in Southern Generations." *The Southern Quarterly* 21.4 (summer 1983): 39–53.

Derrida, Jacques. "At This Very Moment in This Work Here I Am." *Re Reading Levinas.* Edited by R. Bernasconi and S. Critchley. Bloomington: Indiana University Press, 1991.

———. *Writing and Difference.* Translated by Alan Bass. Chicago: University of Chicago Press, 1978.

Ellison, Ralph. *Invisible Man.* New York: Vintage Books, 1989.

———. *Shadow And Act.* New York: Vintage Books, 1972.

Emerson, R. W. *Essays and Lectures.* New York: The Library of America, 1983.

———. "Illusions." *Selected Prose and Poetry.* Edited by Reginald L. Cook. New York: Holt, Rinehart and Winston, 1966.

———. *Selections from R. W. Emerson.* Edited by Stephen E. Whicher. Boston: Houghton Mifflin, 1960.

———. "Spiritual Laws." *The Works of R. W. Emerson*. New York: Tudor Publishing Company, 1968.

Fanon, Frantz. *Black Skin, White Masks*. London: Paladin, 1970.

Faulkner, William. *Light In August*. Harmondsworth: Penguin Books, 1960.

Feeley, Kathleen. *Flannery O'Connor: Voice of the Peacock*. New York: Fordham University Press, 1982.

Foucault, Michel. *The Foucault Reader*. Edited by Paul Rabinow. New York: Pantheon Books, 1984.

———. "Technologies of the Self." *Technologies of the Self: A Seminar with Michel Foucault*. Edited by Luther Martin, Huck Gutman and Patrick Hutton. Amherst: University of Massachusetts Press, 1988.

Freeman, Alma. "Zora Neale Hurston and Alice Walker: A Spiritual Kinship." *SAGE* 2 (spring 1985): 37–40.

Freud, Sigmund. "Family Romances." *On Sexuality*. Translated by James Strachey. London: Penguin Books, 1977.

Friedler, Maya. "An Interview With Grace Paley," *Story Quarterly* 13 (1981): 32–39.

Friedman, Melvin, and Lewis Lawson, eds. *The Added Dimension: The Art and Mind of Flannery O'Connor*. New York: Fordham University Press, 1966.

Gates, Henry Louis. *Loose Canons: Notes on the Culture Wars*. New York: Oxford University Press, 1992.

Giannone, Richard. "Flannery O'Connor Tells Her Desert Story." *Religion & Literature* 27.2 (summer 1995): 47–67.

Gingher, Robert S. "Has John Updike Anything to Say?" *MFS* 37.1 (spring 1991): 97–105.

Goffman, Erving. *Stigma: Notes on the Management of Spoiled Identity*. Harmondsworth: Penguin Books, 1968.

Goldstein, Richard. " 'Go the Way Your Blood Beats': An Interview With James Baldwin." *James Baldwin: The Legacy*. Edited by Quincy Troupe. New York: Simon & Schuster Inc., 1989.

Graham, Maryemma, and Amritjit Singh, eds. *Conversations With Ralph Ellison*. Jackson: University Press of Mississippi, 1995.

Hall, S. and P. Du Gay, eds. *Questions of Cultural Identity*. London: Sage Publications, 1996.

Handelman, Susan. *Fragments of Redemption: Jewish Thought & Literary Theory in Benjamin, Scholem, & Levinas*. Bloomington: Indiana University Press, 1991.

Harris, Trudier. "Folklore in the Fiction of Alice Walker: A Perpetuation of Historical and Literary Traditions." *Black American Literature Forum* 11.1 (1977): 3–8.

Hever, Hannan. "The Struggle over the Canon of Early-Twentieth-Century Hebrew Literature: The Case of Galicia." *Interpreting Judaism In a Postmodern Age*. Edited by S. Kepnes. New York: New York University Press, 1996.

Hulley, Kathleen. "Grace Paley's Resistant Form." *Delta* 14 (1982): 3–18.

———. "Interview with Grace Paley." *Delta* 14 (1982): 19–40.

Humphries, Jefferson. *The Otherness Within*. Baton Rouge: Louisiana State University Press, 1983.

Humy, Nicholas. "A Different Responsibility: Form and Technique in Grace Paley's 'A Conversation With My Father'." *Delta* 14 (May 1982): 85–97.

Hunt, George. *John Updike and the Three Great Secret Things: Sex, Religion and Art.* Grand Rapids: William B. Eerdmans Publishing Company, 1980.

Hurston, Zora Neale. "How It Feels to Be Colored Me." *I Love Myself When I Am Laughing . . . And Then Again When I Am Looking Mean and Impressive: A Zora Neale Hurston Reader.* Edited by Alice Walker. New York: The Feminist Press, 1979.

Isaacs, Neil. *Grace Paley: A Study of the Short Fiction.* Boston: Twayne, 1990.

Iser, Wolfgang. *The Act of Reading.* Baltimore: The Johns Hopkins University Press, 1978.

———. *The Fictive and the Imaginary: Charting Literary Anthropology.* Baltimore: The Johns Hopkins University Press, 1993.

James, William. *The Varieties of Religious Experience.* New York: Collier Books, 1961.

Jameson, Fredric. *The Ideologies of Theory.* Vols. 1, 2. Minneapolis: University of Minnesota Press, 1988.

———. *The Political Unconscious: Narrative as a Socially Symbolic Act.* Ithaca: Cornell University Press, 1981.

———. *Postmodernism, or the Cultural Logic of Late Capitalism.* Durham: Duke University Press, 1991.

Jasper, David. *Readings in the Canon of Scripture: Written for Our Learning.* New York: St. Martin's Press, 1995.

———. *Rhetoric, Power and Community.* Louiseville Kentucky: Westminster John Knox Press, 1993.

Jonas, Hans. *The Gnostic Religion.* 2d Ed. Boston: Beacon Press, 1963.

Katz-Kahane, Claire. "Flannery O'Connor's Rage of Vision." *American Literature* 46.1 (March 1974): 54–67.

Kaufmann, Walter, edited by *Existentialism From Dostoevsky to Sartre.* Cleveland and New York: Meridian Books, 1956.

Kauvar, Elaine. "An Interview With Cynthia Ozick." *Contemporary Literature.* 34.3 (1993): 359–94.

Kierkegaard, Soren. *Fear and Trembling.* Translated by Walter Loweie. Princeton: Princeton University Press, 1941.

Kristeva, Julia. *Strangers to Ourselves.* Translated by Leon S. Roudiez. New York: Columbia University Press, 1991.

Levinas, Emmanuel. *Basic Philosophical Writings.* Edited by Adrian Peperzak, Simon Critchley, and Robert Bernasconi. Bloomington: Indiana University Press, 1996.

———. *Beyond the Verse.* Translated by Gary D. Mole. London: Athlone Press, 1982.

———. *Collected Philosophical Papers.* Translated by Alphonso Lingis. The Hague: Martinus Nijhoff, 1987.

———. *Difficile Liberte: Essays sur le Judaisme.* Paris: Editions Albin Michel, 1963.

———. *Difficult Freedom.* Translated by Sean Hand. Baltimore: The Johns Hopkins University Press, 1990.

———. *Existence and Existents.* Translated by Alphonso Lingis. Dordrecht/Boston/London: Kluwer Academic Publishers, 1988.

———. *In the Time of the Nations.* Translated by Michael B. Smith. London: The Athlone Press, 1994.

———. *Of God Who Comes to Mind.* Translated by Bettina Bergo. Stanford: Stanford University Press, 1998.

———. *Otherwise Than Being.* Translated by Alphonso Lingis. The Hague: Martinus Nijhoff, 1981.

———. *Outside the Subject.* Translated by Michael B. Smith. Stanford: Stanford University Press, 1993.

———. *Proper Names.* Translated by Michael Smith. Stanford: Stanford University Press, 1996.

———. *Totality and Infinity.* Translated by Alphonso Lingis. Pittsburgh: Duquesne University Press, 1969.

———. "The Trace Of The Other." *Deconstruction in Context: Literature and Philosophy.* Edited by Mark Taylor. Chicago: University of Chicago Press, 1986.

Lidoff, Joan. "Clearing Her Throat: An Interview With Grace Paley." *Shenandoah* 32.3 (1981): 3–26.

Lincoln, Eric, and Lawrence Maniya. *The Black Church in the African American Experience.* Durham: Duke University Press, 1990.

Lyons, Bonnie."Grace Paley's Jewish Miniatures." *Studies In American Jewish Literature* 8.1 (spring 1989): 26–33.

Mandel, Dena. "Keeping Up With Faith: Grace Paley's Sturdy American Jewess." *Studies In American Jewish Literature* 3 (1983): 85–98.

Marchant, Peter, and Earl Ingersoll. "A Conversation With Grace Paley." *The Massachusetts Review* 26 (winter 1985): 606–14.

McDowell, Deborah. " 'The Changing Same': Generational Connections and Black Women Novelists." *New Literary History* 18.2 (winter 1987): 281–302.

———. "The Self in Bloom: Alice Walker's *Meridian.*" *CLA* 24.3 (1980): 262–75.

Mead, Margaret, and James Baldwin. *A Rap On Race.* Philadelphia: J. B. Lippincott Company, 1971.

Meier, Joyce. "The Subversion of the Father in the Tales of Grace Paley." *Delta* 14 (May 1982): 115–27.

Melville, Herman. *Moby Dick.* New York: Macmillan, 1962.

Michaels, Walter Benn. *Our America: Nativism, Modernism and Pluralism.* Durham: Duke University Press, 1995.

Miller-Budick, Emily. *Engendering Romance: Women Writers and the Hawthorne Tradition, 1850–1990.* New Haven: Yale University Press, 1994.

———. *Fiction and Historical Consciousness: The American Romance Tradition.* New Haven: Yale University Press, 1989.

———. *Nineteenth-Century American Romance: Genre and the Construction of Democratic Culture.* New York: Twayne Publishers, 1996.

Morrison, Toni. "Life in His Language." *James Baldwin: The Legacy.* Edited by Quincy Troupe. New York: Simon & Schuster, 1989.

Moynihan, Robert. *A Recent Imagining: Interviews with H. Bloom, G. Hartman, J. Hillis Miller, P. De Man.* Archon Books, 1986.

Munk, Linda. "Understanding Understatement: Biblical Typology and 'The Displaced Person'." *Literature & Theology* 2.2 (September 1988): 237–53.

Nietzsche, Friedrich. "The Use and Abuse of History." *Untimely Meditation*. Translated by R. S. Hallingdale. Cambridge: Cambridge University Press, 1983.

Nisly, Paul. "The Prison of The Self: Isolation in Flannery O'Connor's Fiction." *Studies in Short Fiction* 12.2 (1974): 49–54.

O'Brien, John. "An Interview With Alice Walker." *Alice Walker: Critical Perspectives Past and Present*. Edited by H. L. Gates and K. A. Appiah. New York: Amistad, 1993.

O'Connor, Flannery. *The Complete Stories*. London and Boston: Faber & Faber, 1990.

———. *The Habit of Being: Letters of Flannery O'Connor*. Edited by Sally Fitzgerald. New York: Farrar, Straus and Giroux, 1988.

———. *Mystery and Manners*. Edited by Sally and Robert Fitzgerald. New York: Farrar, Straus and Giroux, 1989.

———. *The Presence of Grace*. Athens: University of Georgia Press, 1983.

———. *Three by Flannery O'Connor*. New York: Signet Classic, 1983.

O'Sullivan, Rosemary. "Listening and Telling in Counterpoint: A Conversation with Grace Paley." *Plotting Change: Contemporary Women's Fiction*. Edited by L. Anderson. London: Edward Arnold, 1990.

Ozick, Cynthia. *A Cynthia Ozick Reader*. Edited by Elaine Kauvar. Bloomington: Indiana University Press, 1996.

———. "Judaism & Harold Bloom." *Commentary* 67.1 (January 1979): 43–51.

———. *Metaphor & Memory: Essays by Cynthia Ozick*. New York: Alfred A. Knopf, 1989.

Pagels, Elaine. *The Gnostic Gospels*. New York: Random House, 1979.

———. "To the Universe Belongs the Dancer." *Parabola* 4.2 (1979): 7–9.

Paley, Grace. *The Collected Stories*. New York: Farrar, Straus, and Giroux, 1994.

———. Introduction to "A Conversation with my Father." In *Fathers, Reflections by Daughters*. Edited by U. Owen. New York: Pantheon Books, 1985.

———. "Midrash on Happiness." *TriQuarterly* 65 (winter 1986): 151–53.

———. "Of Poetry and Women and the World." *TriQuarterly* 65 (winter 1986): 247–53.

———. "Symposium." *Shenandoah* 2 (winter 1976): 3–31.

Parfit, Derek. *Personal Identity*. Edited by J. Perry. Berkeley and Los Angeles: University of California Press, 1975.

———. *Reasons and Persons*. Oxford: Oxford University Press, 1986.

Parker-Smith, Bettye. "Alice Walker's Women: In Search of Some Peace of Mind." *Black Women Writers, 1950–1980*. Edited by Mari Evans. Garden City, N.Y.: Anchor Doubleday, 1984.

Pease, Donald E. "National Identities, Postmodern Artifacts, and Postnational Narratives." *Boundary 2* 19, no. 1 (spring 1992): 1–13.

Perry, Ruth. "Grace Paley." *Women Writers Talking*. Edited by J. Todd. New York: Holmes and Meir Publishers, 1983.

Petry, Alice Hall. "Walker: The Achievement of the Short Fiction." *Alice Walker: Crit-*

ical Perspectives Past and Present. Edited by Henry L. Gates and K. Antony Appiah. New York: Amistad, 1993.

Peuch, Henri Charles. "Gnosis and Time." *Christian Backgrounds of English and American Literature.* Edited by Zephyra Porat. Dept. of English, Tel Aviv University, Tel Aviv. Photocopy, pp. 224–65.

Pinsker, Sanford. "Joyce's Poldy/Updike's Rabbit." *Cimarron Review* (January 1995): 92–101.

Plath, James, edited by *Conversations With John Updike.* Jackson: University Press of Mississippi, 1994.

Porat, Zephyra. *Prometheus Among the Cannibals: Adventures of the Rebel in Literature* (in Hebrew). Tel Aviv: Am Oved Publishers, 1976.

———. "Towards the Promethean Ledge: Varieties of Skeptic Experience in Melville's *Clarel.*" *Literature & Theology* 8.1 (March 1994): 30–46.

Ricoeur, Paul. *Oneself as Another.* Translated by Kathleen Blamey. Chicago: University of Chicago Press, 1992.

———. *Time and Narrative.* Translated by K. McLaughlin & D. Pellauer. Chicago: University of Chicago Press, 1988.

Robateau, Albert. "Exodus and the American Israel." *African-American Christianity: Essays in History.* Edited by Paul Johnson. Berkeley and Los Angeles: University of California Press, 1994.

Robinson, James M., edited by *The Nag Hammadi Library.* Translated by members of the Coptic Gnostic Library. San Francisco: Harper & Row, 1977.

Rotenstreich, Nathan. *Basic Problems of Marx's Philosophy.* Indianapolis: The Bobbs-Merrill Company Inc., 1965.

Sadoff, Dianne. "Black Matrilineage: The Case of Alice Walker and Zora Neale Hurston." *Signs* 2.1 (1985): 4–26.

Said, Edward. *Orientalism.* London: Penguin Books, 1985.

Sartre, Jean-Paul. *What Is Literature?* Translated by Bernard Frechtman. London: Methuen and Co., 1949.

Schiff, James A. "Updike Ignored: The Contemporary Independent Critic." *American Literature* 67.3 (September 1995): 531–52.

Schleifer, Ronald. "Chaste Compactness." *Contemporary American Women Writers: Narrative Strategies.* Edited by C. Rainwater and W. Scheik. Lexington: University Press of Kentucky, 1985.

Sollors, Werner. *Neither Black Nor White, Yet Both: Thematic Explorations of Interracial Literature.* New York: Oxford University Press, 1997.

Standley, Fred, and Louis Pratt, Eds. *Conversations With James Baldwin.* Jackson: University Press of Mississippi, 1989.

Steinem, Gloria. "Do You Know This Woman? She Knows You." *Ms.* (June 1982): 36–37, 89–93.

Sternberg, Meir. *The Poetics of Biblical Narrative: Ideological Literature and the Drama of Reading.* Bloomington: Indiana University Press, 1987.

Sundquist, Eric. *To Wake the Nations: Race in the Making of American Literature.* Cambridge: Harvard University press, 1993.

Tanner, Tony. *The City of Words: American Fiction 1950–1970*. New York: Harper and Row, 1971.

Tate, Claudia. "An Interview With Alice Walker." *Black Women Writers at Work*. Edited by C. Tate. New York: Continuum, 1983.

Taylor, Jacqueline. *Grace Paley: Illuminating the Dark Lives*. Austin: University of Texas Press, 1990.

Thompson, Lawrence. *Melville's Quarrel with God*. Princeton: Princeton University Press, 1952.

Todorov, Tzvetan. *Mikhail Bakhtin: The Dialogical Principle*. Translated by Wlad Godzich. Minneapolis: University of Minnesota Press, 1984.

Troupe, Quincy. "The Last Interview." *James Baldwin: The Legacy*. Edited by Quincy Troupe. New York: Simon & Schuster, 1989.

Twain, Mark. *The Mysterious Stranger and Other Stories*. New York: Signet Classic, 1962.

Updike, John. *The Afterlife and Other Stories*. New York: Fawcett Crest, 1994.

———. *Assorted Prose*. New York: Fawcett Crest, 1965.

———. *Hugging the Shore*. Harmondsworth: Penguin Books, 1985.

———. *In the Beauty of the Lilies*. New York: Fawcett Crest, 1996.

———. *Midpoint and Other Poems*. New York: Alfred A. Knopf, 1978.

———. *Odd Jobs*. London: Andre Deutsch Ltd., 1992.

———. *Picked Up Pieces*. New York: Fawcett Crest, 1975.

———. *Pigeon Feathers and Other Stories*. New York: Fawcett Crest, 1963.

———. *Self Consciousness: Memoirs*. New York: Fawcett Crest, 1989.

———. *Telephone Poles and Other Poems*. New York: Alfred A. Knopf, 1979.

Vidal, Gore. "Rabbit's Own Burrow: The Comfortable Patriotism of John Updike and His Fiction." *TLS* (April 26, 1996): 3–7.

Wagner, Joseph. "John Updike and Karl Barth: An Insistent 'Yes'." *Cithara* 18.1 (1978): 61–69.

Walker, Alice. *Good Night, Willie Lee, I'll See You in the Morning*. New York: Harcourt Brace & Company, 1984.

———. *In Love and Trouble: Stories of Black Women*. New York: Harcourt Brace & Company, 1973.

———. *In Search of Our Mothers' Gardens: Womanist Prose*. New York: Harcourt Brace & Company, 1984.

———. *Living By The Word: Essays*. New York: Harcourt Brace & Company, 1989.

———. *Revolutionary Petunias & Other Poems*. New York: Harcourt Brace & Company, 1973.

———. *The Same River Twice: Honoring the Difficult*. New York: Scribner, 1996.

———. *The Temple of My Familiar*. New York: Pocket Books, 1989.

———. *The Third Life of Grange Copeland*. New York: Pocket Books. Revised edition, 1988.

———. *You Can't Keep a Good Woman Down*. New York: Harcourt Brace & Company, 1981.

Weinberg, Meyer, ed. *W. E. B. Du Bois: A Reader*. New York: Harper Torchbooks, 1970.

Wells, Joel. "Off the Cuff." *Conversations With Flannery O'Connor.* Edited by Rosemary Magee. Jackson: University Press of Mississippi, 1987.

West, Cornel. *Prophetic Thought in Postmodern Times.* Monroe, Maine: Common Courage Press, 1993.

———. *Race Matters.* New York: Vintage Books, 1994.

Whitman, Walt. *Complete Poetry and Selected Prose by Walt Whitman.* Edited by James Miller. Boston: Houghton Mifflin, 1959.

Wilson, Sharon. "A Conversation With Alice Walker." *Alice Walker: Critical Perspectives Past and Present.* Edited by H. L. Gates and K. A. Appiah. New York: Amistad, 1993.

Wirth-Nesher Hana. "Afterword: Between Mother Tongue and Native Language in *Call It Sleep.*" In Henry Roth, *Call It Sleep.* New York: Farrar, Straus and Giroux, 1991.

———. Ed. *What is Jewish Literature.* Philadelphia and Jerusalem: The Jewish Publication Society, 1994.

Zeigler, Heide. "The Challenge to American Literary History." *Multiculturalism and the Canon of American Culture.* Edited by Hans Bak. Amsterdam: Vu University Press, 1993.

Index